GOD'S COMPANIONS

Challenges in Contemporary Theology

Series Editors: Gareth Jones and Lewis Ayres
Canterbury Christ Church University College, UK and Emory University, US

Challenges in Contemporary Theology is a series aimed at producing clear orientations in, and research on, areas of "challenge" in contemporary theology. These carefully co-ordinated books engage traditional theological concerns with mainstreams in modern thought and culture that challenge those concerns. The "challenges" implied are to be understood in two senses: those presented by society to contemporary theology, and those posed by theology to society.

Published

Forthcoming

GOD'S COMPANIONS

Reimagining Christian Ethics

Samuel Wells

Blackwell
Publishing

For Stephen Wells
1922–2005

God's gentle companion

© 2006 by Samuel Wells

BLACKWELL PUBLISHING
350 Main Street, Malden, MA 02148–5020, USA
9600 Garsington Road, Oxford OX4 2DQ, UK
550 Swanston Street, Carlton, Victoria 3053, Australia

The right of Samuel Wells to be identified as the Author of this Work has been asserted
in accordance with the UK Copyright, Designs, and Patents Act 1988.

First published 2006 by Blackwell Publishing Ltd

4   2009

Library of Congress Cataloging-in-Publication Data
Wells, Samuel, 1965–
   God's companions : reimagining Christian ethics / Samuel Wells.
      p.   cm.—(Challenges in contemporary theology)
   Includes bibliographical references and index.
   ISBN: 978–1–4051–2013–5 (hardcover : alk. paper)
   ISBN: 978–1–4051–2014–2 (paperback : alk. paper)
   1. Christian ethics. I. Title. II. Series.
   BJ1251.W445 2006
241—dc22   2005026434

A catalogue record for this title is available from the British Library.

Set in 10.5pt Bembo
by The Running Head Limited, Cambridge
www.therunninghead.com
Printed and bound in Singapore
by Fabulous Printers Pte Ltd

The publisher's policy is to use permanent paper from mills that operate a sustainable forestry
policy, and which has been manufactured from pulp processed using acid-free and elementary
chlorine-free practices. Furthermore, the publisher ensures that the text paper and cover board
used have met acceptable environmental accreditation standards.

For further information on
Blackwell Publishing, visit our website:
www.blackwellpublishing.com

CONTENTS

PREFACE

It is hard to say where and when a book begins. I recall being delighted to hand my supervisor Ann Loades Chapters 1–4 and 6 of my PhD thesis, and, daunted but relishing the challenge, saying, "Now for Chapter 5 – the time to show how all this talk about ethical theory is embodied in the lives of local congregations!" Ann soberly and wisely said, "You don't need to write Chapter 5 – there's already plenty here to get you through a PhD." Delighted yet deflated, I realized she was right. Ten years later, here at last is that lost Chapter 5.

It never went away. While reflecting on issues of poverty in which I was engaged in Norwich, I read, at Ben Quash's suggestion, John Milbank's essay "Can Morality Be Christian?" (Milbank 1997, 219–32), and for the first time began to realize that what was impoverished was not so much the housing estate on which I lived, but my understanding of God. To my sense of ethics being rooted in local congregations was being added a sense of ethics as plenitude.

I recall sitting in the library at Duke Divinity School. I had been talking excitedly with Stanley Hauerwas about our plans for editing *The Blackwell Companion to Christian Ethics*, and I realized I needed a moment to myself. I sketched out the essay that was to become the second chapter of that book, "The Gift of the Church and the Gifts God Gives It." It was an attempt to unite the authoritative polemics of Hauerwas with the playful orthodoxy of my own book *Improvisation: The Drama of Christian Ethics*. Put that essay together with my essay "How Common Worship Forms Local Character" (Wells 2002), and there seemed to be limitless potential for discovery and exploration. I sensed I had struck a seam that went down and down and down. To local congregations and plenitude I had now added the centrality of the Eucharist.

And then I sat down with my editor Rebecca Harkin and she dared me to gauge how deep that seam might be. She simply suggested I keep digging, and she would publish what treasure I found. That quarry has given me a labor of joy and delight. I dare hope that any reader may find the reward in perusing this book that I have found in writing it. To local congregations, plenitude, and the Eucharist I had finally added a confidence that here was a whole approach to Christian ethics, one that aspired to draw together the different aspects of practical, pastoral, scriptural, dogmatic, liturgical, and moral theology and thus take on some of the conventional assumptions of the discipline. I had a book.

This book is soaked in the environments in which it has been discovered. The parishes of St Luke, Wallsend, St Andrew Cherry Hinton with All Saints Teversham, St Elizabeth, North Earlham, and St Mark, Newnham have shaped what I understand to be the context of Christian ethics. What I have sought to propose here is what I have sought to practice there. The people of those parishes populate the stories of this book. I mention no names because I do not wish the idiosyncrasies of personality to distract from the grace of God. I am grateful also to the staff and students of Ridley Hall, Cambridge, who provided the companionship, warmth, and seclusion to make the writing of this book so enjoyable. I have also learned deeply about the role of the Eucharist in moral formation from the work of Jerome Berryman and others involved in the practice of Godly Play.

There have been countless opportunities to reflect with groups and congregations, and the fruits of those discussions have appeared notably in the following articles, which were earlier forays into this territory, and on which this book draws significantly. "How Seventeenth-Century Evensong Forms Twenty-First-Century Character: An Evocation," *Journal of Anglican Studies* 2/2 (2004): 70–4; "Holiness: Baptism," *The Christian Century* 117/7 (March 1, 2000): 235; "Prayer for the Week: Living and Dying in God," *Church Times* 7334 (September 26, 2003): 12; "Name that Fear," *The Christian Century* 121/12 (June 15, 2004): 18; "More than Enough," *The Christian Century* 121/12 (June 15, 2004): 19; "They All Have the Same Shepherd," *The Tablet* (December 11, 2004): 18; "Gathering in Expectation: Worship: Act One," *Christian Century* 122/7 (April 5, 2005): 9–10; "Hearing God Out: Worship: Act Two," *Christian Century* 122/9 (May 3, 2005): 9–10; "Courage to Respond: Worship: Act Three," *Christian Century* 122/11 (May 31, 2005): 10–11; "Broken and Shared: Worship: Act Four," *Christian Century* 122/13 (June 14, 2005): 8–9; "Sent out: Worship: Act Five," *Christian Century* 122/15 (June 28, 2005): 9–10.

My writing has been enriched by so many good companions who have shared the vision of this book and encouraged it in diverse ways. My wife Jo has constantly expanded my imagination and embodied the gospel of abundance. She knows no scarcity. Our children Laurence and Stephanie have surprised us with joy. Connie the dog has daily reminded me of God's crazy delight and his longing faithfulness. John Inge, Chad Boulton OSB, Andrew McKearney, Kate Litchfield, Nick Garrard, Jana Moravcova, Martina Rehakova, Caroline Worsfold, Robin Steinke, and Neville Black have mapped a journey from scarcity to abundance. My reading companions Phil Jones, Craig Hovey, Marion Drobig, John Kiess, and Beth Barton Schweiger have shared the enterprise of embodying ethics in the practices of community. Stanley Hauerwas, Bernd Wannenwetsch, Bridget Nichols, and Graeme Walker offered timely advice and encouragement.

But the deepest gratitude is to my father, Stephen, whose ministry has never ceased to inspire my own. He read the essay "The Gift of the Church and the Gifts God Gives It." Rather mystified about how such an essay could make such grand claims about the nature of Christian ethics, he said "There's nothing new here." Of course there wasn't – to him: he took for granted that the local church is the principal place where the grace of God is embodied. He had practiced that faith in a ministry of over 50 years. He never read a word of this book. That is a great sadness to me. But he never needed to; because he spent his whole life living everything it proposes. And as long as the Church has witnesses like him, it will hardly need books like this.

INTRODUCTION

God gives his people everything they need to worship him, to be his friends, and to eat with him. A companion is one with whom one shares bread. God calls his people to be his companions, the ones with whom he shares bread – his friends. Christians call sharing bread with God, worship. Thus to follow the God of Jesus Christ means to worship him, to be his friends, and to eat with him: in short, to be his companions.

The purpose of this introduction is to demonstrate the significance of each aspect of this summary statement, and to locate my argument in relation to other understandings of the nature and purpose of Christian ethics.

God

This study is founded on one definitive choice: God's original choice never to be except to be for us in Christ (Barth 1963, 62). Thus ethics assumes a relationship between humanity and God, a relationship epitomized in Jesus, that constitutes human identity and distinguishes humanity from the rest of creation. To be God's companions: that is the nature and destiny of humankind.

There are all sorts of understandable reasons why it has become difficult to talk of God in ethics in the last 300 years. The fragmentation of the Church has not diminished the zeal of many of its competing parts: and since the religious wars of the sixteenth and seventeenth centuries there has always been a lingering assumption that convictions about God lead to violence. The philosopher Immanuel Kant set out an ethic that, if not wholly shorn of the divine, reduced God to the limits of reason alone: no longer could the noumenal deity have a meaningful role in the phenomenal world (Kant 1960). The growth of technology has set up a host of expectations and fears that would have been unknown to those figures that inhabit the narratives of the Bible, and thus it has been easy to assume that God (at least the God of Jesus Christ) has little to say on such issues. The spread and succession of global empires has hastened the pluralization of religious culture, such that in a contemporary democracy it seems to many absurd that one conception of God should have a louder voice than another. The perceived decline of church attendance in the West, together with the supposed triumph of the secular, has perhaps weakened the confidence of the churches themselves. And the hermeneutics of suspicion has become so influential that many assume that every claim involving the word God is not only coercive but also a respectable mask behind which power elites maintain their sometimes subtle but invariably merciless structures of oppression.

For all these reasons and many others, it has frequently been assumed that Jesus Christ no longer constitutes all that Christians might want to say about ethics. And a new discipline has been invented, to fill the gap between what God gave his people in Christ and what people yet feel they still need. Christian ethics is the name of this gap. This book is intended to show that such a gap is an illusion. It is written to bridge the separation between theology and ethics, to insist that theology and ethics are two sides of the same coin. That coin is God, and his will in Christ to make all people his companions. This will is the heart of theological ethics.

Gives

In using the term "gives" I am saying that this book concerns not just God but God's action. This is a significant claim because ethics is usually understood to be the study of *human* action. I maintain that what sustains human life is a pattern of practices – good ways to relate to one another, honed in community and developed by tradition, learned by apprenticeship and embodied in habit. These practices are fundamentally gifts of God. They are the ways his will to companionship is expressed in human life. They not only draw people closer to him but also foster their flourishing.

My argument is not a conventional one – and here I refer to the form, not just to the content. The principal rhetorical device used in this book is the list. I simply intend to overwhelm the reader with examples. I am reluctant to belittle the arguments of others: I would rather display the full implications of my own approach and hope that readers are moved to develop the practices in which they are already engaged and embody others. This is not a paper debate: it is a call for the renewal of the Church.

I perceive three broad ways of writing about ethics. The first is description. Its aim is primarily to render the subject matter meaningful. It seeks to portray the Christian life in terms so illuminating, so beautiful, that it attracts commitment by the sheer acuteness of its own rendering. Like a recipe, it makes one want to cook the meal; like a travel guide, it makes one want to visit the country; like a gospel, it makes one want to follow Christ: not because it tells one to, but because one longs to turn the wonder of the description into lived experience. In short, it captures the imagination.

The second is comparison. This is ethics in critical vein. It is the careful evaluation of different approaches, different arguments, different theories, in order to establish a plausible winner. It is the polemical summoning of evidence that an argument is flawed, a genealogical tracing of another argument to its unexpected and disturbing roots, a conscientious exploration of a third argument's implications if taken to their limit, and a transposition of themes from one context to another in which those themes are reflected in a very different light. This is the substance of the ethics of the academy: in short, it is "the discipline."

The third is persuasion. This is ethics in popular vein. It is always denied but frequently assumed that this is the ethics of unquestioned assumptions seeking hasty endorsements, shaky prejudice in search of validating evidence, deep conviction yearning for a pithy slogan. Of course apologetics has a more honorable tradition: that of seeking a truth that can be expressed in non-theological language and commending that truth beyond the bounds of the Church. But behind apologetics always lies a danger that the particularity of Christianity be translated into the platitudes of contemporary aspirations.

This book is an exercise in the first kind of ethics. The famous claim that "the best apologetics is a good dogmatics" guides my whole approach. Unlike many whose work I deeply admire, my principal task is description. Hence my citing of authors from ancient tradition and contemporary debate is largely confined to those whose descriptions seemed so winning that they have captured my imagination. I have largely left comparison to those who can do it better than me (for example Hauerwas 2001).

In what follows I seek to display the gifts of God in an account of the practices his Gospel entails. My hope is that these practices, rather than theoretical arguments, will come to be seen as the substance of Christian ethics.

His People

By saying "his people" I am accepting a broadly traditional use of pronouns relating to God. This is less because of any commitment to the maleness of such language than out of having failed to find satisfactory alternatives (see the discussion in Ford 2002, 181–4).

More central to my argument, saying "God gives *his people*" means making a specific claim about the status of the Church. (For a discussion of the Jews as still God's people, see Yoder 2003.) Again, one may make a threefold distinction in regard to the imagined location of Christian ethics (see Wells 2004, 33–41).

The most common location may be termed "universal" ethics, or "ethics for everyone." God is the God of the whole creation, so the argument goes, and his will for one part of humankind is no different from his will for another. Ethics is largely about finding common principles or guidelines that can inform and shape public life. It is deeply aware of the context in which a pluralist democracy and a contested public sphere make it difficult to articulate the claims of faith in other than broad and abstract terms. Thus Christianity becomes largely what Kant made of it, a code of behavior with little reference to origin or purpose, specific heritage or ultimate destiny.

A rival approach may be called "subversive" ethics. This subjects the universal version to the aforementioned hermeneutic of suspicion, and finds it wanting. "Universal" is little more than a cover for the way those in power concoct rules to suit their interests, and rewrite history and mythology to fit in with their purposes. In protest, subversive ethics is "ethics for the oppressed." It identifies with – and often emerges from – those whose social location places them almost inevitably outside the power elites. By articulating the suppressed voices, subversive ethics challenges those in power to demonstrate whether they have any authority beyond the implicit threat of violence.

"Ecclesial" ethics, the third understanding, may be termed "ethics for the Church." It shares the subversive approach's critique of the way universal ethics elides particularity, and it agrees that the Church must always be the Church of the poor. But it doubts whether autonomy and self-expression are where true happiness lies, and it seeks in the traditions and practices of the Church, its narrative, and its hope, a more subversive gospel than "subversive" ethics can ever articulate.

This study is an exercise in ecclesial ethics. It believes that God's call is to all people, but it does not take for granted that all people are therefore the same: it locates their sameness in their shared humanity with Christ, rather than in something significant they share with one another. It believes God's call turns the world upside-down, but that that subversion finds its power not in numbers or guile but in running with the grain of the universe, that is along the contours of cross and resurrection, remembering God's surprises and anticipating God's transforming future.

Perhaps most distinctively, this is a study that locates the heart of ethics squarely in the practices of the local church. Through all the descriptions of practices and claims that these constitute God's gifts to the Church for shaping its life, I throughout offer examples that demonstrate the way ordinary Christians have had their characters shaped by these remarkable gifts. These stories are more than illustrations, for in many cases they take the argument forward in ways that could not be perceived except in narrative form. On occasion I have drawn on stories from beyond the local church when that seemed more appropriate. But these cases are rare exceptions, and for each one there is a fairly evident reason. In general, the doggedness of the stories seeks to celebrate the earthiness of the Church. Sometimes I have changed details of characters or events in order to preserve the anonymity of the protagonists. But all the stories derive from actual events. It is not just that throughout the writing of this book I was a parish priest, striving to practice what I am here preaching. It is that I believe the people whose stories are told in this book are truly God's companions, the heart of Christian ethics and the embodiment of the Gospel, and the best form ethics can take is a celebration of what God does through the practices they perform and the people God thus makes them.

Everything They Need

This book displays that ethics is about the action of God embodied in the practices of the Church. But perhaps its most controversial claim is that this action constitutes everything his people need to follow him. Everything they *need* does not mean everything they *want*. And everything they need to *follow* him does not mean everything they need to live a long, healthy life free from suffering, disappointment, frustration, or loneliness and full of achievement, recognition, and contentment. These things may be substituted for the Gospel, may be the aspirations of many Christians, may be welcome blessings in any human life – but they are not to be mistaken for following the God of Jesus Christ. Christians are called to follow and are given everything they need to follow. Following Jesus is living with the grain of the universe. Christian ethics commends those things that run with the grain of the universe, and amplifies those practices that enrich and enable that life; explicitly or implicitly it critiques those things that run against the grain. Following Jesus means learning to want the limitless things God gives us in Jesus.

Throughout the argument I am consciously alternating between two related notions: sufficiency and abundance. On the one hand I argue that

God gives enough: on the other, I suggest that God gives too much. To suggest that God gives enough is a criticism of what I take to be a consistent majority strand in Christian ethics – the assumption that there is not enough, and thus that ethics is the very difficult enterprise of making bricks from straw. Scarcity assumes there is not enough information – we know too little about the human body, about the climate, about what makes wars happen, about how to bring people out of poverty, about what guides the economy. There is not enough wisdom – there are not enough forums for the exchange of understanding, for learning from the past, for bringing people from different disciplines together, and there is not enough intelligence to solve abiding problems. There are not enough resources – world population is growing, and there is insufficient access to education, clean water, food, health care, and the means of political influence. There is not enough revelation – the Bible is a lugubrious and often ambiguous document, locked into its time, unable to address the problems of today with the clarity required. Fundamentally, I suggest, this whole assumption of scarcity rests on there being not enough God. Somehow God, in creation, Israel, Jesus and the Church, and in the promise of the eschaton, has still not done enough, given enough, been enough, such that the imagined ends of Christian ethics are and will always be tantalizingly out of reach.

In contrast to this assumption of scarcity I suggest that God gives enough – everything that his people need. He gives them everything they need in the past: this is heritage; and everything they could possibly imagine in the future; this is destiny. He gives them the Holy Spirit, making past and future present in the life of the Church. He gives them a host of practices – ways in which to form Christians, embody them in Christ, receive all that God, one another, and the world have to give them, be reconciled and restored when things go wrong, and share food as their defining political, economic, and social act. The things he gives are not in short supply: love, joy, peace. The way these gifts are embodied is through the practices of the Church: witness, catechesis, baptism, prayer, friendship, hospitality, admonition, penance, confession, praise, reading scripture, preaching, sharing peace, sharing food, washing feet. These are boundless gifts of God. My complaint with conventional Christian ethics is that it overlooks, ignores, or neglects those things God gives in plenty, and concentrates on those things that are in short supply. In the absence of those things that are plentiful, it experiences life in terms of scarcity. My argument draws attention to those things that God gives his people and resists the temptation to scratch around for more.

On the other hand I argue that God gives his people not just enough, but too much. What I am doing is trying to account for there being more than one kind of problem in ethics. The first kind of problem is simply not wanting, or wilfully disregarding, the gifts of God, and setting about making one's own. But there is another kind of problem, which is primarily about imagination. The "problem" is that there is too much of God. Whereas the first kind sees the difficulty being that God gives the wrong gifts, or not enough gifts, for the second kind the difficulty is that the human imagination is simply not large enough to take in all that God is and has to give. We are overwhelmed. God's inexhaustible creation, limitless grace, relentless mercy, enduring purpose, fathomless love: it is just too much to contemplate, assimilate, understand. This is the language of abundance. And if humans turn away it is sometimes out of a misguided but understandable sense of self-protection, a preservation of identity in the face of a tidal wave of glory. Christian ethics should seek to ride the crest of that wave. It should be a discipline not of earnest striving, but of joy; a study not of the edges of God's ways but of exploring the heart of grace. The practices that I outline in this book are patterns of activity through which God makes his overwhelming mercy a daily digestible discipline. They are ways of embodying his grace so that people of all social locations, all abilities, all ages can be transformed without being drowned.

These two claims, sufficiency and abundance, attract a recurring anxiety. "But surely the world is full of scarcity! Is it not foolhardy, wilfully blind or immoral to talk of sufficiency, let alone abundance?" I would offer two responses to this. One is from personal experience. For several years I was vicar of a church on a socially deprived housing estate in the East of England. For my own reasons I felt quite at home in a context of economic, cultural, social, and emotional deprivation. And then suddenly the estate found itself being offered a vast sum of government money to catalyze the formation of a community-led regeneration process. I found myself in a very influential position in this process for an extended period. What I learned was that poverty is not primarily about money. It is about having no idea what to do and/or having no one with whom to do it. The former I called imagination, the latter I called community. To the extent that our neighborhood had imagination and community, we were not poor. But without imagination and community, no money could help us. I perceived that the role of the local church was to be a *community of imagination*: and what enriched that community and embodied that community were the practices I describe in this book. Living in that deprived community, I discovered the abundance of God.

A second answer would be more analytical. It would ask in return, "What is it that makes starvation wrong? What is it that makes Africa, in the words of Tony Blair, 'a scar on the conscience of the world'?" What makes starvation wrong is not just human suffering and the degree to which it is brought about by the greed and conflict of others. It is that it is a grotesque affront to God's character and purpose, which is for people to flourish in abundant life in companionship with him. Hence abundance is the grain of the universe, and starvation is a symptom of things being badly against the grain. The truth is that the world is not short of food, and the solution to starvation is not making more food (overcoming scarcity); the solution is sharing the food the world already has and reconciling the divisions that lead to ruinous conflict. These are exactly the concerns of the practices I describe as the gifts of God's abundance.

Thus there is no equivalence between God's abundance and human wealth or happiness. This is not a "be happy" or "realize how lucky you are" proclamation. On the contrary, it is a witness that God's gifts are etched most starkly in the face of human poverty and often recognized most distinctly in the face of human suffering. What is the accumulation of wealth but an insulation against dependence on the gifts of God? Is the accumulation of wealth not therefore a proclamation of God's scarcity? What is the absence of wealth but a dependence on the gifts of God – friendship, hospitality, the sharing of food? Is the voluntary absence of wealth not therefore a proclamation of the sufficiency of the gifts God gives in the practices of the Church? This surely is the reason monastic communities have such a treasured place in the Christian story – for they have traditionally been removed from conventional resources of insulation and have depended on the practices of the Church, which have thus been refined in their company. The Rule of St Benedict, for example, emphasizes having enough for one's needs, welcoming guests as though they were Christ, not driving people to undue lengths in manual labor, and praying concisely unless definitely led on by the Spirit (Benedict 1970).

To Worship Him

If God gives his people everything they need to follow him, what does following him entail? I suggest that to follow him means to be God's companions – hence the title of the book. Resolving companionship into three dimensions, it means to worship him, to be his friends, and to eat with him.

The book is divided into three parts, each of which is called "The Body of Christ." This phrase is used in three senses in the New Testament and in the life of the Church. It sometimes means Jesus, the embodied, anointed one, the good news of God yesterday, today, and forever. It sometimes means the Church, with its many limbs and organs, united to Christ in Baptism.

And it sometimes means the living bread of the Eucharist. Each sense informs and amplifies the other two. The shape of the book fills out the three dimensions of the introductory sentence. For the first sense, Jesus, corresponds to the call to worship God; the second sense, the body of companions known as the Church, corresponds to the call to be God's friends; and the third sense, the Eucharist, corresponds to the call to eat with him. Each is retrospective, in that it describes the pattern of the Gospels, in which the disciples worshiped Jesus, were his friends, and ate with him on significant occasions; each is descriptive and prescriptive, in that it describes how the Church lives today, and how it should perceive its role, response and aspiration in relation to the pressing issues of our day; and each is eschatological, in that it describes the ultimate state of companionship with God, worshiping around his throne as his guests at the kingdom banquet.

Worshiping God is thus the theme of the first part of the book. To worship is to recognize that to be God's companion is to be a party to an unequal relationship. God is sovereign and self-sufficient yet also constantly seeking relationship and unceasingly merciful. I have no theory of worship detachable from the conduct of the various practices described in this book. Thus the first part of the book establishes the sovereignty of God and the sufficiency and abundance of his gifts. Scripture signals the way God has given everything needed in the past; kingdom denotes how God will give everything needed in the future; Holy Spirit names the ways God brings his saving past and transforming future into a present characterized by memory and hope.

To Be His Friends

The first part of the book displays the claim that God seeks to be in relationship with his people. The second part of the book specifies the kind of relationship in question: God calls his people to be his friends. The name for those seeking to respond to Jesus' invitation to friendship with God is the Church.

Whereas the emphasis of Part One is on the abundance of God, the emphasis of Part Two is on the sufficiency of his gifts to his people. The governing practice in this section is Baptism. The practices of formation – evangelism and catechesis – are given their orientation by their relation to Baptism. The practices of Baptism – stripping, washing and clothing – display the full dimensions of what God gives the Church through embodying his life in human community. The diverse but not exhaustive pattern of practices that follows all arise from the gift of Baptism. And the recognition

of the fragility of the Church and of the need for forgiveness and reconciliation is nothing but a reassertion of the abiding necessity of renewing the
gifts given in Baptism.

A recurring anxiety is that the Church is not what I claim it to be – the
primary way in which God pursues his purposes and makes himself known
today. To many the Church is mired in sin, complicit in evil, shamed by its
silence on injustice, and exposed as a clumsy, flawed, all-too-human failure
to embody the gracious Gospel of Christ: in short, an earthen vessel. I
nonetheless maintain it contains treasure; and that there is no alternative.
Whether in embarrassment or in exasperation, many writing in Christian
ethics have chosen to make the Church almost invisible in their work: as if
Jesus calls us directly o'er the tumult without the response of people over
2,000 years counting for much one way or the other. I center my account of
Christian ethics on the Church because the Church is, despite all its limitations, nonetheless the place where all the practices that are the abundant
gifts of God are still performed; because bypassing the Church leads only to
some Gnostic fantasy of discipleship without sin; and because in belonging
to several ordinary churches in a variety of unremarkable localities, I have
experienced the kinds of Christians and transformations I describe in this
book. But most of all, I wish to set aside widespread misgivings about the
Church, misgivings that invariably inhibit a display of God's gifts, and, having
done so, to offer an uninhibited account of how the saving mercy of God
inhabits the practices of the Church and shapes the Church's understanding
of every pressing issue that it may encounter.

To Eat with Him

God seeks to be in relationship with his people (Part One), and that relationship is one of friendship (Part Two): and the nature of that friendship is
fundamentally companionship – the friendship of those who break bread
together. That is the theme of Part Three.

Around ten years ago I had been presiding at a service in another part
of the city and arrived at my own church at the point when my colleague
was breaking the bread. I took a seat at the back and watched. For the next
15 minutes a whole pattern of practices and activities took place. People
received communion; some went to a side chapel to receive prayer and the
laying-on of hands; a music group stood up and led some reflective singing;
individuals comforted one another in grief or studied the day's readings for
further wisdom. Yet no one during this time gave any word of instruction
or explanation. It was one of the most beautiful things I have ever seen:

perhaps 150 ordinary people in a working-class community, so schooled and shaped by liturgy that it had become second nature, almost entranced in a seamless flow of offering and receiving love and mercy. I realized that this was the Church's politics: this was an embodiment of everything I was searching for in Christian ethics: humanity at peace with God, sharing the gift of peace; not just talking about eternal life, but living it.

So the five chapters of Part Three outline this renewed politics: they display how the practices of the Eucharist transform society. They describe and prescribe how the Eucharist shapes the character of worshipers so that, like those people I saw for the first time "from behind," they learn to take the right things for granted. Some gifts are received in coming before God and one another; others in hearing God's word; others again in responding to that word. Some are distinctively embodied in the sharing of food; others in being sent out; others pervade the whole.

Is this shape of worship shared by all Christians, or at least by all who may have any interest in Christian ethics? I believe it is. Of course different congregations and different denominations tend to do things in a different sequence. Does every congregation sing the Psalms? Does every congregation say the Creed? Does every congregation wash feet? Clearly not. But more significantly, does every congregation acknowledge the gift of the Psalms, the significance of the Creeds, the dominical institution of foot-washing? This is a better question, one that leads to the kinds of conversations this book wishes to encourage. Such conversations are not about whether it is better to be Anglican or Anabaptist, Catholic or Calvinist, guitar-carrying or eastward-facing, robed or strobed, mission-shaped or antiquarian. They are about what practices embody the Gospel of Christ, how they may be performed faithfully, and what kind of people are shaped by such a life. They are about a constant to and fro between the embodiment of the Gospel after the greeting and the embodiment of the liturgy after the dismissal – about how worship makes disciples faithful and about how faithful disciples renew worship. And, just as I have said about ethics in general, so I say about the Eucharist: if God has given his Church such myriad of gifts for the shaping of its life and for enriching every aspect of its faithful response to him, why would any congregation neglect to receive and use any of those gifts? And if that congregation's experience was one of scarcity, of the impoverishment of faith and the apparent distance of God – and yet they were ignoring these life-giving gifts – whose fault would that be?

The reader eager to get into the heart of the book may wish to start at Part Three. Indeed, the reader could start at almost any point – the book is designed to be circular, rather than linear, in its argument. Just as God continually sends out and draws to himself, and just as the Eucharist is a continuous cycle of being sent and being invited, so this book is intended to be a constant interweaving of display and challenge, enticing to inspire and dismissing to embody. For Christian ethics finally depends for its quality not on well-chosen words, but on holy lives, on faithful communities, and on the abundance of God's grace. And it will not rest until all God's people, from every tribe and denomination, eat with him as his table companions.

How to Read this Book

This is a book to be read with imagination and in community. Imagination and community, as I have noted, are the chief forms abundance takes. But I have also a specific sense in mind.

By "imagination" I mean this book should be read alongside my earlier *Improvisation: The Drama of Christian Ethics* (Wells 2004). There I laid out a number of practices from theatrical improvization that might form the discipline of Christian ethics and the practice of the Church today. *God's Companions* arises out of the first of these, "forming habits," since it is chiefly concerned with how Christians learn to take the right things for granted. The second discussion concerned "status," and in *God's Companions* this reappears in locating ethics principally in the local church and in the prominence given to practices such as footwashing. The third major proposal was that of "overaccepting," and this practice appears everywhere in *God's Companions*. The treatment of Scripture, Baptism and reconciliation assumes that God is constantly fitting the smaller story of human sin and striving into the larger story of grace. The treatment of witness assumes everything in *Improvisation* about the way the Church can neither actively block nor passively accept the "offers" that it receives from society. The liturgical discussion assumes that in the Eucharist God in Christ takes the "loaves and fishes," or "water" of human life and transforms it into the abundant food or "wine" of eternal life. Likewise the fourth proposal, "reincorporation," is also everywhere in *God's Companions*. It is the constant assumption of my treatment of the kingdom that God uses the discarded parts of the world's narrative to provide resolution of the world's story. This appears not only in the chapter "Forever" but constantly in relation to the hearing of God's word in Scripture and in the reassembling of the nations at the Eucharistic table. Reincorporation and overaccepting are both fundamentally ways of understanding how God gives us everything we need in the face of scarcity. If I do not repeatedly interrupt the discussion to highlight these connections it is perhaps because I seek to induce the reader to take the right things for granted before gently acknowledging that these assumptions are not widely held.

By "community" I mean this book should be read alongside *The Blackwell Companion to Christian Ethics*, which I edited with Stanley Hauerwas (Hauerwas and Wells 2004). In some ways this book is a companion to the *Companion*. This is so in three senses. First, the *Companion* is a much longer book, enabling much more detailed treatment of a host of ethical "issues" and concerns. While I have touched on a wide range of such issues in *God's Companions*, I have not tried to be in any way comprehensive or sufficient in addressing such complex themes. The *Companion* does a much better job here. Second, while I believe that on the night before he died, Jesus instituted a pattern of practices that gave his disciples everything they needed to follow him, I appreciate that more needs to be said about how worship connects with other practices of the Church and what this understanding of abundance means theologically. This is exactly what *God's Companions* seeks to address. Third, a book called *God's Companions* should not really be a single-author work. In the cascade of stories that follow I describe those with whom I have shared bread in the power of the Spirit; in the *Companion* one may find many with whose conceptual company I have found inspiration and common cause. Together we seek to make the world a Eucharist.

Part One

THE BODY OF CHRIST
AS JESUS

Chapter One

YESTERDAY

God has given his people everything they need to worship him, to be his friends, and to eat with him. He has done this by giving them the body of Christ. He gives his people the body of Christ in three forms – Jesus, the Church, and the Eucharist. In each case he gives his people more than enough. He overwhelms them by the abundance of his gifts. His people may respond in three ways. They may turn away from his good gifts, and strive to make a life on their own resources. This is the perversity of sin. They may find that their imaginations cannot stretch to the enormity of grace and, fearing that they might drown in the overflowing gifts of God, they reduce God to a manageable size and deal only with the gifts they can comprehend. This is ignorance, the poverty of moral imagination. Or they can open heart and mind, body and soul to discovering and receiving these teeming gifts, and shape their lives and the lives of their communities according to the practice of embodying the abundant gifts of God. This is what it means to be transformed by Jesus, molded by the Church, and sustained by the Eucharist. This is what it means to be God's companions.

The first three chapters consider the gifts God gives his people in Jesus. Jesus is God giving his people everything they need yesterday, today and forever. Later we shall look at the gift of hope, in addressing what Jesus gives forever, and presence, in addressing what Jesus brings today. But first we consider memory – what Jesus offers yesterday.

The key to the memory of God's people is Scripture. Scripture defines what God's people mean by memory. Scripture shows how God's character and purpose are revealed through his relationship with his people. Although he is the creator God who can transcend all known laws of probability, he yearns to share the destiny of his creation with his beloved companions. Scripture thus not only identifies God: it identifies God's people. As God's people look back through the pages of Scripture, they rediscover how awesome was the destiny God had for them. They realize how central to that destiny are the Jews. They perceive how liberation (exodus) and discipline (law) are interdependent and mutually enriching – how the creating and redeeming and covenant-keeping God gives his people everything they need. They acknowledge that in every generation many – perhaps most – were reluctant to receive God's gifts or unable to perceive the treasures they had been offered. These failures frequently reveal as much as the moments of faithfulness. Yet there are regular signposts of constancy – commandments, ark, land, temple, perhaps king – that inspire faith and hope that companionship with God by a whole people is possible. Even in the horror of exile God's transforming purpose is not obscured. And in Jesus, the purposes of God meet the longings of Israel. His life displayed the character of God for all to see, his death and resurrection broke through the barriers of death, sin, and ignorance that still separated God and his people. Jesus repeated the pattern of Israel's prophetic, priestly, and kingly ministry. Likewise the Church repeated the pattern of diaspora and discovery following the empowering commission of Olivet and Pentecost.

Jesus as the Superabundance of God

I shall now explore three passages from John's Gospel. All three are stories about how God gives his people everything – indeed, far too much – to worship him, be his friends, and eat with him. They are stories about true and false worship, the friendship with one another made possible by the companionship of God, and the bread and wine fellowship realized in the nourishment of the Eucharist. They are stories of the three central elements considered in this book: wine, water, and bread.

Too much wine

John's prologue offers itself as a new creation story; "in the beginning" (John 1.1). The calling of the first disciples presents itself as a new presentation of the first "week." John was baptizing (1.28). The "next day" (1.29) he baptizes Jesus. The "next day again" (1.35) his disciples follow Jesus. The "next day" (1.43) Jesus decides to go to Galilee. Finally "on the third day" there is a wedding in Cana of Galilee (2.1).

And at the climax of this first momentous week comes a story that describes salvation history and demonstrates how Jesus fulfills God's purposes in creating the world and calling Israel. The story comes in four stages.

There is good wine. The wine runs short. The wine runs out. Then, stretching the imagination of the steward and the disciples, there is magnificent, abundant wine. Likewise the scriptural story comes in four stages. There is good wine. The creation is good; Israel knows peace with its God. The wine runs short. The creation is bent by sin; Israel strays from God's ways. The wine runs out. Israel is in exile: she has lost land, king, ark, temple. Even after Judah returns from Babylon she has no possession of the land, no king, a temple but no ark. And yet here is Jesus, on the third day, offering better wine than ever. Not restoration – resurrection.

If Cana is the story of Israel, it is the story of Jesus too. There is good wine. He begins his ministry in popularity and with faithful disciples. The wine runs short. He begins to face hostility. The Judean authorities turn decisively against him. His disciples begin to fragment. The wine runs out. He is betrayed, tried, and persecuted. He goes to the cross. And yet, on the third day, the wine is better than ever. Creation is restored and transformed by grace.

This is not a story of the transformation of poison into safe water. It is not a story of a world deformed by sin being converted into a clean and healthy community. It is not a story of the obliteration or extermination of evil by a divine cleanser. It is a story of the inadequacy of fallen creation and the inadequacy of Israel (the six ritual water jars) being transformed by the generosity of God. It is a story of a good creation, become subject to the economy of scarcity, having no resources to help itself, being brought under the economy of abundant grace. It is a story of enough becoming not enough becoming too much. It is a parable of the person and work of Christ. This is the story of the Gospel: God in Christ overwhelms his despondent people by giving them far more than they need.

Too much water

For Jews of Jesus' time, one number epitomized completeness, and that was the number seven. God made the world in seven days. Jacob served seven years for Rachel. Pharaoh's dream had seven fat and seven thin cows. The traditional menorah candlestick had seven lights. Joshua marched around Jericho seven times on the seventh day – and so on, endlessly. Seven was the complete number. Six was just that painful little bit short of seven, as the Cana story exemplifies.

The story of the Samaritan woman (John 4) is a story of a woman who has had five husbands, and is currently living with a man who is not her husband. That makes six. Samaritans and Jews had hated each other for centuries. Samaria was full of all kinds of ethnic groups with their numerous religious cults. It had been since the eighth century, when the Assyrians invaded the northern kingdom of Israel. Over time the Samaritans developed an uneven but bitter contest with the Jews. The Samaritans worshiped God on Mount Gerizim. The Jews insisted that the center of their faith was the Temple in Jerusalem, 50 miles to the south. In 2 Kings 17 there is an account of the Assyrian invasion. It lists five kinds of foreign peoples who worshiped idols in Samaria. Now the story starts to make sense. We can see the Samaritan woman's five husbands as representing the five false gods the Samaritans had worshiped.

And who is the sixth husband, the one to whom the woman is not married? Josephus tells us that Herod the Great turned the capital of Samaria into a Roman city called Sebaste. Sebaste was the Greek name for the Emperor Augustus. Herod filled Sebaste with 6,000 colonial settlers. But Josephus makes an interesting observation. He notes that the Samaritans did not intermarry with the settlers in the way they had under the Assyrians. Hence Jesus' words "and the one you have now is not your husband." So this woman represents the Samaritan people. Jesus is pointing out that the Samaritans are historically and spiritually devoted to five false gods, and now, politically, subjected to Roman power. These are the six husbands (Stibbe 1993, 62–70; Howard-Brook 1994, 101–15).

And at this point we realize that Jesus and the Samaritan woman are enacting a courtship ritual. It is a ritual that is rooted in the foundational stories of Isaac, Jacob and Moses. The point of the courtship scene is quite simple. Jesus is the Samaritan woman's seventh husband. Assyria could not save her; neither could Rome. But Jesus can, and does. He is the completeness, the resolution, the fulfillment of her and her people's restless searching. He is the answer to their unquenchable thirst.

And that brings us to the water. The story starts with a woman who has a bucket, yet no water, and Jesus, who has no bucket, yet is never thirsty. From here develops a conversation that shows exactly who Jesus is and why he is her savior and the savior of the world. The important thing to understand is the nuance of the language. When the woman talks about the well she refers to it as a cistern, containing still, maybe stagnant water. When *Jesus* talks about water he is talking about a gushing, overflowing fountain of life, a bursting geyser shooting up to the skies. The passage that lies behind this interchange is Jeremiah 2.5,13:

> Thus says the Lord: "What wrong did your ancestors find in me that they went far from me, and went after worthless things, and became worthless themselves? . . . My people have committed two evils: they have forsaken me,

the fountain of living water, and dug out cisterns for themselves, cracked cisterns that can hold no water."

The woman has two problems. The first is that the water she is drawing is not very good water. The second is that however much she draws, she remains thirsty. It is just like her situation with her husbands. Her five husbands have not nourished her, and her sixth still leaves her thirsty. Jesus is saying the Samaritans' worship of false gods has been like a stagnant cistern, poisonous and debilitating to their life. And meanwhile their subjection to Rome is leaving them perpetually thirsty, unable to break out of the cycle of hand-to-mouth dependence that occupies their whole existence. Like the woman, they are humiliated on a daily basis. But here is Jesus, in the desert of desire, offering water that never runs out and completeness that quenches all thirst. Jesus is the seventh husband who delivers Samaria from the false worship of Assyria – the five husbands – and political subjection to the sixth husband, Rome. He brings a fountain of living water that exposes the squalor of idolatry and breaks the daily dependence on the oppressor. This is a story about the religious and political transformation all people can find in Christ.

So if neither Assyria nor Rome can save the Samaritans, who can? Jesus and the woman now get into a conversation about correct worship. Jesus makes it clear that anyone who wants to worship God has to reckon with the Jews. But worship will finally transcend the Jews, and be about spirit and truth – God alone. Immediately the woman leaves her water jar. That water jar is the symbol of her daily economic subjection to fetching water for survival, the social humiliation of having to do so in the heat of the noonday, because her life had made her an outcast. She leaves it behind, because now she has found *living* water, and she will never be thirsty again. Then straightaway she becomes an evangelist. She uses the key words that in John 1 brought the first disciples to faith: "Come and see." And through her testimony many people from the city believe in Jesus. And astonishingly, Jesus, the loyal Jew, is invited to stay with the Samaritans for two days. That means he must eat with them – which, it was suggested at the beginning of the story, he would never do. The enmity between Jew and Samaritan is over. The dividing wall of hostility has come tumbling down, and is replaced by communion. A story that begins in scarcity – religious, political, economic, social – ends in the abundance of grace found in Christ. Christ brings too much water – a geyser not a cistern. He brings unimaginable resources of food and a harvest that is always now. This is everything God's people need to worship him, to resolve their divisions and be his friends, and to eat with him. Which is exactly what the Samaritans do.

Too much bread

John 6 provides a third portrayal of the way God in Jesus gives his people more than everything they need. Like John 2 and John 4, the narrative concerns material, in this case bread, that is the stuff of ordinary life and at the heart of the Church's subsequent sacramental life. Like the previous stories, this is a display of the relationship of Jesus to Israel, of the transformation Jesus brings, and of the discipleship this transformation entails. In other words, it is a narrative through which God gives the Church everything it needs to know, and the central thing it needs to know is that God has given it too much.

The story begins with a reference to the sea, the mountain, and the Passover. There is no doubt this is going to be a story about Moses, and about how Jesus is going to liberate Israel. One may suppose that the five barley loaves represent the five books of the Pentateuch, the books of Moses. Perhaps the two fish, symbols of Jesus through the acrostic *ichthus*, represent the humanity and divinity of Christ. This is a story about what happens when the tradition of Moses is transformed by the glory of Christ. Jesus takes, gives thanks, and shares: eucharistic actions that embody appropriate ways for disciples to engage with the "too much" that Jesus offers. Stretching the disciples' and the people's imaginations, Jesus gives the people as much as they want: everything they need. The disciples gather up the food so nothing is wasted: thus they imitate the children of Israel gathering the manna in the wilderness. There are 12 baskets left over. In other words, Jesus fulfills the needs of the 12 tribes of Israel, but also the needs of the teeming mass of humanity from the borderlands of Israel, who may or may not be Jews, but are evidently God's people and look to him as their savior. And yet he will not let them make him king: he returns to the mountain, the place of Moses, the liberator, the lawgiver. He has greater things in store.

This story makes more explicit than the stories of wine and of water what being a disciple entails. It means first of all imitating Jesus in the way he handles the overwhelming gift in his hands. Disciples are to take, give thanks, and share. They do this as they relate to Jesus and as they engage with all the gifts God gives them through him. But second it also means recognizing the different roles played by Jesus and his disciples in the economy of salvation. The disciples begin the story in an economy of scarcity: "Six months' wages would not buy enough bread for each of them to get a little" says Philip (6.7). But Andrew, undaunted, nonetheless brings to Jesus the resources he can find. In the hands of Jesus, these turn out to be more than enough. Jesus does what only Jesus can do. (How much burnout results from disciples trying to do themselves what only Jesus can do?) Then, in distributing the food and in carrying out his instruction to "gather up the fragments left over, so that nothing may be lost" (6.12), the disciples discover the wonder of what Jesus has done. They discover both the "everything" (the satisfied crowd) and the "too much" (the baskets left over) that constitute the salvation brought by Jesus.

Together these three stories epitomize what God gives the Church through the gift of Scripture. God has given his people a heritage that identifies key moments of revelatory presence and action. He has given a cloud of witnesses who have been loved and encountered by God. It offers a tradition that focuses attention on Israel, "for salvation is from the Jews" (John 4.22). It is a legacy of liberation and law, of worship and wonder, of exodus and exile, of faithfulness and folly, of spirit and truth. But Scripture also discloses the gift of Jesus. Jesus identifies with the "water" of Israel's story, brings the story to its turning point, and bursts forth with abundant, glorious, life-giving wine. He reaches across ancient enmities and racial and gender boundaries and offers the Samaritan woman a fountain of living water, bringing her people spiritual, economic, social and political liberation. He reaches into the hinterland beyond the sea, a murky mixture of Jewish and Gentile need and yearning, and brings a transforming meal that offers the new community of Jew and Gentile a picture of who he is, the salvation he brings, and how they can respond to it.

These are among the abundant gifts God gives his people in the gift of Scripture: and these are just three stories.

Sin as Scarcity

The perversity of sin and the abundance of grace

The Gospels portray Jesus as the one who brings the overwhelming grace of God into the intimate companionship of human life. His person and work, his word and deed, the questions he asks and the challenge he presents, the commands he makes and the pleas he answers, the stories he tells and the sacrifice he makes – all are too much for the people he meets. And the abundance of God lays bare the scarcity of sin.

Jesus' presence reveals two kinds of failure amongst those around him. On the one hand are those who *cannot comprehend* the world into which he is inviting them. The disciples, endlessly, fail the test of imagination. Jesus feeds the 5,000 (Mark 6.42) but the disciples are clueless when the 4,000 find themselves hungry (Mark 8.4). The disciples stop the little children coming to Jesus (Mark 10.13), even though he has already alerted them to the way children are parables of his presence (Mark 9.37). James and John assume that places of honor in glory are theirs for the taking (Mark 10.37), even though Jesus has already said the one who wants to be first must be last and servant of all (Mark 9.35). All the disciples flee at the first hint of danger (Mark 14.50), even though Jesus has three times predicted his passion (Mark 8.31, 9.31, 10.33). What Jesus presents is simply too much for the disciples' imagination.

On the other hand, there are those who *set their face against* the gifts that Jesus brings. This is not a failure of the imagination – ignorance. It is deliberate perversity – sin. After Jesus heals the man with a withered hand on the Sabbath, "the Pharisees went out and immediately conspired with the Herodians against him, how to destroy him" (Mark 3.6). The anointing at Bethany (Mark 14.3–9) becomes the defining moment. The nameless woman has the imagination to perceive the extent of Jesus' abundant giving. She knows it is very costly (Mark 14.3); it is poured out (Mark 14.3); it is beautiful (Mark 14.6); it is apparently wasted (Mark 14.4); it leaves the poor apparently no better off (Mark 14.5); it is on the brink of death (Mark 14.8); it has global significance (Mark 14.9). Those present meanwhile are living in an economy of scarcity, and angrily ask why the "true value" of the nard (300 denarii) could not have been realized for the benefit of the poor. And this becomes the point of contrast: for immediately before this scene the chief priests and scribes were looking for a way to arrest Jesus (Mark 14.1); while immediately after this scene Judas went to the chief priests to betray Jesus – ironically, for money.

A miniature version of this scene is played out in the story of the widow's mite (Mark 12.42). Here is a stark yet ironic contrast between the economy of abundance and the economy of scarcity. The widow profoundly believes in the purpose of the temple, and places "everything she had, all she had to live on" (Mark 12.44) into the treasury. She is living out the generosity of God. Meanwhile the rich people "contributed out of their abundance" (Mark 12.44). Yet their comparatively modest contributions enact the economy of scarcity. It is she, not they, who reflects the superabundance of grace. The irony appears in that Jesus has just denounced the meanness of the scribes, particularly toward widows (Mark 12.40) and immediately foretells the destruction of the temple (Mark 13.2), the cause for which the widow gave everything.

The perversity of sin is perhaps definitively expressed by the crowd before Pilate. The chief priests' antipathy to Jesus is attributed to jealousy (Mark 15.10). But for the crowd's hostility, there is no explanation. Pilate asks whether the crowd would have him release Jesus; hearing the answer no, he asks what they would have him do to Jesus; hearing the answer to crucify, he asks what evil he has done: "but they shouted all the more, 'Crucify him'." There is no possibility of explaining sin on this scale.

The parable of the sower is a programmatic story of the perversity of sin and the abundance of grace. The seed that fell on the path represents the perversity of sin. It has no chance whatsoever to grow. "Satan immediately comes and takes away the word" (Mark 4.15). The seed sown among rocks and the seed sown among thorns are different kinds of failure of imagination – of the economy of scarcity eclipsing the abundance of grace. "They have no root" (Mark 4.17); "the cares of the world . . . come in and choke the word" (Mark 4.19). Herod, the disciples, and the rich man who wanted to inherit eternal life (Mark 10.17) are all types of this failure of imagination. But the true wonder of the parable is the extraordinary abundance of the harvest from the good soil – "thirty and sixty and a hundredfold" (Mark 4.20): enough to blow away the bonds of oppression and provide food not just for the sower but for everyone (Myers 1988, 177). The type of this soil is blind Bartimaeus, who throws away his cloak, his only means of income, and readily follows Jesus, the provider of all the gifts he now needs (Mark 10.50).

Thus the central question of the Gospels, as for their readers 21 centuries later, is, can anyone receive the superabundant gifts of God embodied in Jesus, or will their imagination prove too small, or will they reject Jesus and strive for their own gifts?

Reading Genesis through Mark

Having discovered sin and its link to scarcity in the Gospels, one can revisit the story of Eden to find what it is really saying about sin. The Garden of Eden is portrayed as the epitome of abundance. Everything about it is more than enough. There is companionship. There is beauty. There is every kind of animal life. There is a vocation, to till the garden and keep it (Genesis 2.15): there is thus a place for humanity in the garden and a role in creation. There is permission to eat freely of every tree in the garden (2.16): there is almost unlimited freedom. There is just one prohibition – not to eat of the tree of the knowledge of good and evil (2.17) (Brueggemann 1982, 46). This prohibition is for humanity's good – the story makes a contrast not between knowledge and ignorance, but between knowledge and trust. The story demonstrates that greater knowledge is damaging if it comes at the expense of unlimited trust.

Then there is a portrayal of two kinds of sin. The first is the sin of the serpent. There is no explanation for the serpent's craftiness. It is simply perversity. The second kind of sin is the woman's lack of imagination (matched by the man's later in the story). The conversation is undertaken as if God were not a companion – the covenantal language of "Lord God" used hitherto is replaced, at the serpent's instigation, by the creation language of "God." Immediately there is confusion: in the absence of awareness of God's guiding and abiding companionship, the woman quickly regards the serpent as an authority figure. Shortly afterwards, there is seduction: it is significant that the serpent never tells or suggests to the woman that she should eat the apple. She makes that choice entirely herself; as does the man (there is no record of her telling him to eat, only of her giving some to him). But most importantly, the result of the woman's lack of imagination is that she suddenly inhabits a land of scarcity. The garden of abundance is still there, as much as ever. But she cannot see it. All she can see is the one thing in the garden that she cannot eat. This is the effect of the serpent's words. They have transformed a world of abundance into an anxiety about scarcity, a companionship of trust into a web of deceit. Before long the imaginations of all God's people were blighted: "every inclination of the thoughts of their hearts was only evil continually" (Genesis 6.5).

God's Companions through Jesus

Jesus' death and resurrection are not "talents" that Christians can put to work in the marketplace of practiced discipleship; they are events that transform reality – moments that no human power alone could achieve. Beyond all others, these are the superabundant gifts God gives the Church through the written text of Scripture. To examine the significance of these gifts I shall turn to Luke's account of the resurrection, and specifically the story of the encounter on the Emmaus road (Luke 24.13–35).

The first meal described in the Bible is the eating of the apple in the Garden of Eden – the meal that crystallizes humanity's estrangement from God. Perhaps the definitive meal in the Old Testament is the Passover, the meal that unites faith in God as the Lord of heaven and earth – who can move the seas – with faith in God as the savior who liberates his people from slavery. The tradition of a meal as the communal commemoration of liberation is picked up elsewhere, particularly in the book of Esther, which is arranged as a series of ten banquets (Fox 1991, 157). The role of the meal as the test of God's people's faith in his abundance and their constant temptation to perceive life in terms of scarcity is epitomized by the story of the manna in the desert (Numbers 11). Eating is so much at the heart of the

Scripture that one can almost say "Christ is a sort of book inscribed on human flesh, and eating the body of Christ is like eating a sort of book" (Loughlin 1996, 244).

Luke's Gospel gives an account of a series of meals in which Jesus transforms alienation into companionship. Levi the tax collector has a banquet for Jesus at which a large crowd of tax collectors and others join them (5.29). Simon the Pharisee hosts a dinner at which a sinful woman washes Jesus' feet with her tears and proceeds to kiss and anoint his feet (7.36). Jesus takes five loaves and two fish, blesses, breaks and gives them, filling the crowd of 5,000 and leaving 12 baskets over (9.16). A Pharisee invites Jesus to dinner and then is amazed that Jesus did not wash before the meal (11.37). Jesus is going to the house of a leader of the Pharisees to eat a meal on the Sabbath when he meets and heals a man with dropsy (14.1). Jesus meets Zacchaeus in Jericho and tells him to come down from the sycamore tree, because Jesus will eat at his house that day; whereupon Zacchaeus begins a radical program of welfare and restoration (19.8). Here are six meals. They invariably begin in scarcity – the economy of farmed taxation, the hunger of the crowd, the Pharisaic obsession with ritual details, the experience of impurity and debilitating illness. They become occasions of abundance – the filled crowd and baskets of leftovers, the new life for the sick man, the limitless forgiveness toward the sinful woman, the new-found bounty of Zacchaeus. These meals are a paradigm of the Gospel, epitomized by Jesus' words in celebration of the sixth story, "Today salvation has come to this house" (19.9).

The seventh meal is the Last Supper (22.14). It looks forward to the fulfillment of all Passovers, of all meals, in the kingdom of God (22.16). The Last Supper is surrounded by scarcity. There is scarcity of trust (22.21 – as in Eden, the meal is the moment of betrayal), of understanding (22.24 – the squabble over which disciple was the greatest), of faithfulness (22.34 – the prediction of Peter's denial), and of wakefulness (22.45). All around is "the power of darkness" (22.53).

And the eighth meal, on the first day of the week, is at Emmaus. Here is a host of Eucharistic elements. There is a gathering ("Jesus came near," 24.15). There is a recalling of the sacred story ("a prophet mighty in deed and word . . . condemned to death . . . but we had hoped . . . some women astounded us . . . angels said that he was alive . . .," 24.18–24). There is a reinterpretation and opening of the Scriptures, during which the disciples' hearts were burning within them (24. 25–7, 32). There is the fourfold action of taking, blessing, breaking, and giving bread (24.30). There is a moment of revelation, of eyes being opened (24.31). And there is a departure with renewed mission and good news to share (24.33). This is a restoration of companionship lost in Eden, and lost again after the Last Supper. It is a story of how God gives Cleopas and his companion everything they need to worship him, to be (restored as) his friends, and to eat with him.

The transformation comes as Jesus shows the disheartened disciples that what they took to be scarcity (their loss of Jesus) was in fact glorious abundance – the "necessity" (24.26) of the Messiah's suffering and the fulfillment of prophecies stretching back to Moses (24.27), and the corresponding "necessity" of the Messiah's death and resurrection (prefigured in 9.22). The definitive experience of scarcity had been exile – hence the significance of the hope that "he was the one to redeem Israel" (24.21). And as the series of meals throughout Luke's Gospel demonstrates, he does see himself as the one to redeem Israel: he redeems Israel not through political restoration but by gathering those whose lives epitomize exile, taking on the groaning of creation and exile on the cross, bringing about a new creation in his resurrection, and, beyond the ascension, by sending them out to witness to him "in Jerusalem, in all Judea and Samaria, and to the ends of the earth" (Acts 1.8).

The Emmaus road story affirms that in the Old Testament God gives the Church everything it needs to understand the significance of Jesus' life, death, and resurrection. Jesus fulfills the yearnings of Israel. All the promises of the Hebrew scriptures find their yes in him. The story affirms also that in his death Jesus has more than amply faced the "necessity" of fulfilling whatever it was – epitomized by exile – that was lacking in the relationship between God and his people, whatever inhibited their full companionship. In this sense Jesus' way to the cross becomes the definitive pattern of how Christians are to address every issue that jeopardizes God's full companionship with his people. The story finally affirms that in his resurrection Jesus once again – more than ever – shares companionship with his people. This companionship is expressed definitively in eating together. At this resurrection meal disciples rediscover that in Jesus, God has given them everything they need to follow him, and that following him means to worship, to be his friends, and to eat with him.

Chapter Two

FOREVER

If Scripture names God's people's heritage, kingdom names their destiny. The purpose of this chapter is to show that in the gift of the coming kingdom and in the promissory note of its contemporary signs, God gives his people everything they need to follow him forever; and that the destiny of God's people is to worship him, be his friends, and eat with him.

The following passage demonstrates the way the themes of this chapter echo and build on the shape of the first chapter.

> I pray that the God of our Lord Jesus Christ, the Father of glory, may give you a spirit of wisdom and revelation as you come to know him, so that, with the eyes of your heart enlightened, you may know what is the hope to which he has called you, what are the riches of his glorious inheritance among the saints, and what is the immeasurable greatness of his power for us who believe, according to the working of his great power. God put this power to work in Christ when he raised him from the dead and seated him at his right hand in the heavenly places, far above all rule and authority and power and dominion, and above every name that is named, not only in this age but also in the age to come. And he has put all things under his feet and has made him the head over all things for the church, which is his body, the fullness of him who fills all in all.
>
> (Ephesians 1.17–23)

This prayer shows that the Trinitarian God gives his people vital gifts. Prominent among these gifts is that of imagination ("wisdom and revelation") that grows over time. This is not simply a cognitive or intellectual gift ("with the eyes of your heart enlightened"). It focuses on a promise of what God has in store ("the hope to which he has called you"). It is an abundant, indeed a superabundant gift ("the riches of his glorious inheritance . . ., the immeasurable greatness of his power . . ."). It is not simply a given, but depends on election and faith ("to which he has called you . . . for us who believe"). It is focused on and through Christ, definitively on his death and resurrection ("God put this power to work in Christ when he raised him from the dead"). Yet it is channeled through the Church, the body of Christ ("the fullness of him who fills all in all"). One of the recurrent words in the Pauline epistles is "all" (it occurs over 250 times). In the first chapter of Ephesians this "all" is prominent, combining the "all" that is the fullness of God with the "all" that is the completeness of his revelation in Christ and the "all" that is his eschatological purpose.

Thus this passage shows that the moral imagination is crucial, that it is a corporate, shared gift, and that it is an embodied, enacted pattern of construing reality. It is always a gift to the "saints," not to an individual detached from the body. It is always about a reality that is breaking in, and is therefore a hopeful quality. But it is always also about the way human interaction reflects and rehearses the prior activity of God, and is thus not just a cognitive process.

A second, closely related, passage sets out the shape of this chapter.

> With all wisdom and insight he has made known to us the mystery of his will, according to his good pleasure that he set forth in Christ, as a plan for the fullness of time, to gather up all things in him, things in heaven and things on earth. In Christ we have also obtained an inheritance, having been destined according to the purpose of him who accomplishes all things according to his counsel and will, so that we, who were the first to set our hope on Christ, might live for the praise of his glory.
>
> (Ephesians 1.8b-12)

The two sentences of this passage distinguish two aspects of the gifts God gives his people in the gift of the kingdom. Thus the first half of this chapter concerns the *coming* of the kingdom ("the mystery of his will . . . to gather up all things in him"). The second half of this chapter concerns the *life* of the kingdom ("we have also obtained an inheritance . . . so that we . . . might live for the praise of his glory"). In other words, God gives his people everything they need ("he gathers up all things in him") so that they might live for and with him ("live for the praise of his glory").

The Coming of the Kingdom

The coming of the kingdom is fundamentally the setting right of the two dimensions of estrangement from God. These two dimensions, perversity and lack of imagination (more commonly described as sin and ignorance), are prominent in the narrative of the Fall, as we saw in Chapter One. They are definitively identified and addressed in the life, death, and resurrection of Christ. The sower parable identifies them as distinct destroyers or inhibitors of discipleship. Other parables tease listeners to expand their imagination (the mustard seed, the laborers in the vineyard) or demonstrate the perversity of avoiding God's gifts (the rich man and Lazarus, the prodigal's brother). Likewise Jesus' miracles portray and embody the coming of the kingdom, but evoke both kinds of alienation in response. Jesus' passion is consistently hastened through the perversity of the Judean authorities and compounded by the lack of imagination of his followers. And yet his resurrection finally overwhelms the forces that put him to death and demands a transformed imagination to take in the new reality his kingdom brings.

Thus there are two aspects to the coming of the kingdom: the overcoming of sin and the fulfillment of potential.

The overcoming of sin

The key gifts of God in the defeat of sin are the dismantling of the powers of oppression and the vindication of the oppressed. The story of Legion (Luke 8.26–39) demonstrates the significance of these two dimensions of the defeat of sin.

A man lives in dire straits; naked, among the dead. When he breaks the shackles it leads to worse torment from the demon. He recognizes Jesus, but sees him as a threat. Jesus, curiously, asks him his name. His name is Legion. This name is the key to the story. Why are there so many pigs, when Jews would have no use for pigs? Why are they described as a "herd" (or "band"), when pigs don't move in herds? These are baffling questions in the story as it stands. But when the simple meaning of Legion is allowed to dictate the shape of the story, all becomes clear. This is a story about Rome. Roman legions possessed Israel. Israel lived in internal exile – "he did not live in a house" (v. 27). Pigs had one purpose only – to feed the bands of Roman recruits. Exegesis obsessed by Jewish custom or eschatological expectation or charismatic gifts or psychological states may miss the highly political significance of what the Gospel writer is recording. This is a coded identification of Jesus the liberator.

And it retells the story of Jesus' ministry. He arrives at the "far country" – far from his heavenly home. As he begins his ministry ("steps out on land") he meets with conflict straightaway. Those who confront him are exiles from their true home. They find themselves unclean – defiled by death, as Israel is defiled by Gentile rule. And these people have an impossible choice before them, daily. Confront Rome, and find that either their shackles be fastened more tightly or they be "driven into the wilds" into a new diaspora; or allow the Romans to possess them, and lose their identity. Jesus faces the question of identity head on: "What is your name?" The man has lost his identity: he says "My name is Rome."

Drastic action is needed. Jesus delivers the people. The transformation is terrifying: less fascinated by the sane and clothed state of the man, the people are horrified by the costs and consequences of the salvation Jesus brings. Their imagination falls far short of being able to encompass the kingdom Jesus brings. They cannot imagine living without pigs. They ask Jesus to leave. The last scene of the story anticipates the last scene of the Gospel: just as later the disciples are "continually in the Temple, blessing God," so here the former demoniac proclaims throughout the city how much Jesus has done for him. Oppression is over: the new life of the kingdom has begun.

Gerasa is significant because while its customs, adventures, and challenges vary from Jesus' heartland, its real significance is as a portrayal of what is taking place at home. Before arriving, Jesus calms a storm, thereby allaying fears that the land of the Gentiles is a land of deathly abomination. When he returns from Gerasa, he heals two women whose place in the unity of Israel (the number 12 is repeated) is blocked by the impurity of blood and death. Now, on the other side of the lake, a great drama is played out that mirrors and parodies and mimics the drama being played out in Israel. I have pointed out the similarities. But there is one key difference. On the far side of the lake, in Gerasa, many die so that one man can be saved. On this side of the lake, in Jerusalem, it is the other way round: one man is to die so that many can be saved. Whether salvation comes in the casting out of evil, as in Gerasa, or in Jesus taking the evil onto himself and himself being cast out of the city on a defiled cross, as in Jerusalem, the point is the same: the kingdom means God in Christ defeating oppression.

What this means is that it is in the context of greatest scarcity that God's people expect God to be revealed in his greatest abundance. The most ghastly, the most heinous, the most unwarranted moment of oppression in history – the crucifixion of the Son of God – was also the definitive, abiding moment of the presence of God: "Truly this man was God's Son!" (Mark 15.39). The moment of greatest scarcity – "My God, my God, why have you forsaken me?" (Mark 15.34) – was also the moment of deepest fulfillment – "It is finished" (John 19.30). And so God's people experience and enter situations of great oppression and scarcity looking to God not just for "enough," but for abundance: not just for mercy, but for revelation. Like Jesus, they assume that affliction is not simply a result of sin, but an opportunity "that the works of God might be revealed" (John 9.3). They assume that sickness "does not lead to death; rather it is for God's glory, so that the Son of God may be glorified through it" (John 11.4). They pray that, like Stephen, in their time of trial they will "see the heavens opened and the Son of Man standing at the right hand of God!" (Acts 7.56).

Thus the participation of God's people in movements for justice, or initiatives for freeing the oppressed, is rooted in abundance in two senses. On the one hand it is rooted in the abundance of God's kingdom, that the things that matter are things that everyone can have, that freedom for one does not automatically imply oppression for another, that the glory of God is a human being fully alive. On the other hand it is rooted in the abundance of God, that he reveals himself especially to those who need him most, that those who hunger and thirst for righteousness, those who are persecuted for righteousness' sake – the meek, the poor in spirit, the mournful, the peacemakers – are especially blessed. The gift of the kingdom is the gift of the abundance of God in the context of human scarcity.

One local congregation met together in a building just a stone's throw from a large shipyard. The building of ships had dominated the town's life for a century, especially since the closure of the local coalmine. And yet the shipyard seemed in perpetual crisis: the number of local people who had once worked there far exceeded the numbers who still did; shipbuilding was moving to the other side of the world. One day the much-feared news came. Closure loomed. The congregation rallied. Several went to picket the official receivers at the office in the city. Others joined a huge meeting outside the shipyard gates. Others again arranged an act of worship that celebrated the dignity and skill of those who had given their working lives to the yard. Some voices queried whether a new era in which battleships were not needed and men were no longer sent down mines was so much to be mourned. Others doubted what would become of the vibrant community spirit and cohesion of the proud and resilient town. Like Jeremiah, the congregation earnestly sought the welfare of the city, for in its welfare they anticipated finding their welfare. But like Ezekiel, they went into "exile" expecting to find a new revelation of God, and like Isaiah, they realized that this revelation might entail his suffering – and theirs.

The fulfillment of potential

If the overcoming of sin is God's word on perversity, the fulfillment of potential is God's word on lack of imagination. And if God's people have to realize that in the overcoming of sin, a great deal of that sin is their own, then they likewise have to acknowledge that in the fulfillment of potential, a great deal of the kindled imagination in the world lies beyond them.

This is the place to recognize that, while the Church is the body of Christ, the definitive embodiment of God's purposes in Christ, and the incorporation of those who shape their lives in response to the kingdom made possible in Christ, the Church by no means exhausts the kingdom. The failures of the Church have been many. Institutionally it has countless times mistaken an intermediate good – nation, security, race, affluence, influence, gender, "civilization" – for the goodness of God. (Some of these were not goods at all.) Pastorally it has too often misused its power, preferring coercion to persuasion, developing habits of oppression, subjection, and abuse. Personally its officers and members, clergy and people, have proved as fallible and flawed as the original 12 disciples and the foundational 12 tribes. If nothing is impossible for God, it seems likewise no sin is beyond the bounds of possibility for his people.

But the reason the Church does not exhaust the kingdom is not just because of the failures of the Church. More significantly, the life-giving, restoring, reconciling gifts of the kingdom appear like the first flowers of spring, budding all over God's good creation. The gift of imagination is not about the scarcity of the Church but about the abundance of God. The Church does not need to ponder morosely its own shortcomings in order to explain the breadth of the kingdom: the gift of imagination beyond the Church is not because God so resented the Church but because God so loved the world. Awareness of its own failures should increase the Church's humility, but not jaundice its vision so it cannot see the buds and sounds of God's spring elsewhere.

The signs of the kingdom in the world are a constant challenge to the Church to renew its practices and to keep its heart open to receiving new gifts from God. One local congregation lived and worshiped in a notorious neighborhood. The neighborhood became subject to a large-scale government-sponsored community-led regeneration initiative. The congregation looked at the New Testament together. In the Gospels they found a Jesus who was similarly concerned with regeneration – rebirth. He too was a resident of a deprived area: Palestine was a land deprived of self-government, liberty, and justice – and Galilee was second-class in the Palestine of its day. Jesus called a committed group of 12 people to change society from within. Together, they made themselves familiar with the needs and hopes of all the people in the regeneration area (Israel), especially the most needy, and filled their hearts with the hope of redemption. He challenged the people who were making the nation's oppression worse, those who withheld resources from the poor and those who sought their own well-being without regard to God's justice and mercy. He embodied what he propounded, and took opportunities to show people how they could live in the new era that was breaking in (the kingdom). He paused to address particular crises, especially when they had symbolic significance, and when they demonstrated his underlying purpose (miracles), even when doing so seemed to break traditional practice. All this time he was teaching and training his key partners so that they might later be able to follow in his steps. He taught and showed them what it meant to depend utterly on God and prepare for the time of trial. After his ascension the disciples were empowered by his Holy Spirit to do remarkable things like him. They fully used the gifts they had been given, and in the process discovered gifts they never knew they had. Christ gave his followers a Great Commission – to continue his work in his authority. Some while later, they were clothed with the power to carry this commission through.

The local congregation then compared Jesus' example with the practice of those local people most closely involved with the estate regeneration initiative. They too lived in a deprived area. They too became well informed about the perspectives of the entire neighborhood, for example through regular large-participation surveys. They too stayed close to the poorest, challenging those (whether employers, consumers, service providers, or unruly neighbors) whose practice exacerbated the problem. And they too sometimes addressed extreme cases of need rapidly without using a complex instrument of authority. Meanwhile they sought encouragement, training, and formation to grow into the leadership of the neighborhood long after the injection of government funding had passed. They sometimes failed, and the burden of personal failure was the greater for the knowledge that it brought discredit on the regeneration process as a whole. But most of the people involved in the process could look back on their involvement with considerable pride. The lasting benefits of such regeneration would depend on these people, just as the early Church depended on the disciples. The local congregation wondered whether they, or any other church they knew, were truly as close as this to local needs and concerns, and as committed as this to local empowerment.

The congregation then compared the local estate regeneration process with the Acts of the Apostles. They realized that the residents who led the regeneration process were very much like a church in significant ways. There was a commitment to meeting regularly. There was a regular pattern to which these meetings generally conformed. There was a constant retelling of the story by which the development trust came to be formed, and the values and common purpose that underlay it. The initial sense of grievance was gradually displaced by the increasing record of finding solutions through new partnerships. There was a commitment to, and an increasingly formalized process of, the cordial resolution of differences. There was a strong desire to spread the good news, and to include the most marginalized members of the community in the deliberations and results. There was a constant determination to point local residents in the direction of hope. Most impressively, there was an extraordinary ability to tolerate hurt, anger, abuse, and humiliation, to seek to understand, to work beyond, and even to forgive. The congregation realized that in these ways, especially the last, the regeneration initiative would put many, perhaps most, churches to shame (see Wells 2003, 13–14).

In all these ways God's action in the kingdom beyond the Church was a gift to his people. It did not mean he had given up on the Church, as if the Church were Saul and the estate regeneration process were David. It was rather more that the congregation discovered what the disciples had recognized in Acts 15: that God was at work in the world in ways and through people they had never expected. Like Jacob, they realized "Surely the Lord is in this place – and I did not know it!" (Genesis 28.16). Like Jesus, they looked to the unexpected people – the centurion ("Truly I tell you, in no one in Israel have I found such faith": Matthew 8.10) and the Syrophoenician woman (Mark 7.26) and found gifts to build up the faithful.

This second aspect of the coming of the kingdom, the fulfillment of potential, is thus not the sentimentalizing of the world or the passing-over of the Church. It is a recognition that the coming of the kingdom is not just about the defeat of sin. It is about the fostering of the imagination, about the opening-out of the Church to receive superabundant gifts of God from every possible source. It is about seeing every person, event, and context in creation as a potential gift that presages a transformed Church and renewed world. The new heaven and the new earth are not a statement about the irremediable character of the old; they are a promise of the transformation of the abundant gifts of God into a flood of grace, a hope of the fulfillment of the kingdom's signs in the kingdom's arrival, a restoration of all that seemed lost in the old by its resurrection in the new.

The Life of the Kingdom

The life of the kingdom is the glory to which God calls his people and the purpose for which he created the world. This glory, this purpose, is for his people to worship him, to be his friends, and to eat with him. Worship, friendship and table fellowship constitute the plot, character, and setting of God's story. Each embodies the abundance of the kingdom. Table fellowship embodies the superabundance of life in the kingdom. Friendship embodies the superabundance of creation in the kingdom. And worship embodies the superabundance of God in the kingdom. Together, they comprise the hope of God's people.

Perfect service: worship

There are three dimensions to the perception of worship as the life of the kingdom, the experience of the superabundance of God, the embodiment of Christ as all in all.

The first dimension is of the Trinity as being sufficient in itself. There is no question of the Trinity needing the world or of the frailty and contingency of the creation taking anything away from the abundance of God. In the creation narratives (Genesis 1–2) the initiative lies wholly with God. Matthew's double account of the "genesis" of Jesus – his linear creation story of Matthew 1.1–17 and his human creation story of Matthew 1.18–25 – affirms that, in this new creation, crystallized in the virginal conception of Jesus, God is again the principal character. Likewise in the "third creation," the resurrection on the first day of the week, the initiative lies entirely with God. So holy is this moment that, not only is it not explicitly narrated by any of the Gospel writers, but it seems almost that Jesus' human nature had no distinct agency in bringing it about: the emphasis is always that "God raised Jesus from the dead" – never that Jesus raised himself. There is a new man and woman in the garden in John 20, as in Genesis 2: but there is nothing the woman can do to effect the reversal of the fall in the earlier story: she simply has to let go (John 20.17) and let God do it.

The second dimension is that the embodiment of perfect service, of the abundance of God, of freedom in obedience, is Jesus. His relationship with the Father is the epitome of perfect service. This is true in circumstances of scarcity ("Father, if you are willing, remove this cup from me; yet, not my will but yours be done": Luke 22.42) as much as in circumstances of abundance ("Everything that the Father gives me will come to me": John 6.37; "The Father judges no one but has given all judgment to the Son, so that all may honor the Son just as they honor the Father": John 5.22–3; "I do nothing on my own, but I speak these things as the Father instructed me. And the one who sent me is with me; he has not left me alone, for I always do what is pleasing to him": John 8.28–9). Through his abundant presence in the perfect service of Jesus, God achieves everything in his purposes: "For in him all the fullness of God was pleased to dwell, and through him God was pleased to reconcile to himself all things, whether on earth or in heaven, by making peace through the blood of his cross" (Colossians 1.19–20). God's people long for a time of perfect service, because they have seen perfect service in Jesus.

The third dimension is that it is possible, through grace, to embody that perfect service in the worship of God. Mary is perhaps the most striking example: "Here am I, the servant of the Lord; let it be with me according to your word" (Luke 1.38). Paul knows what it means to carry out God's will, and to experience the joy of doing so: "by the grace of God I am what I am, and his grace toward me has not been in vain. On the contrary, I worked harder than any of them – though it was not I, but the grace of God that is with me" (1 Corinthians 15.10). Jesus has no doubt that a life of perfect service is possible: "If you continue in my word, you are truly my disciples; and you will know the truth, and the truth will make you free" (John 8.31–2); although God's continuing grace will always be required:

> Very truly, I tell you, the one who believes in me will also do the works that I do and, in fact, will do greater works than these, because I am going to the Father. I will do whatever you ask in my name, so that the Father may be glorified in the Son. If in my name you ask me for anything, I will do it. If you love me, you will keep my commandments. And I will ask the Father, and he will give you another Advocate, to be with you forever.
>
> (John 14.12–16)

So this is the mystery of worship as perfect service. God has done everything that needs to be done, and requires no assistance or praise; yet in Christ he embodies perfect service as the praise of his glory; thus it is possible for God's people to live lives – eternal lives – of service, made possible by grace not by need, in which obedience is perfect freedom. This is the life to which God's people aspire when they engage in worship. In worship they pray for the full, evident and complete coming of God's reign. They affirm the superabundance of God – more creativity, life, love, compassion, forgiveness, strength, grace than they can possibly imagine or need. They seek to imitate the God-filled service of God embodied in Jesus. And they pursue the gifts of attention and joy, the presence and engagement, the completeness of offering and receiving gifts that can only deepen over eternity. In these ways the perfect service of worship in the kingdom expresses the superabundance of God.

Harmonious relationship: friendship

There are four dimensions to the perception of friendship as the life of the kingdom, the experience of the superabundance of God's gifts, the embodiment of companionship with God.

The first dimension is of the perichoresis of the Trinity, the mutual coinherence and codependence of Father, Son and Holy Spirit. It is not necessary to have an elaborate social understanding of the Trinity, an extensive conception of the inner-trinitarian relationships as a model for society, for the Trinity nonetheless to constitute the beginning of a notion of the life of the kingdom as harmonious relationship. There is no doubt that the relationship of the Father and the Son is intimate: "The Father and I are one . . . The Father is in me and I am in the Father" (John 10.30, 38); "Do you not believe that I am in the Father and the Father is in me? . . . Believe me that I am in the Father and the Father is in me" (John 14.10–11); "a voice from heaven said, 'This is my Son, the Beloved, with whom I am well pleased'" (Matthew 3.17). Likewise the relationships between Father and Spirit and Son and Spirit are similarly close:

> If you love me, you will keep my commandments. And I will ask the Father, and he will give you another Advocate, to be with you forever. This is the Spirit of truth, whom the world cannot receive, because it neither sees him nor knows him. You know him, because he abides with you, and he will be in you.
> (John 14.15–17)

The doctrine of the Trinity is the way God's people understand the self-sufficiency of God – the way God is not just more than enough for them, he is more than enough for himself.

The second dimension of friendship as the life of the kingdom is of the good creation. In the Eden account, the man is given three instructions in relation to the garden. He is to till it and keep it; he is to eat freely of every tree in the garden; but he is not to eat of the tree of the knowledge of good and evil (Genesis 2.15–17). Here is vocation, permission, and prohibition: a kingdom ethic in miniature. Again the account is one of abundance. Harmonious relationship with the creation is a vital dimension of the life of the kingdom. It begins with the abundance of creation in extent and detail and beauty and glory: with its goodness in itself, beyond any instrumental good it might have for humanity or the Church. It develops into the theater of God's glory, the place of encounter between God and his people, the scene of redemption. The abundance of creation is an indicator of all other aspects of friendship, for the majority of creation has no instrumental good to offer God's people: the way they cherish it therefore demonstrates their trust that God gives them more than enough. Jesus' words to his disciples are the definitive affirmation of the non-instrumental good of God's abundant creation and the relationship between friendship with creation and friendship with God:

> Therefore I tell you, do not worry about your life, what you will eat or what you will drink, or about your body, what you will wear. Is not life more than food, and the body more than clothing? Look at the birds of the air; they neither sow nor reap nor gather into barns, and yet your heavenly Father feeds them. Are you not of more value than they? And can any of you by worrying add a single hour to your span of life? And why do you worry about clothing? Consider the lilies of the field, how they grow; they neither toil nor spin, yet I tell you, even Solomon in all his glory was not clothed like one of these. But if God so clothes the grass of the field, which is alive today and tomorrow is thrown into the oven, will he not much more clothe you – you of little faith? Therefore do not worry, saying, "What will we eat?" or "What will we drink?" or "What will we wear?" For it is the Gentiles who strive for all these things; and indeed your heavenly Father knows that you need all these things. But strive first for the kingdom of God and his righteousness, and all these things will be given to you as well.
>
> (Matthew 6.25–33)

The third dimension of friendship as the life of the kingdom is the relationship between diverse strangers. Frances Young describes this dimension vividly in setting her own experience of parenting a child with severe special needs alongside her developing vocation to ministry in a hospital for adults with similar needs.

> It was a sharing of peace and friendship and simplicity, entering a community in which there was a remarkable atmosphere of simple gratitude, a capacity to receive, a delight in little treasures, like photographs, shown off with great pride. A little old lady, deaf and speechless, played peep-bo with a cuddly scarf . . . Another more capable lady . . . pointed to a poster of Our Lady and said "She's my friend." . . . Here were some of the most vulnerable persons in our society, yet each was a self, each had value, and before God we were all equally vulnerable human beings in need of his grace . . .
>
> There is something about the communion of saints, the fellowship of all God's people, transcending space and time, which comes across to me here . . . I feel like I would like to go to the average prosperous congregation and say, ". . . Come and rejoice . . . You'll find a lot of noise and unpredictable movement . . . But if your eyes and your hearts are open, you will find something quite extraordinary, a miracle of grace . . ."

In sharing the confession and absolution, the communion and celebration
of the handicapped, and of people very different from myself, I have experienced a foretaste of the heavenly banquet.

(Young 1990, 100–5, 147)

What Frances Young is describing is an earthly experience of heavenly fellowship – the communion of saints. The significant dimension of her
account is the way it demonstrates that difference leads not to conflict – to
scarcity – but to harmony – abundance. In the life of the kingdom, even
those differences that are assumed to denote scarcity – "special needs," or
disabilities – are transformed into gifts, and even those who are often perceived as a drain on society and a burden to their caregivers are truly seen as
integral to overflowing life.

The fourth dimension of friendship as the life of the kingdom is its unique
combination of breadth and depth of fellowship. Whereas in earthly human
friendship, intimate acquaintance invariably discloses unaddressed fragility,
unresolved grief, and unquenched need, intimate knowledge of God discloses only awesome, sacrificial love. One thief, in the intimacy of the
cross, exposes and ridicules Christ's humiliation; the other, by contrast, recognizes, in that intimacy of death and suffering, the awesome love and
power of Jesus (Luke 23.39–43). Only God combines awe and intimacy in
this way. The life of the kingdom is the unfolding of awe and intimacy on
all creation. Meanwhile in earthly human friendship it is impossible to
know everyone, still less to care or genuinely to love more than a limited
number or range of people. Yet Jesus is the good shepherd, who knows all
of his sheep and calls them each by name; he lays down his life for them.
He is prepared to leave the great mass of them to seek and find just one. He
has other sheep, "not of this fold," whom he knows just as well (John
10.1–16, Luke 15.3–7). In other words, in the life of the kingdom it is possible to love all with the intensity with which one might aspire on earth to
love one; and that love and attention do not disclose deep flaws but evoke
profound awe.

Likewise the kingdom offers a relationship that unites love and knowledge. When Jesus meets Peter by the lakeside, the charcoal fire (John 21.9)
and the threefold conversation remind the reader that this is a restoration
scene after the betrayal in the high priest's courtyard. It is clear that Jesus
knows about the betrayal: but can he still love, given that he knows? The
commissioning of Peter demonstrates that Jesus can and does. This is the
friendship of the kingdom – a relationship of being fully known, yet fully
loved, of uniting awe and intimacy, of loving all with the intensity previously reserved for one.

Joyful communion: eating with him

If in the kingdom the life of worship constitutes the joy that there is an abundance of God, and the life of friendship constitutes the joy that there is an abundance of creation – human, sensate, and insensate – then the life of sharing food constitutes the joy that there is an abundance of purpose, activity, and growth.

Once again this joyful communion begins with the inner-communion of God. The most influential portrayal of the Trinity, the Rublev icon, known as "The Hospitality of Abraham," depicts the three divine persons gathered around a table for a meal together. There is an empty place on the viewer's side of the table: it seems there is an invitation to take up this place, and commune with the Trinity. The heavenly banquet is perhaps the most characteristic scriptural depiction of the life of the kingdom. Jesus enacts these banquets himself in his many significant meals with sinners, strangers, crowds, and disciples. These are invitations to join the inner-communion of God.

Yet they make it clear that the inner-communion of God has a special place for outcasts. Food is at the heart of conflict about the nature and breadth of the kingdom (particularly in Acts, where the incorporation of the Gentiles (perhaps the most significant outcasts of all) is triggered by an instruction to Peter to "eat" (Acts 10.13). The first sin was at the first meal (Genesis 3.6). The first to worship Jesus were shepherds (whose lifestyle excluded them from ritual purification and abrogated dietary laws) and Gentile magi (with whom Jews did not eat). The first miracle was at a wedding banquet (John 2.1). Jesus declares all foods clean (Mark 7.19). His parables depict heaven as a banquet to which all are invited, "the poor, the crippled, the blind, and the lame" (Luke 14.21), and he instructs his disciples to invite the same people when they host banquets of their own (Luke 14.13). It is in a conversation about food with the Gentile woman that Jesus appears to change his mind about the place of outsiders in the kingdom (Mark 7.29). The first thing Jesus does after bringing Jairus' daughter back to life is to direct the bystanders to give her something to eat (Mark 5.43). The Last Supper is the place of revelation and betrayal, and the post-resurrection appearances revolve around meals (Luke 24, John 21). There is a place at this resurrection table for the bewildered Cleopas, the doubting Thomas, and the denying Peter. Thus food comes to define communion.

Food is a development on the notion of friendship because the preparation, sharing, and clearing of meals provide a paradigm of the dynamic, nourishing, and purposeful practices of the kingdom. In short, the practice of eating together delivers the depiction of the kingdom from any sense that it is simply disembodied immobile reverie. There are things to do. These things define friendship and characterize worship. They order the new creation and shape time. They affirm continued growth and offer reward and satisfaction for joyful labor. Perhaps most significantly, the sharing of food epitomizes the way in which God meets his people's deepest need, now and eternally. No need is more basic than the need for food. And yet the heavenly banquet is a depiction of the way God does not simply meet his people's basic needs: he goes much further, giving them far more than they need, surrounding them with food, friends, and his own abundant presence, all in all. This is the purpose of creation, cross, and resurrection: to make possible this everlasting friendship with God – rehearsed in worship and practiced in the sharing of food.

Chapter Three

TODAY

The first chapter argued that God has given his people everything they need to follow him. It suggested that God has given not only enough, but more than enough – indeed, too much. The use of the term "yesterday" names the theological claim that God has been fully revealed in history – in creation, in his dealings with his people, in his Church, but definitively in Jesus Christ. What the Church needs is not "more" from God, but the grace to receive the "everything" that God has already given. This requires conversion from the perversity that rejects the gifts of God and an expansion of the imagination to receive God's abundance. The second chapter changed the perspective from past to future, from yesterday to forever. It suggested that in the coming of the kingdom God will complete the work that Scripture identifies as his; that that work fulfills his eternal purpose, which is that his people live the life of the kingdom, answering his call to worship him, be his friends, and eat with him; and that just as Jesus Christ definitively names what God has done "yesterday," so Jesus Christ similarly identifies what God will do "forever."

The current chapter shifts the focus again, this time to the present tense. This "yesterday" and "forever" come together in "today" – the way God in Christ is acting in the present. The key term in expressing God's action in Jesus "today" is Holy Spirit. The chapter will look at the way the Spirit brings what God *has done* into the present, and at the way the Spirit brings what God *will do* into the present. It will then go on to identify the gifts of the Spirit and the work of the Spirit.

The Holy Spirit Brings Scripture to Life

The Holy Spirit makes the past into a gift of God to the Church. If the Church imagines its task as walking forwards into an unknown future, it may experience its life as one of uncertainty, anxiety, and bewilderment: in short, scarcity. Yet the Holy Spirit enables the Church to reconceive its form of life as *walking backwards* (see Wells 2004, 148). When the Church looks backwards it finds a myriad of examples, warnings, saints, parallel contexts, moments of deliverance, epiphanies of grace. Its experience is no longer one of scarcity, but one of abundance. Church history is theology teaching by examples. Christian ethics belongs more in the history department than in the philosophy department. It is seeking to learn from what God has done and to furnish its life with the good and bad examples of how the Church has embodied this Gospel. The Church thus seeks to reincorporate the lost and stray stories of how forgotten witnesses have displayed the grace of God, have shown courage and wisdom and perseverance and patience, have incarnated the imagination of the kingdom. Until the seventeenth century there was great rejoicing when a lost document or relic from antiquity was discovered, because antiquity was taken to be the summit of civilization to which all subsequent ages sought to return. In just the same way the Church rejoices when an unheralded tale is told of a long-neglected saint resting in an unvisited grave whose witness now challenges or clarifies the Church's mission.

One local church was deeply overshadowed by its history. It had been built through the energy of a remarkable leader, whose character became inseparable from the identity of the congregation. He had led the church for no less than 60 years, and each successor over the next 40 years found it impossible to help the congregation establish deep roots beyond this weight of tradition. Finally an interim leader was appointed, and during his 18-month stay he initiated a large display of photographs and memories from the church's 100-year history. In putting these treasures together, the congregation discovered that the history was more complex than they had ever before realized, and that far from being a burden, it offered them a fountain of abundant examples and gifts on which they could ceaselessly draw. To the astonishment of congregations in the neighborhood who had regarded them as stuck in the past, they took a new direction, appointed their first woman leader, and embarked on a new sense of mission in their community. Here was the Spirit offering the past as a gift to the Church.

Scripture is the key word the Church uses to describe the past, because it is the account of how God has done everything needed to enable his people to worship him, be his friends, and eat with him. Thus the skills the Church learns in reading Scripture shape the way the Church reads the past as a whole. The gift of Scripture is an introduction to reading the gift of Church history and the gift of history in general. For example, in learning to read Scripture, Christians realize that some parts are more important than others, that there is a story emerging in relation to which each element finds its meaning, that lifting one part out of the story can distort both that part and the whole narrative, that reading the story on one's own can make one vulnerable to partial understandings and thus that one needs to read in the company of worshipers seeking faithful discipleship. Learned in relation to Scripture, these discoveries may apply to the reading of history more generally.

The activity of the Spirit in bringing Scripture – and thus the past – to life is witnessed in Scripture itself. Nathan tells David the story of a rich man who, reluctant to slaughter one of his own lambs to provide hospitality, seizes a poor man's only beloved lamb. When David is angry, and denounces the rich man as one who deserves to die, Nathan exclaims, "You are the man!" (2 Samuel 12.1–14). Thus does Nathan draw on David's history as a shepherd-boy and bring that history stunningly into the present, bringing repentance and contrition. This is the Holy Spirit bringing the past to life. Jesus enters the synagogue in Nazareth on the Sabbath, opens the scroll and reads from Isaiah, "The Spirit of the Lord is upon me, because he has anointed me." He goes on to set out his mission to set free the poor, the prisoner, and those crippled by physical disability or debt. Then, to widespread amazement, he says, "Today this scripture has been fulfilled in your hearing" (Luke 4.16–22). Here again is a dazzling moment of the Holy Spirit bringing the heritage of prophecy to life in the presence of Christ – in this case bringing both wonder and dismay. These words, "Today!," "You!," are the words that ring out from proclamations that bring the past and Scripture to life, such as the Barmen Declaration, published by the Confessing Church in Germany in 1934, and the Kairos Document, issued by a group of theologians in South Africa in 1985. Thus the Holy Spirit transforms the present by bringing the abundant revelation of the past to life today.

This chapter is the last of the part of the book called "Jesus" and comes immediately before the part of the book called "Church." That demonstrates how the work of the Holy Spirit involves interpretation. The Holy Spirit interprets the word of Scripture into the practice of the Church, the stories of Church history into the habits of contemporary Christians, the ideas of the world into the embodied grace of faithful disciples. On the night before he died Christ washed the feet of his disciples, an action akin to changing the clothes of a chronically incontinent person today. St Laurence gathered the poor, the blind, and the lame together in the church in Rome and brought in the rapacious Roman authorities, proclaiming, "Here are the riches of the Church!" Whenever Christians refuse to use the word "Church" as a synonym for "those in prominent roles in the clergy hierarchy," but instead assume and take for granted that "Church" means principally the uncelebrated, the downtrodden, and the poor, the Holy Spirit is active in making the stories of Church history live in the habits of Christian speech. Jesus proclaimed good news to the poor. When a coalition of non-governmental organizations adopts the slogan "Make Poverty History" and local churches humbly respond by displaying banners, sending letters, joining marches, and choosing different brands on supermarket aisles, as took place in Britain in 2005, the Holy Spirit is active in translating the ideas of the world into the embodied grace of faithful disciples. These are among the ways the Holy Spirit brings Scripture to life.

The Holy Spirit Transforms the Hope of the Kingdom into Action

The Holy Spirit makes Jesus present by bringing all that God *has done* into the lived experience of today. But the Holy Spirit also makes the kingdom present by bringing all that God *will do* into the lived experience of today. This has several significant consequences for an understanding of Christian ethics, of which three may be noted here.

First, the hope in a future final consummation gives Christian ethics a provisional quality. Christian ethics does not seek to identify, catalog, and commend God's principles for human life for all time: it seeks to celebrate faithful Christian practice appropriate to the time between the times – between Resurrection and final Revelation, between Pentecost and Parousia. The reason why ethics may be different in some respects for Christians in South Africa today from what they were for Jews in Persia in Esther's day is not so much the decline in belief in a three-decker universe or the availability of the vote or the bomb or the pill: it is that for Christians in South Africa today God has definitively revealed himself in Christ and has disarmed the powers through his cross and resurrection and has empowered the Church through Pentecost and has promised fulfillment in the eschaton – whereas Esther's people knew none of these things. The point about Christian ethics being provisional is fundamentally that it is not about human beings but about God. Time will indeed tell if one's actions have been faithful or unfaithful, but that time is not a limited span of time until biographies are published or public (or private) documents are released: it is an eschatological time in which hearts are opened, all desires known, and no secrets are hid, and when those who set Christ at naught shall be deeply wailing when they see their true Messiah. To say the Holy Spirit brings the kingdom into the present is to point out how all human judgments are relativized in eschatological perspective.

Second, if Christian ethics in the light of the kingdom is provisional, it is also teleological. Actions are good or bad to the extent that they tend to make good or bad people. A sanctified person is a person made holy by the power of the Holy Spirit. That is to say, a sanctified person is a person in whom the fullness of what God has done in Christ is made visible by the Holy Spirit, and in whom the fulfillment of what God will do in the coming of the kingdom is also made visible by the Holy Spirit. This is the goal of Christian ethics: to seek God's sanctification of his people through the action of Christ made present by the Holy Spirit. In the case of many people one perhaps sees the action of God as it were through a dark window. But in the case of some, one can see as it were through a clear pane of glass. A sanctified life is one in which justification is made visible and salvation is made present. Christians seek to let the form and content of their practice be transformed by the anticipated character of life with God.

Third, the Holy Spirit makes the future visible in the present by offering the Church constant examples of what God has in store. Like the two previous dimensions of the kingdom-incarnating work of the Holy Spirit, this is really an affirmation of the sovereignty of God. One of God's abundant gifts to his people is to give them countless signs of his willingness to let his kingdom break into the world, often without any self-conscious activity on the part of Christians. Some of these signs become icons for a generation seeking hope: a defenseless man standing defiant before a tank in Tiananmen Square in 1989, for example, or a firefighter running up the steps of the World Trade Center to seek the lost as hundreds bolted in the other direction in 2001. Others are gestures quietly made, easily missed, often forgotten: the time offered by a surgeon to perform an extra operation, because it might just work, or a stranger running a hundred yards to reunite a fellow customer with a purchase they had unwittingly left on the counter. The world is a theater of the grace of God, and Christians are often largely spectators. Christian ethics should never forget that.

The Holy Spirit Gives God's People Everything They Need

"The fruit of the Spirit is love, joy, peace, patience, kindness, generosity, faithfulness, gentleness, and self-control. There is no law against such things" (Galatians 5.22–3). Here lies perhaps the most commanding statement that Christian ethics is about embodying the abundance of God. Paul says "There is no law against such things." He could equally well have said "there is no shortage of these things." It is a lengthy list – designed not to be exhaustive but to be persuasive. These are the things that matter most in the lives of people and communities, and they are not commodities in short supply or resources requiring just distribution but fruit that simply bursts forth wherever the Spirit is at work. There is no need for an unseemly scrap over the sharing-out of these things, because they are not about to run short. A person can have enormous sums of money – as many clothes, houses, cars, university degrees, registered patents, football clubs, or weapons as he or she might like – but if they do not have the things St Paul is talking about, the other things are no good to them. And yet if they have love, joy, peace, and the like, how much they have of the other things hardly matters.

Part of the reason for this is that the fruit Paul commends is salutary in a community-building sense. Most of the words in his list are words that underwrite common life: faithfulness, for example, is vital if people are to trust one another and anticipate that confidences and promises will be kept; gentleness is vital if anger is neither to be so suppressed that it turns to long-lasting poison nor so unleashed that it leads to immediate devastation (Paul's list of vices is similarly community-focused). Moreover it is important to note that Paul talks of "fruit" rather than "fruits." This may not be an exhaustive list but it is a definitive one. The presence of one of these fruits is not to be taken as an emblem of them all. They come en bloc. They are not an expensive series of items that no community could afford in their entirety: they are one colossal unearned gift. There is no question of any competition over which of these fruits is the most significant, or whether priority should be given to one over another: the test of whether one is genuine is the presence of the others.

Paul's list and his wistful observation that there is no law against such things make it clear that Christian ethics is not fundamentally about establishing principles, guidelines or laws. It is about embodying the fruit of the Spirit. The obsession in some cultures for seeking solutions to all tragedies or quandaries through the law court is not endorsed by Paul. The law court epitomizes the culture in which for every winner there must be a loser. But who loses from an embodiment of the fruit of the Spirit? Embodying the fruit of the Spirit is another way of saying following Jesus and anticipating the kingdom. Paul's list is perhaps the closest he comes to describing the character of Christ (Witherington 1998, 407). What Paul is saying is that if the Spirit is at work among believers, their life will come to look increasingly like the life of Christ. We might add, in the light of comments in the previous section and chapter, " . . . and increasingly like the life of God's people in the coming kingdom." Believers empowered by the Spirit will therefore, like Christ, show fruits, be given gifts, and find plenty of opportunity to exercise them: and in exercising them, they will become the catalyst for the revelation of the true character of God and of God's creation.

This is the context in which it becomes helpful to employ the language of virtue and character in Christian ethics. The whole argument of this book is that the practices of the Church, most notably the practices of worship, embody the abundant gifts of God. To talk of virtue in the context of the Holy Spirit therefore means three things. It means, first, that ethics is largely about the shaping of character over time. The assumption that ethics is about decisions in a crisis is rather like the assumption that the work of the Holy Spirit is about moments of ecstatic experience. Doubtless decisions do need to be made and ecstasy may be infused, but God's people are not to be constantly at the mercy of arbitrary interventions: instead they are built up in the image of Christ over time and come to show the fruit of the Spirit. Second, it must always be clear that the practices of the Church are embodiments of the work of the *Spirit*; they are not merely human operations. They are not a Pelagian mechanism for making humanity holy without recourse to the grace of God: they are, on the contrary, a pattern of making that dependence regular and faithful over time. Practices are always gifts, and never become powers. Third, Christian virtue is always about transformation, albeit often gradual transformation. The Holy Spirit transforms all Christian striving, all desire, through making present the sufficiency of the past and the abundance of the future. Virtue is never a static possession, but always a dynamic process of transformation. Hence it never loses its link with baptism.

It is time to consider the purposes for which the gifts of the Spirit are given. This takes us to a second, equally vital, Pauline passage concerning the Holy Spirit, 1 Corinthians 12–14, which offers some familiar words:

> To each is given the manifestation of the Spirit for the common good. To one is given through the Spirit the utterance of wisdom, and to another the utterance of knowledge according to the same Spirit, to another faith by the same Spirit, to another gifts of healing by the one Spirit, to another the working of miracles, to another prophecy, to another the discernment of spirits, to another various kinds of tongues, to another the interpretation of tongues. All these are activated by one and the same Spirit, who allots to each one individually just as the Spirit chooses. For just as the body is one and has many members, and all the members of the body, though many, are one body, so it is with Christ.
>
> (1 Corinthians 12.7–12)

This short passage expresses three highly significant principles that inform the argument of this chapter. The first is that the Spirit gives God's people an abundance of gifts. Paul's inventory is evidently illustrative rather than exhaustive: but it displays the rhetorical device of the list, which stops at the point where the reader is persuaded that the cup runneth over. There simply are too many spiritual gifts to detail in full: the very exercise could be taken as an expression of anxiety (rather like the gathering of bread in the wilderness on the Sabbath day in fear that there would not be enough). The point is that there are too many to mention – wisdom, knowledge, faith, healing, miracles, prophecy, discernment of spirits, tongues, interpretation – it goes on and on. God gives his people everything they need to follow him.

The second dimension of the gifts of the Spirit made clear in this passage is that "as the body is one and has many members, and all the members of the body, though many, are one body, so it is with Christ." The gifts of the Spirit are given to one body, not to one individual. If the Church is disunited, it is almost bound to experience a certain scarcity of gifts: this is part of the consequence, and scandal, of disunity. A single individual is similarly likely to experience a scarcity of gifts and a bewilderment about how best to use their gifts: for gifts are given to the Church, and their shape and purpose cannot become clear until they find their proper place. Likewise "The eye cannot say to the hand, I have no need of you" (1 Corinthians 12.21). Gifts operate best when used together – when the orchestra employs all its instruments. There can be no question of the gifts coming into conflict, for they "are activated by one and the same Spirit." That is a spirit characterized principally by love (1 Corinthians 13.13). God gives everything that is needed, but his gifts must be used in the spirit in which they are given.

The third significant dimension supplied by this passage and developed more explicitly in 1 Corinthians 14, is that the Spirit gives these gifts "for the common good." Over and over again Paul insists that this is what gives the interpretation priority over the ecstatic utterance. "Those who prophesy speak to other people for their upbuilding and encouragement and consolation" (14.3); "Those who prophesy build up the church" (14.4); "One who prophesies is greater than one who speaks in tongues . . . so that the church may be built up" (14.5); "Since you are eager for spiritual gifts, strive to excel in them for the building up of the church" (14.12), and so on.

These principles extend way beyond the ordering of charismatic worship. These are principles that may shape Christian ethics as a whole. Christian ethics is concerned fundamentally with gifts of God that are not in short supply – Christ, the kingdom, the Holy Spirit. In the words of Lanza del Vasto, the Italian follower of Gandhi, "Strive to be what only you can be. Strive to want what everyone can have as well." Christian ethics strives for gifts that everyone can have. And if these are genuinely the gifts of God, they cannot conflict with one another. The ethics of scarcity corresponds with the ethics of tragedy: in the former, the gifts run short; in the latter, the gifts conflict. This is not to say all Christian stories have happy endings: only to point out that in the light of the Christian story, no human story, set in its full eschatological context, can ever be simply a tragedy. Perhaps most significantly, Christian ethics is fundamentally concerned with what builds up the Church. It is not so much seeking whether things are right or wrong in themselves; it is not so much assessing which course of action is likely to produce the most benevolent outcome (in an inevitably abbreviated time-frame); it is about what builds up the Church, which actions foster the kind of character that builds the body of Christ up into the likeness of Christ. It is not just ecstatic utterance that is to be judged in this way: it is all creation.

The Holy Spirit Offers Abundance in the Face of Scarcity

We have seen how the Holy Spirit brings the revelation of God in the past to life, brings the promises of God in the future into the present, and gives God's people everything they need through fruits and gifts. The final test of this gracious provision is whether it abides in the face of adversity. There is no doubt from the New Testament that Christ's followers can expect setbacks, hardships and persecutions. What does it mean in such contexts to say they have been given everything they need?

The moment to address this question is in the farewell discourses in John's Gospel. Jesus says he "will ask the Father, and he will give you another Advocate, to be with you forever" (John 14.16). The work of the Advocate is to subvert the hardship and despair – the scarcity – of the present by supplying witness about the past and counsel about the future. In other words the Holy Spirit again suffuses the Church with abundance by bringing the past to life and bringing the promised future into the present. The Christian story – the story of the abundance of God's grace at every turn – outnarrates the scarcity of momentary Christian experience. Witness and counsel are distinct but complementary themes.

On the one hand the Spirit empowers Christian witness in the face of persecution by bringing the past to life. This is the work of the Advocate. Jesus promises "The Holy Spirit, whom the Father will send in my name, will teach you everything, and remind you of all that I have said to you" (John 14.26). In other words, the Spirit will bring the past – Jesus' words to the disciples – to life at the necessary time. This is a message of abundance, because it stresses that the Spirit will teach *everything*, and remind the disciples of *all* that Jesus has said to them. This is not the language of "some" or even "enough." Jesus goes on to anticipate the oppression that awaits the disciples.

> If they persecuted me, they will persecute you; if they kept my word, they will keep yours also. When the Advocate comes, whom I will send to you from the Father, the Spirit of truth who comes from the Father, he will testify on my behalf. You also are to testify because you have been with me from the beginning.
>
> (John 15.20, 26–7)

Again the role of the Spirit is to provide words and memories for the disciples when their own recall or experience of what Jesus *has already done* falls short. Jesus further talks of the way the Spirit brings the past to life.

> It is to your advantage that I go away, for if I do not go away, the Advocate will not come to you; but if I go, I will send him to you. And when he comes, he will prove the world wrong about sin and righteousness and judgment: about sin, because they do not believe in me; about righteousness, because I am going to the Father and you will see me no longer; about judgment, because the ruler of this world has been condemned.
>
> (John 16.7–11)

All these things either have happened when Jesus is speaking or will have happened before the persecution takes place.

The same point is made explicitly in Mark's "mini apocalypse," where Jesus anticipates times of persecution ahead. The disciples will be empowered to witness by the Holy Spirit providing them with the gift of what God has already done.

> As for yourselves, beware; for they will hand you over to councils; and you will be beaten in synagogues; and you will stand before governors and kings because of me, as a testimony to them. And the good news must first be proclaimed to all nations. When they bring you to trial and hand you over, do not worry beforehand about what you are to say; but say whatever is given you at that time, for it is not you who speak, but the Holy Spirit.
>
> (Mark 13.9–11)

This is what it means to be a witness – to be a martyr: to speak of what God has done in Christ. And it is the Holy Spirit that gives Christians everything they need to say in the face of the "scarcity" of persecution.

On the other hand the Holy Spirit encourages Christian perseverance in the face of hardship by making present the future promises of God. This is the work of the Counselor. (Counselor and Advocate are both names for the one Spirit but using the two names can help to demonstrate the two dimensions of its work.) Jesus recognizes that there will be times of hardship, and his words of counsel offer hope that joy lies beyond pain. A striking image is that of labor:

> When a woman is in labor, she has pain, because her hour has come. But when her child is born, she no longer remembers the anguish because of the joy of having brought a human being into the world. So you have pain now; but I will see you again, and your hearts will rejoice, and no one will take your joy from you.
>
> (John 16.21–2)

Here is the Holy Spirit bringing the promises of the future into the present. Likewise Jesus declares that there will come a time when all that is currently mysterious will become clear:

> I still have many things to say to you, but you cannot bear them now. When the Spirit of truth comes, he will guide you into all the truth; for he will not speak on his own, but will speak whatever he hears, and he will declare to you the things that are to come. He will glorify me, because he will take what is mine and declare it to you. All that the Father has is mine. For this reason I said that he will take what is mine and declare it to you.
>
> (John 16.12–15)

Again the language is of abundance – "*many* things," "*all* the truth," "*all* that the Father has." The whole of the Book of Revelation may be read as the Spirit speaking words of counsel to the Church to abide in the face of hardship. Meanwhile Romans 8 is perhaps the most familiar embodiment of the way the Spirit counsels Christians in their weakness – interceding for them with sighs too deep for words according to the will of God (Romans 8.26–7). This is what counsel means: placing the pressing present in the context of the plentiful past and the superabundant future of the grace of God.

Thus the theological argument of the first three chapters is complete. These are the foundations on which Christian ethics sits. God *has given* his people everything they need to worship him, be his friends, and eat with him. Indeed, he has given them more than enough – too much. This is the witness of Scripture. God will fully reveal himself and *will institute* his abundant life in which his people worship him, are his friends and eat with him. This is the counsel of the kingdom – also witnessed in Scripture (for yesterday and forever are always today with God). And now, between resurrection and full revelation, between Pentecost and Parousia, the Holy Spirit *brings* the story of Scripture to life and *makes* the promise of the kingdom present. Christian ethics is truly the practice of abundance.

Part Two

THE BODY OF CHRIST
AS THE CHURCH

Chapter Four

FORMING

Baptism names the distinction between Church and world, and the distinction between Church and Israel. It is the practice that marks the passing over from a narrative bounded by birth and death to a narrative bounded by creation and eschaton; and it is the practice that marks the breaking-down of the dividing wall of hostility between Jew and Gentile and the formation of a new people. Baptism therefore defines the Church. This second part of the book is therefore characterized by Baptism in the way the first part is characterized by Scripture and the third by Communion.

But just as eating with God carries with it a host of associated practices that embody its significance and establish its context, so being part of the body of Christ involves more than Baptism itself. Being baptized becomes the signal moment that provides both the goal and the starting-point for all the practices of friendship that make up the Church. The current chapter considers those practices that logically precede Baptism. Then comes a chapter on Baptism itself, after which follow two chapters on the life of the Church, made possible by Baptism – one on what happens when it goes right, and another on what happens when it goes wrong.

Evangelism

Evangelism names a variety of practices by which the Church invites all people to worship God, to be his friends, and to eat with him. Straightaway the significance of defining the Church in relation to Baptism becomes clear. In relation to Baptism, evangelism names the routes through which a person comes to the point of being a catechumen, that is, a person who has declared a desire to be baptized. Evangelism is the name for all those conversations, events, communications, gestures, encounters through which a person comes to hear and receive that invitation made by God through the Church.

I shall consider two kinds of evangelism: "prophetic" evangelism, that is, activity whose principal or entire purpose is to bring people face to face with God, especially when such people have forgotten or never known what it means to worship him, to be his friends, and eat with him; and "priestly" evangelism, that is, activity that falls appropriately within the common life of the Church, and is conducted for its own sake, but through which the grace of God may nonetheless touch a person and inspire them to discover more of the hope that is in the hearts of Christians. I shall then complete my treatment by dwelling on whether or not evangelism – and the Church – has a "kingly" dimension.

Evangelism is prophetic when it points to the sovereignty of Christ's person. It is priestly when it points to the pattern of his work. The distinction between prophetic and priestly evangelism (which roughly corresponds to the emphases of Parts I and II of this book) is more helpful than the familiar distinction between "humanitarian" mission that seeks the welfare of people's bodies and "evangelistic" mission that seeks the salvation of their souls. There are various reasons why the more familiar distinction is useful – not least that it makes explicit where Christian mission can seek support from the wider public and where its support can come from Christians alone. However the term "prophetic," and the recognition that prophetic and priestly refer to the sovereignty and ministry of Christ, add an extra dimension. They make clear that when the Church calls, for example, for a change to sentencing policy in the courts, or for a transformation in the structures of world trade, this is a call not simply for justice but for conversion. It is not a deviation from the pressing business of bringing individuals face to face with God; it is a call to governments, just as much as individuals, to "turn from your ways and live." Prophetic speech always assumes a narrative – a story of original blessing and the goodness of life, a story of the transformation of evil in the cross and resurrection of Christ, and a final judgment in which sin will be brought to account and the oppressed vindicated. It has no power other than the rhetorical power of this narrative and its ability to illustrate it in the priestly embodiment of the narrative in the daily practices of the Church's common life. Thus prophetic and priestly evangelism are not alternatives but mutually indispensable aspects of the way the whole of the Church's life is oriented toward bringing persons and peoples to worship God, be his friends, and eat with him.

The Church is a prophet in two respects. The first is that it points people to God. This is the traditional purpose of a spire on a church building. But there may be more subtle expressions of this ministry. One much-loved cathedral has a famous sequence of roof bosses along the length of the nave, depicting salvation history from the tree of knowledge in Genesis 2 to the tree of the Lamb in Revelation 22. It would be too easy for the worshiper or visitor to miss them, so in the aisle are several mirrors, facing heavenwards. Lest the viewer peer into the mirror and become distracted or fascinated by his or her own image, the mirrors are slightly tilted. Those mirrors are an apt analogy for the prophetic ministry of the Church. Without them, few would look up at all, and fewer still would realize what beauty and order lay above. With them, all will have an opportunity to see, some will take time to look in detail, and others will be inspired to look heavenwards for themselves. The work of the mirrors is not ruined even when their glass is badly damaged or broken: for even a small piece of glass can help to highlight a part of the roof, and the existence of the mirror will eventually provoke the viewer to look up. This is the role of the witness.

One local church served a community that was undergoing a considerable period of government-sponsored community-led estate regeneration. Each year an opportunity arose for local residents to stand for election to the board of the local development trust. Those interested in standing were invited to a briefing day where they were given an opportunity to discover how the organization worked and what their role might be. They were encouraged to reflect on their experience of community regeneration and their reasons for wanting to become more involved in the process. Each candidate was asked to write a short summary of their background and priorities to be printed in the election literature and circulated to each house in the neighborhood. One member of the church decided to stand. In her election address she described how she had come across this particular church during a period of personal turmoil and mental distress. Even though she lived a long walk away from the church she had begun to attend services there because they had touched the child within her which was longing for expression, affirmation, and love. She then moved into the neighborhood to live near the church and now she wanted to be part of the community regeneration scheme because she wanted others to have a chance to discover some of the transformation she had experienced – and perhaps to meet their child too. Like the tilted mirrors in the cathedral, her witness was prophetic: it pointed others to the sovereignty and activity of God in Christ.

The second role of the prophet goes beyond the analogy of the tilted mirror. If all prophets were as subtle as that, few would have died horrible deaths. Prophets have died horrible deaths because they have pointed out to the world that it is not the Church. The world is all that in God's creation that has taken the opportunity of God's patience not yet to believe in him

(Yoder 1971, 114). But that unbelief in the God of Jesus Christ does not inhibit misplaced confidence in the abiding power or truth of other theories, practices, or stories. And it is against these idolatries that the prophetic ministry of the Church speaks. The choice is not always a stark one: the Church may work with a great variety of movements in the world, valuing their wisdom, courage and insight; but a point invariably comes when a faith that hinges on cross and resurrection must challenge other models of formation and transformation. A culture pervaded by the management of limited resources must eventually contradict the limitless goods of God; a society sustained by the benevolent models of therapy must eventually be challenged by the foolishness and wisdom of the cross; an economy that depends on the competition of the market must eventually confront the perpetual communion of the Trinity.

If the first kind of prophet is the witness, the second kind is the martyr. The two words literally mean the same thing – but they denote different emphases. The ministry of witness opens the Church and its members to scrutiny, misunderstanding, ridicule. But the ministry of the martyr opens Christians to the prospect of humiliation, violence, even death.

During the community-led estate regeneration process described earlier, a number of local people and agencies involved in health issues came together and put together proposals for a healthy living center. This center would bring together primary health care in the form of offices for doctors and nurses with ancillary and complementary initiatives such as welfare rights, counseling, and aromatherapy. The group approached the local church, which had an excellent site, a modern building, and a small congregation. A partnership between the healthy living center and the church promised to guarantee financial security for the church while offering ideal premises for the healthcare agencies. The church pondered the proposal. It decided Christianity was not just another form of therapy: that (in a "priestly" way) it offered the neighborhood a series of practices that embodied wholesale transformation, not piecemeal health improvement. It was better to continue as a fragile witness to genuine glory than to become invisible among a host of benevolent expressions of humanism. The only way to maintain a prophetic claim that truth was bounded not by birth and death but by creation and eschaton was to retain a distinct but friendly identity as a separate building and organization. This was the martyr's costly witness that the world was not the Church, that the water of health was not the same as the wine of salvation.

If the prophetic ministry of the Church is directed chiefly to those outside it, in the form of witness, the priestly ministry of the Church is principally concerned with ordering the life of those inside the body. The prophet exposes what is impossible without God; the priest demonstrates what is possible with him. The priestly role of the Church is to model sustainable life before God – to show what God makes possible for those who love him, and thus to live a life that surpasses secular understanding.

Like the prophetic aspect of evangelism, the priestly aspect has two dimensions. The first is to live a life that follows the pattern of Christ's work in such a way that it captures the imagination of the world with which it interacts. In the film *When Harry Met Sally*, one couple are ordering dinner at a restaurant when they become aware that the woman sitting opposite her partner at the next table is (pretending to be) experiencing such a peak of sexual ecstasy that she is groaning and shrieking in an apparently involuntary manner. When the waiter asks what the original couple would like to eat, they say, "We'd like some of whatever she is having." This is an analogy for the "priestly" evangelism of the Church: to offer unselfconscious lives of sacrificial, reconciling discipleship that inspire the watching world to consider the hope that is in these people's hearts. Just as the parables of the synoptic Gospels provoke the reader to wonder what kind of a world it might be in which prodigals are forgiven, late-in-the-day laborers receive the same pay as those who began early, and slaves are applauded for taking risks rather than playing safe, so the Church seeks to make its life a provocative parable that opens out an imaginative space in which people can wonder and tentatively begin to live lives rooted in wonder and joy rather than envy and fear.

In one neighborhood that had experienced decades of hostility and mistrust, the church was about to experience a change of leadership, and invited a number of prominent local people to join in an act of worship to mark a significant threshold in the church's life. Adults and children, around 60 in number, sat together. The service began with an opportunity for people to acknowledge mistakes and frustrations, and ended with a washing of feet for renewed service. Before the scripture reading a candle was passed around every member of the congregation and each had an opportunity to say a sentence on the theme "what I have discovered in the last five or six years." One person on the fringe of the church who had experienced a good deal of conflict said "I have discovered that the things we have in common are much greater than the things that divide us." Another person, one of the most controversial and outspoken leaders in the neighborhood, looked around at the way adults and children listened to one another and the space that was given to people's imaginations, and said, to everyone's amazement, "I have discovered that this church is the soul of this community."

The second dimension of priestly evangelism is the pattern of partnership and dialogue that emerges from the humble and compassionate participation

of the Church in the ordinary joys and struggles of neighborhoods and localities. Humility in this instance means acknowledging weakness and admitting
mistakes, penitently recognizing past sin and engaging in discussion about
experience and aspiration with genuine interest. One prominent politician
was asked how he could account for taking senior office in an institution
whose establishment he had campaigned against a generation earlier. "When
I realize I am in the wrong," he said, "I admit it and change my mind. What
do you do?" In a similar spirit of generosity and eagerness to learn the Church
enters every practice of mercy or coalition of goodwill seeking not only "the
welfare of the city" but also to enrich the practices of its own common life
by finding analogies wherever people meet to heal, reconcile and share
resources, to form, maintain, and restore community.

How therefore may this comforting dimension of priestly evangelism be
balanced against the discomforting emphasis of prophetic witness? How
does a local church decide whether a partnership is a humble priestly act of
dialogue and service or a deceptive temptation toward making the Church
invisible? In a modest sense, the prophetic evangelism and priestly evangelism of the Church operate as a check on one other. Evidence that priestly
partnership is making prophetic witness impossible, or evidence that stri-
dent witness is inhibiting the common practices of the Church, is a healthy
guide that things are out of balance.

But a more significant test of whether a form of priestly or prophetic
evangelism is faithful is whether it promises or threatens to take on a kingly
dimension. The prospect of rule, of a significant or dominant share in the
ordering of society, may appear to offer a marvelous vantage point from
which to proclaim prophetic witness more clearly or deliver priestly practices more widely. But the throne is perhaps the hardest place from which
to evangelize – to point to the sovereignty of Christ. Jesus embodied the
memory and hope of Israel by enacting the roles of prophet, priest and
king. The Church, the body of Christ, is called to imitate Jesus in some
respects – but not all. It follows much of the prophetic and priestly aspects
of Jesus' ministry, and should share some of their cost. But it goes seriously
awry when it takes on a kingly role. Assuming a kingly role invariably
directs attention away from Christ and toward itself. The Church thus has a
twofold ministry, pointing to both the sovereignty of Christ's person and
the pattern of his work. In short, the Church is a prophet and priest that
points to a king.

The Church does not have a kingly ministry. Its task is, through prophetic
and priestly witness, to point to the kingship of Christ. The kingship of
Christ is, indeed, exercised in a prophetic and priestly way; but the Church
worships Christ because of his sovereignty not because of his style. He is

king not because he is good, but because he is God; not because he is just, but because he is true. Christ achieved things the Church could never have achieved, and because Christ achieved them the Church does not need to. To take upon itself a kingly ministry thus assumes either that Christ was not victorious, or that he no longer reigns. Either way, it points away from and inhibits the prophetic and priestly ministry. The Church's role is like the role of the disciples at the feeding of the 5,000: to plead for the people, to bring their resources to Christ, to wonder at his work, to distribute his gifts, and to ensure nothing is wasted by gathering up what is left over. But Christ alone presides and multiplies.

One Christian responded to his knowledge and experience of the imbalance of world trade and the hazards faced by small businesses by joining with colleagues and setting up a new organization. The aim of the organization was to encourage people in the UK to invest several thousand pounds each of their own money, while seeking a reduced or zero rate of interest. The surplus interest from these sums would then be used to provide loans to small businesses in developing countries, giving them a new level of security and the ability to make long-term plans and investments. The new organization also had ties to a purchasing and distribution wholesale company in the UK that would often buy and retail the products of the same small business. The founders carefully set up their new organization to follow theological principles they derived from their Christian understanding and experience, but also welcomed involvement and investment – and before long, leadership – from those far beyond the bounds of the Church. The organization flourished. One day a remarkable proposal came. A famous financier who had notoriously made a vast sum of money by speculating on the currency markets at a turbulent time offered the organization an investment that far outstripped any previous figure. Such a swelling of deposits would make the organization a far more powerful force in world trade. But the founder and his colleagues decided not to accept the large investment. Their purpose was not power, but example: not control, but subtle subversion. By accepting the huge deposit they would have become subject to the whim of the donor, and implicitly to the fluctuations of his wider projects, with all their fluidity and uncertain integrity.

In the terms of evangelism I have been using, this organization carried out the first and second kinds of priestly evangelism, and the integrity and imagination of their work brought about initially the first but later the second kind of prophetic evangelism. The decisive moment came when they were offered the attraction of kingly evangelism, and they realized that the security it offered was in something other than Christ. This realization clarified the organization's purpose and renewed its practice. It demonstrated that in prophetic and priestly ministry, God has given his people everything they need to witness to him.

Catechesis

If evangelism names the countless ways the Church in the power of the Spirit seeks out the lost sheep, catechesis names the countless routes by which the Church seeks to bring the lost sheep home. And home means worshiping God, being his friends, and eating with him.

It is in the practice of catechesis that the Church learns the significance of character. Character is the point where nature meets nurture, where the bold outlines of the gift of life meet the subtle disciplines of the habits of eternal life, where the energy and challenge of the world meet the grace and truth of the Gospel. Catechesis is the process by which the Church invites the Holy Spirit to form the character of its catechumens and to prepare them for Baptism. Those catechumens are a gift to the Church partly because they ask the most penetrating questions and subject the practices of the Church to the most honest scrutiny. "If Jesus says 'You should call no man 'Father', why do we call Fr Robert 'Father'?" "If Jesus says 'if I, your Lord and Teacher, have washed your feet, you also ought to wash one another's feet', why don't we?" "If Jesus says 'When you give a luncheon or a dinner, do not invite your friends or your brothers or your relatives or rich neighbors, in case they may invite you in return, and you would be repaid. But when you give a banquet, invite the poor, the crippled, the lame, and the blind', why do we all just invite our friends?"

The gift of the catechumen is displayed in the story of 14-year-old Max and the person who was assigned to be his Confirmation Guide, or mentor, during his preparation – 24-year-old Joe (see Hauerwas and Willimon 1989, 108–9).

> Joe took his Confirmation Guide responsibilities seriously, inviting Max to consider him "an older brother" and to stop by his apartment whenever he wanted to "goof off."
>
> About three weeks after the Confirmation procedures began, the pastor received a call from Joe, who was extremely agitated. "You've got to give me a new person to guide. Max and I just aren't working out."
>
> The pastor was surprised and asked why. At first, Joe was evasive. Then he said, "Well, it came to a head yesterday when Max dropped by unannounced. My girlfriend was visiting me and, well, Max put some things together, and it was obvious that we had been in bed together. Max then blurted out, "How did you two decide that this was OK? I thought people were not supposed to

have sex before they got married." Can you believe that? I told him it was none of his business. Then Max got smart-mouthed and said he and his girl-friend had been talking about sleeping together, too. "If it's OK for you, it's OK for me," he said.

"What did you say to him?" asked the pastor.

"I told him it was none of his damn business and that it was a lot different for me to do this at my age than for a fourteen-year-old to do it before he is ready."

"And Max said?"

"And Max said, 'I am just as ready as you are.' Can you believe this kid?" he shouted.

This story demonstrates how both adult and child are, in different ways, archetypal catechumens. The child is the archetypal catechumen because, like Max, the child is a mass of unformed urges and skills and ideas and desires, and the role of catechesis is to shape these gifts into membership of the body of Christ, to train, educate, form, discipline, encourage, inspire, and mold so that the child may grow in discipleship. By contrast the adult is the archetypal catechumen, because, like Joe, the adult has already made commitments and developed dispositions and formed habits and fostered relationships that reflect the partial and fallen nature of a life spent, like Jacob, wrestling for identity with the angel of God. Thus for an adult the role of catechesis is to lead the catechumen to repentance, to recognizing the lies and deceit wrapped up in a story that seeks to airbrush God out, and to bring about not just formation but transformation, not so much life but new life, not so much nurture but death and resurrection. Thus the child and the adult are a gift to one another in catechesis, for together they repre-sent the perseverance of formation and the necessity of transformation, both of which constitute Christian character.

An appropriate emphasis on catechesis has two broad implications for Christian ethics. It shifts the Church's perception of the key moment, the "when" of ethics. And it considerably influences how the Church under-stands important dimensions of life, such as marriage.

Catechesis is central to the Church's understanding of the "when" of Christian ethics. A major part of the formation of catechumens is to help them discover where they are in God's story. They live after the central moment in history, the death and resurrection of Christ, which in turn came after creation, fall, and the calling of Israel; but they live before the final moment of history, the full embrace of earth by heaven, the trans-formation of the whole earth into a Eucharist. Catechumens learn that they live after the most important events but before the final ones: that the eschaton will affirm all that was faithful to Christ and will complete and transform all that was unfinished or unfaithful. So the first dimension of the "when" of Christian ethics is that it takes place between resurrection and eschaton.

The second dimension of the "when" of Christian ethics is to tell a smaller story that fits within this larger one. That smaller story is like a tree whose stump or cross-section customarily appears as an ethical "dilemma" or "situation." The so-called dilemma, like a tree, has trunk and branches stretching high and wide, and roots sinking deep and broad. If the larger story of the Gospel is the world, the smaller story is the tree. Both constitute wider dimensions of the context than the stump, or "situation." All situations presuppose a story, of where the key players are respectively coming from, where they suppose they are going, and where this contested moment fits in relation to other significant moments in those narratives. If the first "when" of Christian ethics draws attention to the key events in history in relation to which all other events find their meaning, the second "when" tries to tell a coherent story that at least restores a sense of "tree" to what the dilemma would render as a baffling "stump." Likewise in catechesis, catechumens learn to renarrate their lives with a new understanding of their key moments – seen now, not in the terms of success and failure, sadness and joy, but in relation to what they have discovered to be the key moments in history.

The third dimension of the "when" of Christian ethics is most explicitly related to catechesis. Once the second dimension has become clear, and the "dilemma" is placed within an extended narrative, it invariably becomes clear that the dilemma only arises out of what the parties involved have already taken for granted. Indeed the clash of principles that characterizes the conventional dilemma (whether to switch off the life-support machine, have the abortion, kill Hitler given the chance, and so on) transpires to be a clash of narratives, or a controversy in how to tell the story. And so the most significant "when," the vital moment in ethics, is revealed to be not the moment of the dilemma, the negotiation of imponderable forces, but much further back. The vital moment is the period when the parties involved learned what things to take for granted – learned, in fact, how to tell stories. This is the period of the formation of character – the period that the Church calls catechesis.

As catechesis clarifies ethics, so ethics clarifies catechesis. Catechesis is where these three dimensions of Christian ethics come together. It is the process by which Christians have their characters formed and transformed and learn to take the right things for granted (the third dimension) by learning to renarrate their own stories (the second dimension) in the light of the Gospel story (the first dimension). This is how they discover what it means to be disciples, members of the body of Christ, God's companions. In catechesis catechumens learn to perform the practices of the Church, practices that embody the Gospel story. Thus learning and performing these practices – the heart of catechesis – is the heart of Christian ethics.

Catechesis not only identifies the key moment in Christian ethics: it also has a significant influence on how the Church understands a number of "issues." Such an issue is marriage. A theological understanding of marriage turns the attention of Christian ethics toward the practice of catechesis.

One Christian educator sat down for an hour with 26 eight-year-olds in a local school. He said "Marriage is about three things. It's about a powerful, scary feeling, bigger than you are, like a tidal wave. It's about one person telling another, 'While I'm alive, you never have to be on your own.' And it's about having a safe place to bring up children." He checked they knew what each one meant. They all knew about huge feelings – most knew a lot about drugs. They all knew about being alone – many had been locked in the house while their parents went out for an evening. Being safe was more difficult. Six children could not name a single place where they felt safe. The lesson finished with a vote. "Which is the most important part of marriage – the feeling, the never being alone, or the safe place?" One child said the feeling. Nine children said the saying "while I'm alive, you never have to be on your own." And 16 children said the most important thing about marriage is being a safe place to bring up children. The educator came away thinking these eight-year-olds knew more about marriage than he did.

What they demonstrated is that the most important purpose of marriage is the protection of the most vulnerable people in society. That largely means young children, although increasingly it can also mean the frail elderly parent. This is a different argument from saying that the purpose of marriage is *having* children. This is a claim that the primary purpose of marriage is the *protection* of children. This claim is grounded in seeing catechesis as the heart of Christian ethics. If catechesis is so vital, it is important to recognize how much of the formation of a person's character takes place in the home. This view of marriage sees its primary purpose as the catechesis of children. This is an unusual argument today. It is usually assumed that at the heart of marriage lies a quality of relationship. Marriage is taken to be about love – or at least about companionship. But this is an unstable basis for marriage. The quality of a relationship can come and go: at times one partner may feel they have a better quality of relationship with someone else than they do with their partner. But children do not come and go. Once they are born, they are generally there for a long time. The true identity of the child is discovered in Baptism. The principal role of the parent is to shape the child's character according to the formation of catechesis and the transformation of Baptism.

In all the controversies within the Church about marriage – whether sex should be confined to marriage, whether marriages can sometimes end in divorce, whether gay people may sometimes marry, and so on – the various sides in the debate appeal frequently to the New Testament. But throughout the New Testament there is a sustained critique of the centrality of one-to-one relationships and the nuclear family. "Whoever comes to me and does not hate father and mother, wife and children, . . . cannot be my disciple" says Jesus (Luke 14.26). Better not to marry, but better to marry than to burn, says Paul. Set against these kinds of commands, the contemporary obsession with personal fulfillment through sexual relationships seems like a fairly recent invention. There is a whole host of injunctions on what consti-tutes a holy life – peacemaking, being merciful, loving your enemy, visiting the sick and the prisoner, being faithful, forgiving those who hurt you, and the expectation of being poor, hungry, hated, and grieving. Alongside those injunctions is Paul's conviction that the body that matters is not the individ-ual body so much as the body of Christ, which he identifies as the Church. So perhaps the key question in relation to marriage is not to address its primary purpose directly, but to ask what kinds of relationships amongst its members make the Church best able to act justly, love mercy, and walk humbly with its God. Do the relationships in question build up the Church in its mission to and presence with the hungry, the thirsty, the homeless, and the stranger? Rather than trying to get back to an idealized era of faithful marriages and domestic bliss, perhaps the Church should set its eyes and hearts on a future society of generosity to the outsider and hospitality to the outcast, a society that looks remarkably like Jesus' ministry. Such a commit-ment would lead every person, not just a controversial social group, to repentance, renewal, and a transformed set of social relationships.

Thus every issue, when seen as a question of character rather than deci-sion, becomes a potential source of transformation for the Church – and turns the attention of the Church back to what it takes for granted, what it sees as essential to its formation. These are the questions of catechesis. Cate-chesis therefore emerges as central to an understanding of Christian ethics.

Chapter Five

INCORPORATING

I shall look at three aspects of Baptismal transformation: the anticipation of judgment, in which a person comes face to face with God, "without one plea," which I shall call "stripping"; the moment of transformation itself, which I shall call "washing"; and the practices that immediately follow that transformation, in which the person's new identity is characterized, which I shall call "clothing."

Stripping

Because Baptism is the establishment of a new identity – a new creation – it begins with a process that establishes the truth about the old identity. That old identity is good, but fallen; created, yet destined for death. And so the candidate is stripped of all that is fallen and destined for death. This stripping has three dimensions: body, mind and spirit. I shall consider them in reverse order.

In one local church a woman who lived in the neighborhood approached the vicar with a view to his baptizing her three daughters. He spent a good deal of time with the family, looking at the shape of the Old Testament story, perceiving how it was largely repeated in the ministry of Jesus, with one distinct difference: the God who had acted to deliver his people in the Exodus and had yet allowed his people to go into Exile, and his Son to go to the cross, had now acted decisively in the resurrection and the sending of his Holy Spirit. The mother and her daughters took the opportunity to see similarities between the scriptural story and their own stories and to begin to renarrate their stories in the light of what they were discovering. Eventually the vicar asked the mother why it was she wanted something for her daughters she was not going to receive for herself. She said she thought she might make this step one day, but not today. Two years later she came to the vicar again and asked if he could baptize the child of a friend of hers. The preparation classes again took place at her house. During the classes she said to the vicar, "Is it OK if you baptize me this time too?" He raised an eyebrow. "Do you mind me asking what's different from two years ago?" he said. "There was someone I couldn't forgive," she said. "And what has changed?" asked the vicar. "He's died now," said the woman, with relief.

This is what the spiritual aspect of stripping involves. The woman in this story knew that if she was to come before God and seek his forgiveness, she had to be prepared to forgive in turn herself. And while she was still afraid, she knew she could not forgive. The candidate comes to the moment of transformation as they will later come to the moment of death: it is time to leave sin behind, to acknowledge the distorted shape of their passions and desires, their unhealed resentments and remorseless self-pity. This is the traditional moment of exorcism. It is the point in the Church's life where it comes closest to defining evil. Evil is everything that holds the candidate back from the transformation achieved in Christ's birth, ministry, death and resurrection and embodied in Baptism, and all that inhibits the practice of renewed life thereafter. It is expressed in false pride about the past, unfounded fears about the future, and the absence of trust in the present. It sees the water as poisoned, because evil poisons all that it touches; it casts suspicion over all promises, because it undermines every territory it enters; it perceives the embrace of God as a suffocation, because it cannot cherish, only destroy.

In the face of the water of Baptism the candidate discovers the way the false heart and soul of evil translate into the false mind of a jaundiced narrative. Thus the second stripping is the stripping of the mind. For this mental nakedness the Exodus narrative provides a helpful paradigm. The candidate comes to the water of Baptism as the Israelites came to the Red Sea. To come to the Red Sea they had to admit, first of all, that *their lives were chained by slavery*. They had to admit, second, that there was no hope in going on as they were – the burden was intolerable and the only outcome was death – and thus they had to *resolve to leave* Egypt and slavery. They had to recognize, third, that God had a destiny for them that would constitute their flourishing as never before, and that *their only future lay in his hands*. And then, finally, confronted by the daunting water in front of them and the raging chariots of slavery and death behind them, but strengthened by the events of the Passover in which God's plan had begun to be revealed, they had to believe that *God alone had the power to take them across the sea*, to transform their situation from slavery and death to liberation and rebirth – from fate to destiny.

This is the role of Creed and testimony, of Gospel proclamation of promise and fulfillment, of declarations and promises. In testimony the candidate acknowledges the slavery and orientation toward death that perhaps took time to be seen for what it was, the poverty of their efforts to rescue the situation, the discovery that God was at work in their life and had unimaginable gifts in store for them, and the growing trust in the signs that God has already shown and in the new companions that faith has brought. Creed is the other half of testimony, for it names the conviction of a myriad of testimonies no one can number, and offers the ordered series of declarations through which the Church affirms that the redeeming Lord is one with the creator God, that the empowering Spirit is one with the earthly Jesus. Gospel and Creed affirm that this is not merely a personal experience, but an instantiation of God's purpose for all the world: that the same mind that parted the waters to make dry land in Genesis parted the Red Sea to make dry land in Exodus – that creation and salvation are all of a piece, that the murderous Pharaoh and the unforgiving waves and the unknown land beyond are all subject to God's reign, and that his relentless destiny is for his people to worship him, be his friends, and eat with him.

In one congregation an adult came for Baptism after many years attending worship without having been baptized. When eventually she felt able to talk about why she had stepped back from this threshold, she explained that she knew the strictures of Christian discipleship were very severe, and she doubted whether she had the character to live up to them. When it came to her Baptism, the reading for the day was the giving of the Ten Commandments. The congregation got into groups of people of all ages, and each group composed an Eleventh Commandment, drawn from the collective wisdom of the group. When the time came to give the candidate her commandments, representatives from each group went to the lectern, read out their respective commandment, then walked over to the candidate, gave it to her, and sealed the gift with a kiss. Each group was saying that the commandments were a gift not a burden, that God would expect far more of her than just this, but that he would give her everything she needed, and she would be surrounded by supporters and fellow disciples on the way.

This leads on to the third stripping, the stripping of the body. The nakedness of Baptism is an encounter with the nakedness of God in Christ – the nakedness of his birth at Bethlehem, the nakedness of his death on Calvary. Today nakedness may evoke the rippling muscles of the Olympiad and health club, the desire and ecstasy of the cinema, the frailty and neediness of the nursing home. Clothes provide not just warmth but pockets – places for the necessities of life, the marks of independence – wallet, diary, keys, handkerchief, make-up, contraceptives, mobile phone. In the stable and on the tree Christ was without the comfort of clothing and the necessities of independent life. In the stripping of the body for Baptism, the candidate comes face to face with God, face to face with his frail nakedness, realizes all the lies we tell ourselves about our body. He has no clothes, to make him look better than he is. He has no pockets, in which to store secrets or vital necessities. And he smells.

If the stripping of the spirit was a confrontation with judgment and the mercy of God, and the stripping of the mind was a confrontation with slavery and the liberating purpose of God, then the stripping of the body is a confrontation with death and the power of God. Handing a body over for Baptism, whether one is handing over one's own body or one's son or daughter's body, is a profound anticipation of death. It is the end of a story in which one can talk in the same way about "my" body or even "my" child: for the body that matters is henceforth the body of Christ. It is the end of an identity achieved through one's isolated striving, and the defining moment of an identity given by grace and conferred through Baptism. No longer is the body characterized by beauty or strength or age or fitness: henceforth what matters is its membership of Christ's body, which is always youthful but walking the way of the cross, resurrected but poured out in service. This is the death that shapes all theological thinking about death; and this is the new life that shapes all of the Church's thinking about new life. Often at this moment in the liturgy of Baptism the candidate's forehead is marked with the sign of the cross, the symbol and instrument of the new identity.

Having been stripped in body at Baptism, the Christian can never see death in the same light again. The stripping of the body at Baptism is thus the heart of a theological response to September 11. On the one hand, the power of the suicide pilots on that day was precisely that they were not afraid to die. The defenses and the imagination of the United States were powerless in the face of those who embraced a narrative that was by no means concluded by death. The Christian who is delivered of the fear of death through Baptism thus receives extraordinary power. But the suicides of September 11 were a ghastly parody of Baptism. For in Baptism the voluntary confrontation with death – as with Abraham and Isaac – is blessed with participation in the sacrifice of Christ, with participation in the way God in Christ is reconciling the world to himself, and thus becomes a blessing and an act of reconciliation with others that proclaims the gift of life. The suicides of September 11 did none of these things: on the contrary they made a sacrifice that did not take away sin, they distorted the way God reconciles the world to himself, and they brought about discord, grief, and fear rather than blessing and reconciliation. September 11 was many things, but from the perspective of Baptism it was a colossal display of why suicide is wrong.

Likewise in relation to abortion, Baptism takes on tremendous significance as the practice through which the Church understands the subtle language of life and death. The question cannot be one of distinct individuals

– the mother and the fetus – with their competing rights and notion of flourishing: for in the light of Baptism there are no distinct individuals but one body with many members.

> Indeed, the body does not consist of one member but of many. If the foot would say, "Because I am not a hand, I do not belong to the body," that would not make it any less a part of the body . . . The eye cannot say to the hand, "I have no need of you," nor again the head to the feet, "I have no need of you." On the contrary, the members of the body that seem to be weaker are indispensable . . . God has so arranged the body, giving the greater honor to the inferior member, that there may be no dissension within the body, but the members may have the same care for one another. If one member suffers, all suffer together with it; if one member is honored, all rejoice together with it. Now you are the body of Christ and individually members of it.
>
> (1 Corinthians 12.14–27, abridged)

The tragedy of abortion is not just the number of terminations each year, and the percentage of pregnancies that end in this way – it is the invariable isolation of the mother as a moral individual rather than her incorporation into a supportive community. Some of the deepest victims of abortions are the women who have them. If women have abortions because of the financial and physical demands of having a child and because they fear the damage caused to the relationships on which they rely, the Church must be constantly stretching the imagination of those involved by offering ways of assisting with the demands and offering relationships of trust that withstand those demands. "The church, as a society of the liberated, is thus the necessary paradigm that can offer us imaginative possibilities of social relations otherwise not thought possible" (Hauerwas 1986, 76).

In one local church there was a 13-year-old girl who started going out with a 20-year-old man. Her parents were disapproving and fearful. She stopped going to the church youth group. Her behavior changed. Just after her fourteenth birthday she told her parents she was expecting a baby. Her parents despaired, consulted with friends, sought solace and advice from their vicar. They could have sought an abortion and pursued the man through the courts for sexual relations with a minor. They could have, and much of them wanted to – but they did not. They refrained because their friends at the church assured them that they would be available to help with the childcare duties that everyone knew would fall to the grandparents, and that, more sanguinely, if they forced their daughter into such an action they would doubtless find themselves in the same situation again a year later. The girl's parents had a dilemma. But they realized the decisive step had already been taken: they had shared their grief with their friends. It was no longer

the private grief of isolated individuals, but had already become a commu-
nity-forming reconciling reality within the local church. Seeing what was
happening, the girl's attitude to the church changed. No one, it turned out,
was casting the first stone. When the girl, now a mother, brought her baby
to church for Baptism she was welcomed by a congregation every one of
whom knew they had made their mistakes in their time. That child had a
great crowd of godparents.

Washing

The threefold stripping before Baptism gives way to a threefold washing.
And this is not just in the sense of the Trinitarian threefold sprinkling ("I
baptize you in the name of the Father, the Son, and the Holy Spirit"). It
means that three kinds of washing take place in the Baptism itself, corresponding to the three kinds of stripping. (It is important to say at the outset
that these are not three distinct actions, but three parallel understandings of
the same action of Baptism.)

The first kind, corresponding to the stripping of the body, is the washing
of new birth. "If anyone is in Christ, there is a new creation: everything old
has passed away; see, everything has become new!" (2 Corinthians 5.17);
"Very truly, I tell you, no one can enter the kingdom of God without being
born of water and Spirit" (John 3.5). The significance of this for the life of
the Church is that it relocates the key moment in human life from birth to
Baptism. The Church grows by conversion and Baptism rather than by marriage and childbirth. Thus singleness is still the norm against which all other
vocations are to be judged. Likewise strengthening the family is not the
purpose of the Church – instead strengthening the Church is the purpose of
the family. Meanwhile the secrets that determine life are not primarily the
mysterious experiences of early childhood, only to be discovered on the
therapist's couch; instead the secrets that shape life are the decision of God
never to be except to be for us in Jesus and the transformation of reality in
his cross and resurrection. New birth is not discovering (or setting right) the
precognitive patterns of the infant (helpful as this may sometimes be) – it is
being written in to the pattern of Christ's death and resurrection.

> Do you not know that all of us who have been baptized into Christ Jesus
> were baptized into his death? Therefore we have been buried with him by
> baptism into death, so that, just as Christ was raised from the dead by the
> glory of the Father, so we too might walk in newness of life. For if we have
> been united with him in a death like his, we will certainly be united with him
> in a resurrection like his. We know that our old self was crucified with him so
> that the body of sin might be destroyed, and we might no longer be enslaved

to sin. For whoever has died is freed from sin. But if we have died with Christ, we believe that we will also live with him. We know that Christ, being raised from the dead, will never die again; death no longer has dominion over him. The death he died, he died to sin, once for all; but the life he lives, he lives to God. So you also must consider yourselves dead to sin and alive to God in Christ Jesus.

(Romans 6.3–11)

Elsewhere it becomes clear that this new birth is not simply a matter for individuals: it is the creation of a new reality out of the previously hostile Jew and Gentile.

For he is our peace; in his flesh he has made both groups into one and has broken down the dividing wall, that is, the hostility between us. He has abolished the law with its commandments and ordinances, that he might create in himself one new humanity in place of the two, thus making peace, and might reconcile both groups to God in one body through the cross, thus putting to death that hostility through it.

(Ephesians 2.14–16)

Thus fundamentally Baptism is an enactment of death and resurrection. Baptism incorporates death, and its fruit is resurrection, new birth. Just as the embodiment of death in Baptism shapes the Church's understanding suicide, so it characterizes the Christian response to euthanasia. The call for euthanasia comes from several sources – rights over one's own body, the inability to sustain life amid the isolating power of pain, the denial of the moral quality of suffering, the demise of the fear of hell. But the Church's response is rooted at this moment in the baptismal liturgy: "this is not your body any more – it is now a part of the body of Christ, which is not yours to dispose of; it could well be that your endurance amid suffering builds up the Church more than any number of financial legacies and flagship architectural masterpieces; this death that lies ahead of you is not as significant as the death you have already died in Baptism; in Baptism you received the body of Christ as a company of companions, and it is for them to strive to make your life tolerable and hold the cross before your closing eyes."

Not killing does not, of course, mean straining every muscle to keep alive when the zest for life is gone: such straining may come from the fear of death. In such cases the baptismal liturgy proclaims the overcoming of death and the faith of facing death well: but this is not the same as euthanasia. Baptism proclaims, in the face of euthanasia, that life is given to be a blessing not just to the individual but to the whole body, the wider community of faith, the communion of saints. Suffering is to be endured not because it is ennobling – for often it is not – nor because it is a just punishment – for there is no discernible pattern to why some suffer more than others. It is to be endured because enduring proclaims that life is not a possession but a gift, and like many gifts, it requires the support and encouragement of a company of friends, specialist caregivers, fellow sufferers, and surprising strangers (such as children) to learn how best to receive it. Fundamentally, deep physical suffering is a problem more profoundly of companionship than of medicine: seeking a medical "solution" leaves the relationships, which are often the real issue, unaddressed.

The second kind of washing relates to the stripping of the mind, and is an act of cleansing. "Do not be conformed to this world, but be transformed by the renewing of your minds, so that you may discern what is the will of God – what is good and acceptable and perfect" (Romans 12.2). This is about the transformation of the imagination. No one has a more significant role in relation to the imagination of the person undergoing the cleansing of Baptism than the godparent. In one congregation, at the Baptism of twin children, the preacher was also a godparent, and spoke to his fellow god-parents in the following terms, stressing that the heart of the godparent's role was to ensure the renewal of the children's minds was embedded in their growing imaginations:

> We have gathered together for a precious and holy moment. We shall shortly be re-enacting the first public moment of Jesus' ministry. And just as we believe God is especially present when we re-enact Jesus' last meal with his disciples, so we believe he is especially present when we re-enact his baptism in the Jordan. What happens at Baptism is that God places a song in your heart. But it is very important that there are other people present – because it is very easy, especially when you are less than four months old, to forget the tune. So you have godparents. It is up to the godparent to learn the song so well that they can sing it back to you when you forget how it goes (Bausch 1991, 171–2). So, listen carefully godparents: we're relying on you.
>
> And what is the song? Well, the story of Jesus' baptism shows us what the song is. Three things happen in this story. The heavens open; the Spirit descends like a dove; and a voice says "this is my beloved child." Each of these events has great significance.
>
> The beginning of the song goes like this: *heaven is open to you* (see Bruner 1987, 83–94). Look at what happens in the story of Jesus: the Gospel begins with the tearing of the heavens and ends with the tearing of the temple curtain. The veil between you and God has been torn apart. Heaven is open to you. There is no limit to God's purpose for your life: it is an eternal purpose.
>
> Now you may find that your godparents sidle up to you when you are making a choice of career: they may say "Don't dive for cover, don't just do what your parents did or want: *heaven* is open to you. The sky isn't the limit: there is no limit." Or if a time comes when you are facing serious illness, even

death, your godparents, knowing the song in your heart, may say: "The angels are waiting for you, they know you by name: heaven is *open* to you. Death is the gate to the open heaven."

And the second line of the song goes like this: *God's Spirit is in you.* Remember the end of the flood, when the dove brought the twig of new life back to Noah? Well here is the dove descending on Jesus, bringing the gift of the Holy Spirit. You are now the Temple of God's Holy Spirit. You are the place where others will encounter God. God's Spirit is in you.

If a time comes in your life when you feel alone and surrounded by hostility, you may hear a godparent gently whispering a tune: "You may feel evil is all around you, but you can still worship, for God's *Spirit* is in you." Or if a time comes when you are wildly successful, you may hear a sterner song: "*God's* Spirit is in you – everyone may worship you, but don't forget whom *you* worship." You may be cross with your godparent at the time, but they may be singing the song in your heart, and reminding you of your Baptism.

So, heaven is open to you; God's Spirit is in you: and finally, the third line of the song of Baptism: *You mean everything to God.* God's words are "This is my beloved Son." These words mean, "Jesus means everything to God, and everything God gives to Jesus he gives to us." You mean everything to God.

There may come a time in your life when you feel a deep sense of your own sin. Then you should hear your godparent say, "You are everything to *God.* You still are, whatever you have done, however unworthy you feel." Or you may wander away from the Church because God seems so distantly cosmic and ethereally vague, when you long for intimacy and passion. Then you may hear your godparents sing, through their tears, "You are *everything* to God. Remember your song."

So, this is what baptism is: God places a song in your heart. And so your godparents' role is this: to learn that song so well that they can sing it back to you when you forget how it goes. And this is the song: "Heaven is open to you; God's Spirit is in you; you are everything to God." This is the song that makes your heart sing. And what does the song mean? I'll tell you. You are the song in God's heart, and he will never forget how you go.

The third kind of washing relates to the stripping of the spirit: this is not washing at all – it is drowning. This is a death from which there is no resurrection. Its origins are in the Flood of Genesis 6–8, its paradigm is the drowning of the pursuing, enslaving Egyptians in Exodus 14–15, and its allusive symbol is the drowning of the Gadarene swine after the exorcism of Legion in Mark 5 (and Luke 8). This act of drowning prefigures God's eternal purpose for evil. Whereas the willingness of God in Christ to undergo suffering for his creation is embodied in the Eucharist, the determination of God to obliterate evil is fundamentally expressed here, at this moment in the baptismal liturgy. It is perhaps a unique moment, because here God acts not primarily by persuasion or by pouring out his own life or by slow transformation, by the reintegration of the lost or by the outnarration of the foolish. Here, uniquely, he acts by the obliteration of evil.

There is a warning here to three kinds of perversion of the Christian tradition. The first is a dualist perversion, one that maintains that the body is drowned in Baptism because the body is evil. The body is not drowned. Sin is drowned. The story of Legion is the story of how the body is restored. It is in the grip of dark forces. There is good reason in the Gospel accounts to see the name Legion as signaling a reference to the way Rome dominated the land of Israel, and the swine as indicating the food on which the Roman legions would have fed (for Jews would not have eaten pork). The demons infest Legion in the same way Rome infests the land of Israel – the way sin infests the body. Legion, like the people, can either confront his oppressors and find the shackles fastened more tightly, or give in to oppression and lose his identity. Outside help is required. As we saw in Chapter Two, the economy of Gerasa is many-for-one, whereas the economy of Jerusalem is one-for-many. This is the paradoxical link between Baptism and the cross. But for both Legion and the candidate for Baptism, it is not their bodies that drown; it is all that infests them. This is a story and a practice about the original goodness and restoration of the body, and the need for an outside force, God, to drown sin and save his people.

The second perversion is an approach to redemption that baulks at God's anger and hatred toward sin and evil. Evil is inherently absurd: no account can explain why any force in creation should refuse God's invitation to worship him, be his friends, and eat with him. God's anger is the flipside of his love: his will to bring all creation into relationship with him is so strong that nothing can eternally withstand it. Baptism is the moment that epitomizes entry into that relationship, and evil is all that diminishes, inhibits, or undermines that relationship. So the drowning of Baptism is the practice through which the Church continues to recognize the vehemence of God's antagonism toward sin and evil, and his determination to remove all forces that subject creation to its fate rather than draw it to its destiny.

The third perversion is understandings that see sin and evil as forces that are drowned primarily by human endeavor. This is the heart of the question of the "just war" – not just the tragic estimation that wars are inevitable and in certain circumstances unavoidable, but also a comic sense that good can be achieved and a victory for justice can be won, together with a romantic sense that meeting these criteria may be described as following the will of God. On the other hand the pacifist may point out that, when it comes to genuine enemies – those who jeopardize our salvation, our ability to worship God, be his friends, and eat with him – it is God's action that obliterates, not ours. The drowning of sin and evil in Baptism is not a human act: it is an act of God that accompanies the washing in water. A Baptismal view of war may therefore take the (physical) view that we have already died, with Christ, and thus that death from an invader is not to be feared above all things; the (mental) view that the role of the Church is to be a perpetual godparent, using rhetoric and persuasion and priestly gesture and prophetic action to cajole, subvert, disorient, and finally convert the invader; and the (spiritual) view that it is God who fights the fundamental battles, and that the Christian life is constituted by confidence in Christ's victory rather than by striving for our own.

Clothing

After the stripping and the washing comes the clothing. In the liturgy of Baptism this may include the receiving of a candle, the vesting in a suitable robe, an anointing for service, and words of intercession, welcome, and commissioning. All of these consolidate the transformation enacted in the washing. The significance of clothing for the Church is that here the congregation rehearse the three dimensions of the body of Christ – Jesus, the Church, and the Eucharist.

The congregation rehearse their understanding of Jesus through the act of clothing itself. "Put on the Lord Jesus Christ, and make no provision for the flesh, to gratify its desires" (Romans 13.14).

> Do not lie to one another, seeing that you have stripped off the old self with its practices and have clothed yourselves with the new self, which is being renewed in knowledge according to the image of its creator. In that renewal there is no longer Greek and Jew, circumcised and uncircumcised, barbarian, Scythian, slave and free; but Christ is all and in all! As God's chosen ones, holy and beloved, clothe yourselves with compassion, kindness, humility, meekness, and patience. Bear with one another and, if anyone has a complaint against another, forgive each other; just as the Lord has forgiven you, so you also must forgive. Above all, clothe yourselves with love, which binds everything together in perfect harmony. And let the peace of Christ rule in your hearts, to which indeed you were called in the one body.
>
> (Colossians 3.9–15)

This is where the Church defines virtue. For virtue is that quality for which the congregation pray on behalf of the new Christian. In one local congregation a baby was brought for Baptism – a child who had been cherished and prayed for by the whole community from long before conception. The reading for the day was the above passage from Colossians, and, after the reading, the whole assembly divided into groups of around seven people, children and adults together. Even the tearaways intent on disrupting the service joined in. Each group was given a strip of colored towel, and wrote on it the virtue that they believed was the one they were asking God to bestow upon this new young Christian. There was an opportunity for each group to tell the others what they had chosen. The towels were then whisked away, and during the "stripping" – the decisions and promises – they were sewn together. The baby was baptized naked in a large punch bowl, and when he emerged from the water for the third time he was clothed in a huge towel made up of all the virtues for which the congregation had prayed.

An ethic of virtue shifts the ground of Christian ethics from the fragile moment of agonized decision to the permanence of God's everlasting choice never to be except to be for us in Christ. It shifts the center of ethics from the crisis to the period of the formation of character, for it is concerned with making good people who take the right things for granted, not with good decisions that anyone could come to if they applied the right criteria. Baptism affirms God's eternal decision to be for us. It is about his decision far more than it is about the catechumen's. The candidate may think that he or she is like a merchant who went and sold all he had to buy the pearl of great price, but the candidate is wrong, for the candidate is the pearl – the merchant is God.

The clothing in Baptism provides the paradigm for the role of virtue in Christian life. Leonard Wilson, Bishop of Singapore, gave the following account of his internment by the Japanese during the Second World War. It perfectly displays the way the way ethics is primarily about character rather than decision.

> I was interned by the Japanese; I was imprisoned for many months; I suffered many weary hours of beatings and torture. Throughout that time I never turned to God in vain; always he helped and sustained.
>
> I remember reading that, if you pray for any particular virtue, whether it be patience, or courage, or love, one of the answers that God gives to us is an opportunity to exercise that virtue. After my first beating I was almost afraid to pray for courage lest I should have another opportunity for exercising it; but my unspoken prayer was there, and without God's help I doubt whether I would have come through. In the middle of the torture they asked me if I still believed in God. When, by God's help, I said, "I do," they asked me why God did not save me. By the help of his Holy Spirit I said, "God does save me. He does not save me by freeing me from pain or punishment, but he saves me by giving me the strength to bear it"; and when they asked me why I did not curse them I told them that it was because I was a follower of Jesus Christ, who taught us that we were all brothers and sisters.

I did not like to use the words, "Father, forgive them" – it seemed blasphemous to use our Lord's words; but I felt them, and I said, "Father, I know these men are doing their duty. Help them to see that I am innocent." When I muttered "Forgive them," I wondered how far I was being dramatic, and if I really meant it; because I looked at their faces as they stood round, taking it in turns to flog me, and their faces were hard and cruel, and some of them were evidently enjoying their cruelty. But, by the grace of God, I saw those men not as they were, but as they had been. Once they were little children with their brothers and sisters – happy in their parents' love, in those far-off days before they had been conditioned by their false nationalist ideals. And it is hard to hate little children.

So I saw them not as they were, but as they were capable of becoming, redeemed by the power of Christ, and I knew that I should say, "Father, forgive."

I do not know how many of you know what real hunger is, but the temptation to greed is almost overwhelming. There was a young Roman Catholic in the cell. He was a privileged prisoner; he was allowed food from the outside. He could have eaten all of it, but never a day passed without his sharing it with some people of the cell. It raised the whole tone of our life, and it was possible for others to follow his example – to learn to share with one another.

After eight months I was released, and for the first time got into the sunlight. I have never known such joy. It seemed like a foretaste of the Resurrection. For months afterwards I felt at peace with the universe, although I was still interned and had to learn the discipline of joy – how easy it is to forget God and all his benefits! I had known him in a deeper way than I could ever have imagined, but God is to be found in the Resurrection, as well as in the Cross, and it is the Resurrection that has the final word.

(Bowker 1975: 96–7)

Perhaps the key discipline in relation to being clothed in virtue is imitation. Paul insists, "Be imitators of me, as I am of Christ" (1 Corinthians 11.1). "For though you might have ten thousand guardians in Christ, you do not have many fathers. Indeed, in Christ Jesus I became your father through the gospel. I appeal to you, then, be imitators of me" (1 Corinthians 4.15–16). This is the heart of a theological response to the question of human cloning. For while the issues are often discussed in terms of autonomy and medical progress, the genuinely theological questions are about the degree to which Paul sees Baptism and discipleship as the nonsexual reproduction of human beings and the renewal of the species. Clothing is not just a pragmatic addition to the liturgy of Baptism reflecting the varied traditions about the quantity of water involved: it is a practice of tremendous significance in relation to the Church's understanding of the making of new life. Catechesis, Baptism, and discipleship are the Christian technology of reproduction.

If the first dimension of clothing is the congregation's understanding of Jesus, the second dimension of clothing is the congregation's understanding of the Church. This is where the cluster of symbols and practices toward the later part of the liturgy of Baptism – candle, anointing, commissioning, and welcome – tends to gather.

The welcome – like all the habitual practices of the Church – only makes sense if it is a matter of course. Michael was a ten-year-old boy who started coming to his local church through the encouragement of a teacher at his school. After he had been coming a few months, funds were found for him to come on the parish weekend away. But the weekend was marred by complaints that he persistently bullied the younger children. The adults finally had to talk to each other about it. It was pointed out that, being brought up solely by his young and temperamental father, he was a troubled boy looking for security. Allowances were made, patience was maintained, and gradually he began to find his feet. Eventually, nine months later, at a special evening service he was baptized. Around 40 people came, and each member of the congregation was invited to describe to him what they most valued about being members of that church. When he was asked the same question his habitual frown broke, for once, into a smile, and he replied "You didn't throw me out after that weekend."

The commissioning, anointing, and candle are all ways in which the Church roots its notion of vocation in the practice of Baptism. All understanding of vocation is an outworking of the implications of Baptism. But vocation is not a once-for-all thing, like the washing of Baptism: it is an emerging, growing thing, appropriately defined by the clothing aspect of Baptism. The other practices of Baptism shape the understanding of vocation: vocation involves stripping, in body, mind, and spirit, of all pretension, self-deception, and resistance to grace; it requires new birth, cleansing, and the drowning of sin; and it requires clothing in virtue. It is not a mere blessing of an existing state of affairs but an embodiment of transformation. It is not simply an individual path but a ministry bestowed as a member of a body. It is not a response to scarcity ("Africa needs doctors!") but a participation in the abundance of the gifts God is giving to his people.

And the final aspect of clothing is the full incorporation of the new Christian in the definitive practice of the Church, the Eucharist. What this means is set out at length in Part Three. The point here is to make clear that the practices of clothing after Baptism are the moments when the new Christian receives what the Church constantly rediscovers – that God gives his people everything they need to follow him, and that following him is expressed in answering the call to worship him, to be his friends, and to eat with him.

Chapter Six

PERFORMING

Just as throughout the book I am arguing that God gives his people everything they need to follow him, and throughout this section I maintain that
he does so through the practices of the Church, so here I display what those
ordinary practices are. I suggest that these practices are gifts to the Church
not only in themselves, but also in that the Church, in seeking to be the
kind of community that can perform these practices well, discovers the
abundant grace of God in unexpected ways. Most of the practices outlined
in this chapter are commanded in some form in the New Testament: but the
Church finds in carrying them out, not the relief that comes from fulfilling
a command, but the joy that comes from receiving a gift. The Church is
shaped, not by obeying a command, but by being the kind of people who
can receive the gifts that derive from carrying out these practices.

The chapter comes in three parts, corresponding to three kinds of practice. All are expressions of dependence. For to say the Church exists by
grace means that it depends on gifts. These gifts are in three forms – those
who come direct from God, those who come from the fellowship of faith,
and those who come from strangers. There is no hierarchy of gifts – all are
essential to the character of the Church, and the reception of each is a
preparation for the reception of the others.

Dependence on God

Praying

Christians pray. They self-consciously turn to God, seek his mercy, call
upon and open their hearts to him, celebrate and meditate on his wonders,
and place themselves in the company of his creatures and servants. The life

of the Christian disciple is unrecognizable without the moments or pattern, the resort or habit, of personal prayer. Why unrecognizable? Because God gives his people so many gifts this way that the life that does not open itself to receive them is deeply impoverished.

Prayer means petition: it means explicitly looking to God to transform all in life that does not reflect his glory and specifically requesting him to meet needs, heal bodies, and change hearts. Prayer means wonder: it means being taken out of the mundane and routine and being astonished and dazzled by the breadth and detail of creation and the depth and passion of redemption. Prayer means recognition of error: it means painful admission of purposeful sin and participation in widespread evil, and resolve to be done with such ways of thinking and saying and doing and to begin again the new life made possible in Christ. Prayer means gratitude: it means receiving all the contours of life as the gifts of a gracious God, it means renarrating the events of each day as a letter of love from God to oneself, it means expressing love and joyful thanks in return. Prayer means silence: it means humble meditation, the simple offering of time, the stillness that attests to the fundamental priority of God's activity, the simple opening of the ears of the heart. And if prayer means reading the Bible, it does so in the sense that the disciple seeks that the words of Scripture enrich and inform these various modes of prayer, shaping the Christian's understanding of the awesome goodness and grace of God and the mysteriously yet invariably inhibited character of human response, and placing this act of prayer within a great sequence of divine–human conversations.

Becoming the kind of person who can pray

Prayer is an end in itself: it is an experience of God's ultimate purpose that his people should worship him and be his friends. It is not a means. References to the power of prayer are properly a way of referring to the power of God. However prayer is a gift to the Church not just in itself but also in the patterns of life the Church must adopt if its people seek to become people of prayer. These patterns are God's gifts to the Church ancillary to his gift of prayer – gifts that shape the character of disciples and communities. Let me give several examples.

Becoming the kind of person who can make petition to God means becoming incarnate – in other words it pushes the disciple to discover more about the person being prayed for, quite possibly to get to know them or their circumstances personally, to visit their country or learn about their condition, to walk a mile in their shoes and thus to pray with and alongside them rather than from a safe distance. The prayer of petition thus offers the Church the gift of solidarity, the gift of becoming more one body. To pray for the needs of others means also that the disciple searches the depths of their own compassion, naming their own neediness and recalling their experience of having their own needs met. This is the gift of humility, the gift of knowing that we are all disabled, only that in some one cannot see it. Petitionary prayer also shapes the disciple in the gift of discernment. It instills a healthy skepticism in the face of the urgency of the news media: the simple enquiry "who or what might I pray for in this news story?" dismantles the hasty scramble for blame and the thirst for clashing opinion in unyielding conviction. The two-dimensional news "story" becomes instead a multi-dimensional human drama, in which final purpose and meaning are unlikely to emerge fully but need and longing and hope and desire are invariably everywhere. And, last, becoming a person who can intercede means not just responding to the crisis, but methodically anticipating the rhythms of God and the world, of laying out lists of colleagues, old friends, family members, godchildren, congregational members, neighborhood residents, missionary partners, other congregations, so that all are not a teeming mass of responsibility and earnest memory but a careful web of systematic offering to God. The person who prays methodically has accepted God's invitation to order the world in which they live eschatologically, arraying their circle of acquaintance and the extent of their imaginative compassion around the throne of grace, just as they shall be in the kingdom of heaven.

Becoming the kind of person who can wonder means keeping the company of those for whom exultation in the sheer joy of life is a simple habit – whether that company be that of a golden retriever who launches herself into a river in pursuit of a stick or a two-year-old child who gurgles with delight on learning to kick a ball. It gives purpose to idleness and leisure – for every rain shower may be followed by the glory of a rainbow and every sunny day may conclude with a shimmering sunset. Every television program may show another intricate dimension of the created world of flora and fauna, and every journey to a new territory may disturb the complacency of thinking things must always be done the familiar way. The prayer of wonder gives a new definition to the purpose of learning: for the disciple who prays, education is not primarily training in knowledge or skills or even wisdom – the first thought for the disciple in beginning a new course of study or taking up a new book is to inform and amplify the wonder of the heart, to stretch the imagination with the glory of God and the diversity of his revelation. Likewise the enjoyment and creativity of sport and the arts are only secondarily the response of humanity to the talents bestowed by God: they are primarily windows of wonder – yet more channels through which the prayer of awe may be amplified and inspired.

Becoming the kind of person who can confess sin means keeping the imagination open to how a story can look from a perspective other than one's own. Just as Nathan told David a story about the poor man's ewe (2 Samuel 12), and through that story moved David's imagination to perceive his sin in taking Bathsheba and killing her husband, so through fiction, poetry, and biography disciples may learn to see the patterns of human self-deception reflected in their own narratives. An ability to identify and name sin is an indication that other aspects of prayer are healthy: if thanksgiving is plentiful, pride is likely to be the more easily identified. For pride is the tendency to see oneself as the center of the story, rather than a small part in a story that is always about God. And if wonder is abundant, then despair will be shown in sharper relief. For despair is the tendency to see the world as other than the purposeful creation of a just, merciful, and endlessly gracious God. Without thankfulness and wonder, the disciples' ability to confess sin will be confused or limited: they may have an abiding sense of falling short, but they are unlikely to perceive a genuine impediment in a relationship with the God of Jesus Christ. One further gift that may come through developing the habit of confessing sin is the formation of a friendship with a trusted outsider – a soul friend or spiritual director. Such a person, a kind of "coach" in discipleship, is part of what it means for prayer to be a gift to the whole Church.

Becoming the kind of person who can give thanks means, as with intercession, spending time in the company of those less fortunate than oneself. And this is not for their benefit, but for one's own, because it is hard to value a gift – even to realize that something *is* a gift – unless one knows what it means not to have such a thing. And so works of charity, aside from any other benefits that might derive from them, are gifts to the Church in that they make disciples better able to make petition and give thanks. If learning to confess means developing the imagination, learning to give thanks means using one's memory. For memory offers a host of examples of how things were not always this way: valued friendships all began somewhere, fulfilling pursuits all arose from someone's invitation and encouragement, the security blankets of health care, insurance, rapid transport, mass communications, accessible education, let alone comparative peace and security, are all things of relatively recent vintage. Just as God is so often identified in the Old Testament as the one who brought your forebears out of Egypt, so the witness of memory must characterize God today. And the rhythm of thankfulness peaks appropriately at moments of sharing food: for "fast food" is but a commodity that seeks to concertina the elaborate process of planting,

growing, harvesting, transporting, selling, transporting again, storing, preparing, eating, digesting, and clearing that constitutes a genuine process of
being fed; and thankfulness, perhaps in the form of saying grace, is a reassertion of understanding of all the labor and relationships and the gift of life
and growth involved in bringing food to a table.

Becoming the kind of person who can be silent before God means
realigning one's notions of efficiency, of productivity, and of time in
general. For contemplation, meditation and stillness are by any conventional
definition a "waste" of time. But if time is a gift, rather than a possession,
and time is a friend, rather than a commodity, then appropriate time spent
in contemplation is an affirmation that time in God's dispensation is not in
short supply. Silence and stillness refine disciples' understandings of how
God works and their role in his providence. If disciples are to listen to God
they must learn to be attentive in other relationships too: and thus life
becomes a ministry of listening (and watching) for revelation, rather than
merely passing on observation. Contemplation shapes the Church's notion
of atonement: for the disciples who do not trust that God in Christ has reconciled the world to himself will never pause long enough to contemplate
because they assume that the reconciliation must come from them.

Becoming the kind of community that can pray

So much for personal prayer: but personal prayer is simply an introduction
to the way God gives his people everything they need when they depend on
him. Since prayer is always in the company of the saints, in the power of the
Spirit and in union with Christ, it is somewhat strange to use the term "personal" prayer at all. But my argument that personal prayer implies becoming
the kind of person who can pray is incomplete without looking at the
implication of corporate prayer – which is becoming the kind of community in which people can pray together.

Becoming the kind of community that can pray is something that is
bound to emerge over time: but its ground rules are simply put. They are no
more than an extension of becoming the kind of person who can pray. The
latter requires that one become the kind of person who can make petition.
The former entails that members of the community learn the habit of
making petition to one another – of asking one another "how can I help?"
and of responding with honest acknowledgement of need when the question is addressed to them. To be a person who can pray requires that one
learn to wonder. To be a community that can pray correspondingly means
that members must be prepared to share their joys, humble and great, and to

treasure and celebrate the joys of others. Birthdays are particularly important in communities because they mark the sheer gift of a created person,
uncluttered by the clothing of achievement or complications of character.
To be a person who can pray means that one must learn to confess sin. To be
a community that can pray means that members must positively seek to discover the ways in which they have wronged one another, never being
surprised that misunderstanding and hurt occur, but seeing each instance as
a prelude to reconciliation, grace, and deeper relationship. As with petition,
members who seek to make confession together must explicitly ask "have I
wronged you in any way?" and expect the answer yes, and honestly respond
when the question is addressed to them. Members must learn not to say to
God what they should be saying to each other. To be a person who can pray
means learning to give thanks. Likewise to be a community that can pray
means that members must carefully consider those things for which they
want or need to thank one another and how best to express that thanks in
such a way that it genuinely lifts the hearer rather than simply discharges an
urge or duty from the speaker. Finally, becoming a person who can pray
means learning to be still and silent before God. Likewise becoming a community that can pray means making spaces where the members are silent
and still together, where the corporate practice of the community affirms
the priority of the action of God, where all come together and share the
intimacy and vulnerability of resting for both their urgent present as well as
their eternal future in nothing other than in the grace of God.

To become such a community requires that its members should aspire.
Such a community is a gift of God to those who seek to pray together. It is a
great deal more than an expression of mutual tolerance. Tolerance expresses
no statement of final purpose. Christian community presupposes a greater
goal, but it is important that members express at appropriate moments what
that greater goal is. On the other hand, it is important that the members of
the community do not have impossibly high standards. The health of the
body is so that it may carry out the vocation that comes from God: it is not
an end in itself. The point is faithfulness, not excellence. If high standards
get in the way of members expressing needs, joys, hurts, and thanks to one
another, then those standards have gone beyond their usefulness. God's gift
to Christian community is divine: but the divine gift is a gift that makes the
community human.

One local congregation had been through a traumatic period in which
high hopes had been dashed, relationships of trust had been damaged, and a
prominent marriage had ended in bewildered separation. The members of
the congregation went away together, and through careful facilitation spent
the morning articulating need and regret. At one point the isolation of

bereavement overcame one of those present. The facilitator asked the person sitting beside the one who was bathed in tears to offer comfort on behalf of everyone else, ensuring that the grief was kept within the body, not taken elsewhere. Unknown to the facilitator, the person called upon had been dealing with significant problems of mental health, problems that would commonly be seen as alienating a person from local society – so this momentary ministry was especially poignant, and could not be refused. After a cathartic period that acknowledged the darkness of the previous few months, members began to express a sense of thankfulness for one another's faithfulness and embodied hope. At the end of the morning they began to talk of high points in the last year, and one member referred to the annual Passover meal, traditionally held each Maundy Thursday. "We really enjoy that night – having the Last Supper together," she said. "But I've begun to wonder recently, did *Jesus* enjoy the Last Supper? Did he enjoy it in the way we do?" An awed silence followed. Her words turned petition and confession into wonder, revealed that a period of grief had been an encounter with the God of Jesus Christ, and transformed what could simply have been a therapy session into an experience of corporate prayer.

Dependence on One Another

Sharing life – being one body

There are four dimensions to the way God gives his people everything they need through the practices of dependence on one another. Here I explore first, the ordinary habits of common life, next, the particular practices of sharing faith and finally the commitments involved in bearing one another's burdens. In the next chapter I discuss the fourth dimension – admonition, forgiveness and restoration.

The first dimension, the simple sharing of life, is rooted in Baptism and most fully expressed in the Eucharist. For the general experience of sharing life covers all aspects of discipleship that are not covered by vocation – and vocation emerges from the clothing stage of Baptism. Meanwhile the defining experience of common life is the sharing of daily bread, and the epitome of sharing food is the Eucharist. Here I outline three of the contours of the ordinary habits of common life: friendship, money, and play: but each is defined by the sharing of food.

Friendship offers a bridge between the somewhat lonely pursuit of a personal vocation and the somewhat self-denying participation in a community's common life. Friendships may arise through either shared vocation or shared experience of community. In either case, they may enable disciples to enjoy some of the benefits of vocation and common life with less of a sense of their constraints. For example, vocation may be a lonely and dispiriting experience. The workplace may be hostile, the campaigning ground may be unfertile, the results and achievements of labor may be hard to perceive. In such circumstances a friend may share deeply held and seldom articulated convictions, understand the poignancy of apparently trivial incidents, and suggest new approaches and methods in a context of broad encouragement. Thus a friend may alleviate the constraints of pursuing what may be an unrewarding vocation, while affirming through a shared sense of vision that the vocation is nonetheless genuine. Likewise the experience of common life may require a good deal of self-denial. The church leader may be unsympathetic and insensitive, the shared worship may be uninspiring and exclusive, the values and example of many fellow disciples may seem hard to reconcile with the Gospel. In such circumstances a friend may bring patience and endurance, discernment and compassion, humor, and a sense of irony, enabling the disciple to engage with the human aspects of the congregation even when the divine are hard to see. Thus again a friend may alleviate the constraints of an inhibiting experience of community, while affirming that the disciple should nonetheless continue to grow where he or she is planted.

In short, a friendship may offer a more intimate, focused, rewarding experience of what pursuit of a personal vocation or a participation in community may offer in a more challenging or less intense way. In so doing friendship may sustain the disciple through lean times and offer encouragement and inspiration for better times. Meanwhile the confidence that there are friendships that offer trust and affirmation and stimulating company and a depth of feeling and practical support may prevent disciples looking for such things in inappropriate places, and thus strengthen their vocations and communities.

Of course friends may offer distraction, amusement, and adventure, a vehicle for projections and attractions, and a transitory opportunity to experiment in mutual trust, the sharing of affection, the testing of opinion, the filling of empty, purposeless periods of leisure. None of these need necessarily be wrong. But the sense in which friendship is a gift of God to the Church to build up its shared life lies in harmonizing what could be two discordant themes: the pursuit of vocation and the disciplines of common life. Friendship offers disciples opportunities for mutual encouragement, renewal, accountability, and understanding outside the expectations and responsibilities of the working, domestic, or Church environment. It is a gift oriented toward both the sustenance and the abundance of life.

If friendship is a gift to make sometimes contradictory commitments reconcilable, the common purse is a gift to make commitments concrete. "Where your treasure is, there your heart will be also" (Matthew 6.21). The degree of commitment to the shared life of discipleship is less about words than about money.

> All who believed were together and had all things in common; they would sell their possessions and goods and distribute the proceeds to all, as any had need . . . Now the whole group of those who believed were of one heart and soul, and no one claimed private ownership of any possessions, but everything they owned was held in common . . . There was not a needy person among them, for as many as owned lands or houses sold them and brought the proceeds of what was sold. They laid it at the apostles' feet, and it was distributed to each as any had need.
>
> (Acts 2.44–5, 4.32, 34–5)

These are words in relation to which any Christian community must define itself.

The common purse is a practice that defines money, community, and the relation of the community to the state. It defines money because it makes money always a gift, always an instrument, to serve a greater end – never a goal, never an end in itself. Money becomes a means of establishing and maintaining relationships, rather than a method of bypassing relationships, or an insurance in case relationships go wrong. The parable of the dishonest manager portrays a man who capitalizes on the time lag between news of his impending dismissal and the moment when his dismissal takes effect by writing off the debts of his master's creditors and thus buying their good favor for the time when he will need it (Luke 16.1–9). The parable demonstrates that it is much easier to be generous when one is spending someone else's money, that the people who matter are those who owe God the most, that generosity is the best investment, and that God is charmed when we are more generous than he is. The common purse accordingly affirms that money is always God's, not ours, that the more one gives, the more one cares, and that giving makes the relationships of community essential. Giving the first, significant, percentage of one's income certainly pays for the administration of the Christian community, underwriting its expenses, supporting its mission, and alleviating hardship; and such giving frequently demonstrates sacrificial love, answering and echoing the sacrificial love of God: but these are not its primary purpose. Its primary purpose is to engraft disciples in community, by transforming their politics from the politics of scarcity (paying the bills) to a politics of abundance. In deliberating over how to invest the surplus gifts of God the community learns to identify the places and ways God works in the world, and how best to follow where he has led. The translation of common faith and common vision into a common purse concentrates the minds and hearts of disciples so that every gift they make is evaluated for faithfulness and accompanied by prayer.

Meanwhile such a view of investment in the ways of God, founded on generosity as the purpose of capital, which itself is founded on the discovery that it is God's money all along, shapes the relationship of the community to the state and to other organizations. The biggest witness of Christians to their neighbors, families and friends is the way they spend their money. And the common purse affirms that they use their money by supporting communities of trust and love that show what kind of life is possible when people believe that God is sovereign, when they place their trust and security in him. Those communities do not need to be invented because they already exist. And the common purse proclaims that there is no better way to spend money than to support them. It does not proclaim that Christians should not pay their taxes, because taxes help to provide basic necessities and security for needy people. It does not suggest that Christians should not give to charities, because charities pay for things for which a majority in a democracy would not vote. It does not imply that Christians should give to less economically developed countries through the way they shop, because trade gives the recipient both money and dignity. But it does affirm that the Church is the principal way in which God chooses to make himself known in the world. It does transform money from a source of division and isolation to a bond of peace. And it does make gratitude and generosity the center of the Christian common life, offering some protection against all the deceptions money can foster.

One local church received a large sum of money from its diocese to help it erect a new building. For the first three years after the new building opened the church was not asked to make any contribution toward the diocesan common purse (which paid the clergy and covered other shared expenses). Thereafter its contributions to the diocese were restored, but at a discounted rate, taking account of its missionary status and the relative economic hardship of local residents. When the members of the church gathered together to discuss money issues, they resolved to send to the diocese more money than was asked for. This was a sign of gratitude. But it was also a twofold message to Christians elsewhere: first, that the church believed an indication of maturity in discipleship was the habit of generosity; second, a challenge that if this church, with all its disadvantages, could contribute above and beyond the "need," then surely others might be moved to do the same. Through the practice of the common purse, the church was saying, "Don't pity us: copy us."

If friendship and finance provide the fiber of shared life, fun puts the spring in its step. The gift of play is rooted in the Sabbath command. The crown of creation is not so much humanity (the sixth day) as rest (the seventh day); and in the resurrection Christians come to see the Sabbath as not the last but the first day of the week. Just as Latin regards leisure, *otium*, as normative and names business, *negotium*, only as the opposite of leisure, so the Sabbath is a gift to the Church to shape its life around play. Why play? First, because play is sheer exultation in the goodness of being alive. It is not purposeful, productive, efficient, economical, measured, effective, or strategic. It is exuberant, passionate, joyful, reckless, wholehearted, and un-selfconscious. It is a corrective to any solemn Gospel that seeks to make disciples more earnest than God. Second, because play, like rest, affirms the providential hand of God. He who works even while we sleep gives disciples time to play. By taking time to play Christians demonstrate their faith that fundamentally it is in God's hands, not theirs, that the future of creation is cradled. Third, because play invariably practices the manners and disciplines of common life and vocation. Just as children need to learn to share their toys, and just as friends on the sports field need to balance their desire to win the game with their wish to build up their friendship, so play becomes a time of experimentation and training in virtue. And fourth, the undisputed masters of play are young children, and if adults need to relearn how to play, they do so in a spirit of humility, for they remember that Jesus took a little child, put it among them, and took it in his arms, and that later he said "whoever does not receive the kingdom of God as a little child will never enter it" (Mark 10.15; Berryman 2004).

The paradigmatic practice of shared life is the common meal. While the Eucharist is the meal that defines all other meals, the simple sharing of food is the most time-honored bond of a common life. The sharing of food turns physical need into an occasion for deepening fellowship. It brings together all the themes of dependence on one another. For the essence of friendship is to be a companion – a person with whom one shares bread. And it is this companionship that Jesus extends to Simon the Pharisee, Zacchaeus the tax collector, and most especially to the disciples, including Peter, and even the betrayer Judas, at the Last Supper. And at the Last Supper Jesus says to the disciples "I do not call you servants any longer, because the servant does not know what the master is doing; but I have called you friends, because I have made known to you everything that I have heard from my Father" (John 15.15). Likewise the common purse crystallizes in the common meal. When a group of friends go out for a meal together, the most poignant moment comes when they have to address the question of how the bill is to be paid. Somehow the amount required is always a little more than the sum of all the contributions each of the diners felt was due to them. The common purse is a joyful expression of abundance before the meal, rather than a resentful experience of scarcity at the end. It is generosity become routine, the anticipation of common need and the commitment to transform common need into an experience of grace. Thus money, through the lens of food, becomes an instrument of community, a gift of God for the building-up of the Church. Meanwhile play and food come together in that most significant moment of common life, the celebration. Just as the common purse represents the healthy routine aspects of sharing food in community, so play represents the spontaneous, joyful, even anarchic excitement of celebrating a birthday, a church festival, the crossing of a threshold in the life of the community or one or more members of it. It is hard to imagine such a celebration without food: the father of the prodigal son slays the fatted calf and invites the whole village to share his joy: likewise the shepherd and the woman in preceding parables say "let the party begin." The discipline of celebration is such that if the community cannot find occasions of joy in the world around them, they must seek all the harder to rejoice in one another, looking deeper into the gifts God has given them in giving them such friends.

In one local church the congregation found that local children were turning up an hour or more before the service, looking for company, entertainment, or mischief. For a few years two members of the congregation opened the doors an hour before the service began and tried to offer a mixture of conversation, education, and encouragement, together with a little bit of discipline. Slowly they began to notice that one explanation for the children's behavior was that they were hungry. So a pattern began of holding a breakfast 45 minutes before the service began, and during that time weaving into the conversation some high and low points in the week, encouragements and discouragements to faith, and hopes and fears for the near future. Gradually this breakfast extended so that it became not just for the children but for the whole congregation: and three or four times a year instead of breakfast everyone would set about getting ready for a celebratory lunch that would follow the service, and would be made up of contributions, great and small, from almost every member. Thus were human need and a point of aggravation transformed into an occasion of celebration, fellowship, and grace. The need of the human body became an experience of the body of Christ.

Sharing life thus includes friendship, finance, fun, and food. And this is why it is the appropriate place to identify an understanding of marriage. Throughout the New Testament there is a tension between the community of faith and the household of faith: the *transforming* call to go, sell, give, come, follow, dispensing with the fishing nets and leaving the dead to bury their dead, and the *renewing* call to be a good husband, wife, parent, even slave. This study, in emphasizing the practices of the whole body, inevitably stresses the transforming, communal aspect of faith. But not in order to dispense with the household: for marriage is an instantiation – perhaps the most important – of the practices of dependence on one another.

An understanding of sexuality begins with a healthy understanding of play. The description of play offered earlier is an entirely bodily one: and it is vital that an understanding of sexuality be bodily, lest the quest for sexual excitement become an attempt to transcend the body in a moment of ecstasy. Play involves sheer enjoyment of the physical being and presence and movement and gift of the other.

If play is to be more than an occasional series of pleasurable encounters between strangers, it must be disciplined by the habits of friendship. Following the portrayal offered earlier, friendship strengthens the sometimes tenuous bond between vocation and community, by providing a more intimate experience of each, while affirming the underlying purpose of both. Friendship between two partners in a sexual relationship should not only offer an intimate experience of common life, but strengthen each partner's commitment to the common life of the body of Christ. Meanwhile their friendship should not only offer an intimate experience of sharing a joint vocation, but also refine and renew their respective callings. For neither a marriage nor a friendship is an achievement, but a gift enhanced by building up friendships with others.

If such a friendship is to be sustainable over the long term, if it is to be an experience of abundance rather than scarcity, of gift rather than duty, it must be shaped by the practice of the common purse. It is sometimes said that commitment to a marriage is less about sharing a bed than about sharing a bank account. And in this new society made possible by the sharing of goods arises a safe place in which children may be born and reared. Play, friendship, and money create a new body, a body that transforms scarcity into abundance. And this affirms the central place of marriage in an understanding of the Church's practices of dependence on one another: for marriage, as much or more than any other single one of those practices, is about becoming one body.

And central to the practice of marriage is food. Just as it does for the Church in general, so for the married couple in particular, sharing food becomes the practice by which they come to understand play, friendship, and the common purse. By learning to eat the same food at the same time they learn the gift of bodily presence with one another. By learning to share the attendant pattern of planning, purchasing, preparing, clearing, washing, and putting away they learn the disciplines of partnership. And by making the family table the place where manners are articulated and rehearsed, they discover what it means to become a new community with a particular vocation.

Marriage is the great proclamation of abundance. All is focused on a single other – but the truth is that, far from being not enough, that one person is more than enough. Here is the mystery of another person – another mind, another imagination, another myriad of experiences and energies and enthusiasms and enjoyments. Could one ever exhaust that person? And to embody the truth that the good of one half of the marriage can never be in conflict with the good of the other partner, we call them one flesh. They become one body. What is good for the hand is good for the foot. What hurts the knee can never be good for the ear. They are one flesh, and the things that are good for them are things they each can have. This is the politics of love: not the calculation of how in this world of scarcity, each partner can get a fair share out of life together; instead, the discernment together of how all the gifts they have been blessed with may be enjoyed for their mutual flourishing and the service of others.

Marriage is not a zero-sum game, where one person sacrifices their career, or their friends, or their creativity, or their deepest needs, so that the other can be the hero, or be the star, or never have to lose the argument. It is an adventure, in which a new body can be together what neither of them could have been apart, and the only thing that might stop them would be any sense that they could somehow get there on their own. One other person is always more than enough, when you believe that that person will listen to you until you run out of things to say, when you trust that that person will wait for as long as it takes for you to understand why you are the way you are, when you realize that that person will always impute the best of motives to your actions however clumsy you feel inside. You don't need to grab the biggest piece of cake any more, because you are one body, and her eating it is as good as you eating it. You don't have to have all the witty punch lines yourself any more, because it is not a competition for attention that only one of you can win.

Thus the end of a marriage, even if there are no children involved, is a process of great sadness. For an inability or lack of inclination to play together is a denial of the exuberance of creation. Meanwhile estrangement proclaims that this friendship has not sustained either pursuit of vocation or participation in community – or both. And adultery, so often a symptom rather than a cause, is not so much a defilement of the purity of the marriage bed as a proclamation of a message of scarcity – that this partner is not enough – that reduces everyone to poverty.

Sharing faith – a body destined for friendship with God

The second dimension of the way God gives his people everything they need through the practices of dependence on one another is the way disciples build one another up in faith. If the first dimension concerns the sheer goodness of being one body, the second concerns the regular reminders and discoveries of what it means for that body to be constituted by and destined for friendship with God. If the ordinary habits of common life are rooted in Baptism and most fully expressed in the Eucharist, the faith-sharing habits are self-consciously so. Sharing faith requires and depends on the same practices and virtues as sharing life: it is a shared life lived consciously in the presence and company of God.

Paul repeatedly stresses the importance of the practices of shared faith. "Wait for one another" (1 Corinthians 11. 33); "through love become slaves to one another" (Galatians 5.13); "encourage one another and build up each other" (1 Thessalonians 5.11); "lead a life worthy of the calling to which you have been called, with all humility and gentleness, with patience, bearing with one another in love" (Ephesians 4.1–2) (Lohfink 1984, 99–100). Of these many patterns of sharing faith, four stand out for consideration here: rearing children, recognizing gifts, studying the tradition, and marking thresholds.

To include rearing children is to state that "sharing faith" is the right place to discuss the family. The family is the principal, but by no means the only, context in which children are reared. All Christians, not just parents, have a responsibility for the care of children and their growth in faith and discipleship. Children are a gift to a church in several ways. They help Christians understand creation. Creation remains God's possession, despite human language about property and control. Children are not the direct result of parental choice – they are gifts that bring with them surprises, challenges, needs, and joys. Because they take time, they teach Christians to see time also as a gift. Those sharing faith with children are relieved of the responsibility that marriage and procreation are the principal way the Church is to grow: that emphasis lies with conversion and Baptism. But the ordinary and sometimes trivial activities of rearing children remind Christians that salvation is *within* time, not *from* time. Meanwhile having children is a significant gesture of hope. Like worship, caring for children is a time-consuming activity that reduces the time available for making the world a better place. But both are activities that affirm that it is fundamentally in God's hands that the world's destiny lies, and that God gives his people time to do the things that celebrate the sovereignty and manner of his reign.

Children are also a gift to a community in that the business of raising them, particularly shaping their faith and character, makes the community face up to questions about its own character. One leader of a local church went to visit a very elderly member of the congregation, now confined to a nursing home. The elderly woman started talking about her father. "He was one of the old school" she said. "Manners," he used to shout. "I *will* have *manners*" – and he used to bang the table. "Manners have gone out of fashion," she added, reflectively. "People only want things you can have straightaway." Her visitor said to her, "Is there any way of teaching manners without banging the table?" He was shortly to become a parent himself, and sensed there might be some wisdom to be found here. "How do you bring a child up to value, to respect, to treasure, to cherish? How do you teach a young person to be grateful, generous, and thoughtful? I don't want to get into endless arguments; and I don't want to bang the table. I fear it's going to be beyond me." The old lady purred for a while. "There is another way," she said. "You're not going like it, because it's not easy." She leaned forward, and whispered in her visitor's ear: "Example." She sat back. "Told you you wouldn't like it," she said.

If example is one half of sharing faith with children, the other half is trust. The Church demonstrates, by the way it opens its life to children, the nature of the God it believes in. The Church displays trust when it recognizes that God speaks to children, when it creates environments in which children can discover God for themselves, when it believes that children can perceive something about God beyond what the adults already know. It is not a matter of giving children so much information, or activity, or excitement, that they will agree that Christianity is lively, busy, and fun. It is about giving children space and safety and support and trusting that God will do the rest.

Recognizing gifts is a second practice of sharing faith. God gives his people everything they need to follow him. These gifts are primarily in Jesus and the practices of the Church. But there are also particular gifts, or charisms, that God gives to disciples for the building-up of the body. And the Church receives these gifts by recognizing them and putting them to work. Paul identifies and lists several spiritual gifts: he speaks of the prophet, the minister, the teacher, the exhorter, the giver, the leader, the person who shows compassion, the apostle, the evangelist, the pastor, the one who utters wisdom, the one who utters knowledge, the one who has faith, the healer, the miracle-worker, the one who discerns spirits, the one who speaks in tongues, the one who interprets tongues, the one who does deeds of power, the one who assists (Romans 12. 6–8; Ephesians 4.11; 1 Corinthians 12.8–10, 28). In broad terms we may summarize these gifts in terms of the roles needed to sustain the community: speaking the truth, making the truth comprehensible to the congregation, embodying the truth in deeds of love, ensuring faithfulness over time through records and memory, and ensuring every gift has its due opportunity and reception (Yoder 1984, 15–45). None of these is an end in itself, or an embellishment of a single disciple's vocation: they are gifts to the whole Church, cherished in the heart and life of particular Christians. As Paul repeatedly says, the gifts are for "other people for their upbuilding and encouragement and consolation" (1 Corinthians 14.3).

This diversity of gifts names the variety of ways in which God makes himself known to his people. Its breadth and depth speak of abundance, of the inexhaustible will of God to communicate his offer of friendship to his Church, and of the diversity of the voices and lives through which he speaks. In addition to the gifts themselves, the discernment and affirmation of gifts shape the Church in two further ways. On the one hand they motivate the Church's outreach, for Christians seek in the new member not only a new friend, a new companion, but also a fresh and challenging range of gifts to build up the body. On the other hand, in the process of discerning whether these new gifts are true gifts, they push the Church back to the heart of its tradition to identify the characteristic and unwavering patterns of God's activity. If there is no love, joy, or peace in evidence, no patience, kindness or goodness to be found, no sign of faithfulness, gentleness, or self-control, this is unlikely to be God's grace at work.

A third practice of sharing faith is studying the tradition. In this the "how" is as important as the "what." The "what" is the whole panorama of Bible and Church: law, prophets and writings, Gospels and epistles, doctrine and philosophy, church history and ethics, liturgy, and pastoral studies. Through the diversity of ways of engaging with the subjects and methods of theology, the disciples come to find their place within the communion of saints, and understand the tradition as a gift. The "how" of sharing faith refers to the vista of home groups, short study series, education hours, weekends away, and recommended reading, together with formal award-bearing courses and vocational training, that make up the way the wisdom of the ancients and the challenge of the moderns (who quickly become the ancients) are distilled and passed on to new generations. And the gift to the Church embodied in studying the tradition is the constant relationship between the "what" and the "how." For as disciples discover more about the voices in which God speaks in the Bible, or the great figures and movements of Church history, or the shape of the liturgy, they seek to make their church communities more faithful and courageous and prayerful in accordance with what they have learned. And meanwhile the contexts in which disciples make these discoveries – the lecture preceded by a prayer and followed by searching questions sympathetically answered, the home group in which study follows the common meal and precedes the sharing of burdens and prayers, the evening service with hymns of faith and Psalms of struggle and the discipline of saying the Creed – challenge any notion of education divorced from the worshiping, practicing, and reflecting community. Disciples seek to straighten out their thoughts because their thoughts affect their performance of vital practices; and meanwhile they seek to straighten out their practices because their practices shape the way they think. Christian education never stands alone, for the sake of amusement, mild interest, or cultural appreciation. It is always standing in the company of worship, of the habits of common life and the care of those in need, of the desire to proclaim truth and share practices, and to extend God's friendship to those who need it most and know it least. But none of those activities whose company Christian education keeps is self-authenticating or self-explanatory: each requires the communicating and refining process constituted by studying the tradition.

A fourth practice that constitutes a gift to the Church for sharing faith is the practice of marking thresholds. In a sense this is an extension of the practice of celebration, discussed earlier in the sharing life section under the headings of food and play. But some of the most significant thresholds cannot be appropriately described as celebrations. Nonetheless they are central to the way the community narrates its life as a story of faith. I refer to moments of public tragedy, and the communal grief of a funeral.

Like many other churches, one local congregation deliberated how best to serve its neighborhood during the fervid week that followed the sudden death of Diana, Princess of Wales. It decided to open its doors on the night before the funeral, project a large photograph of the princess onto a screen, play suitable meditative classical music, and make space available for people to light a candle, to say a prayer, to sign a book, and to sit for a moment in silence. Hundreds of local people took up the opportunity, and toward the end of the evening the floor of the church building was a bobbing sea of dizzy candle flames. In a quiet moment, one elderly member of the regular congregation said to her neighbor, "Diana was six weeks older than Mozart when she died." In one simple sentence she affirmed the genuineness of the tragedy, and yet contrasted a short life of much goodness and great complexity with a life of equal brevity and complexity but a legacy of astonishing music that will continue to move millions to glorify God for as long as anyone can imagine. She gently contrasted the dramatic and sentimental with the truly profound and significant, in a subtle but timely way. It was a word of prophecy.

If public tragedy is a moment when a local church may support its neighborhood while identifying subtle ways in which its hope differs from that found elsewhere, funerals offer a Christian community opportunities to name the ways God expresses himself through the lives of those around them. There is such a thing as a good funeral: one that names and acknowledges the invariable incompleteness of life and the ache and horror of grief, yet sets them in the context of how God has worked, is working, and will complete his work in the world, and identifies precisely how this life was part of that pattern of God's work, thus disclosing an aspect of God's character. Such a funeral can be a genuine gift of God to build up the faith of his Church. At one such occasion, marking the passing of a sturdy-hearted man who lived among straightforward folk, the preacher simply said, "George was carried into this building as a baby, for Baptism; he was carried in again today, for his funeral. In between, he carried pretty well all of us, at times, when we thought we couldn't walk any further. Jesus was carried too, into the Temple for purification by Simeon, and from the cross to the tomb by Mary and Joseph of Arimathaea. And in between, and most of all on the cross – and especially now – he carries us." Little else needed to be said. But in those few words he had affirmed the work of God in the dead man and renewed the mission of God in those who remained.

Sharing troubles: being the broken body

The third dimension of the way God gives his people everything they need through the practices of dependence on one another is the way disciples bear one another's burdens. These are moments when Christians discover whether the habits developed in sharing life and sharing faith count for much or melt away when the heat is on: moments when the life of abundance is challenged by the threat of scarcity. While these practices are undoubtedly gifts to the Church in their own right, they also provide the substance of the Church's response to many pressing issues in biotechnology and healthcare.

Perhaps the most immediate aspect of bearing one another's burdens is the practice of caring for the sick and the dying. A visitor to France may be struck by a medieval building near the center of numerous towns or cities described as the "Hôtel de Dieu," clearly appearing to have been a hospital. Even allowing for the difference in the French and English meanings of "hotel," this is a challenging title: it indicates that the hospital is the place where God comes to stay when he is in town. The most important gesture Christians make in relation to healthcare is not to give up on people when they cease to be economically active or in measurable ways productive. To the extent that this principle is embedded in the assumptions of public healthcare, Christians may applaud and honor its great traditions. But they must never conclude that healthcare professionals can provide everything that is needed for the sick or dying person. There is an important role, of course, for those with medical training and skill; there may well be a role for those with complementary skills to offer, such as a social worker; there is commonly a role for the family, in sharing information and decisions about interventions, prognosis, and convalescence. But there is a vital neglected role of the friend – the one who does not know what the matter is, who has no techniques for alleviation or distraction, who does not have a financial or practical interest in the outcome of the treatment, but who still has an eye for the patient's pursuit of their vocation and participation in community – a simple enjoyment of another person created and called by God and destined to be his friend for ever.

And this is a friendship that does not give up even when the patient enters the valley of the shadow of death. In one congregation there was a woman who developed terminal cancer. Over six months one friend went to visit her five times. The first time she told him of all the things that meant most to her – family, music, work, garden, faith. The second time he asked her, if she had just a few weeks, what were the key things she wanted to do, to say, to complete? She pondered, and planned, and in the days and weeks that followed, acted. Letters were written, significant conversations took place, presents were bought for birthdays she would not live to see, a journal was completed that contained wisdom and reflections. On the third visit she spent a while letting go of the one or two things that still lay uneasy on her heart, and together she and her friend allowed God to release her from the burden of them. Three days before she died they prayed together a fourth time, and her friend commended each part of her life, body, mind, and spirit, to the God who had made and so much cherished her. And finally, shortly after her death, her friend had the opportunity to sit with others beside her body and recognize before God everything that had happened. And afterwards there was only one word spoken: and that word was "beautiful." The friendship had been a discovery of the power Christians are given when they are given mundane ways of encountering the unfathomable.

Those committed to the bearing of one another's burdens discover the subtle distinctions between different kinds of need. Whereas care of the sick and dying usually presupposes a time-frame – the duration of the illness, or the limited period before the illness causes death – the care of the confused and dependent is less about time than about sustainability. These are situations that time is not going to heal. And yet such situations can still be a gift to the Church. In one local congregation there was a man with special educational needs who found himself in a vulnerable social and economic position. Members of his church met together to discuss how they could best serve him, and when they had settled on a level and pattern of support they felt they could sustain they included him in a subsequent discussion of what kinds of activities and opportunities they could share together. However, in the weeks that followed a dispute arose over the extent to which these conversations should be kept confidential. Some felt that the best practice from the caring professions was to keep matters entirely between the interested parties, and certainly not to let it be known that here was a person open to being mistreated by those looking to prey on the vulnerable. Others felt that bearing one another's burdens was at the heart of church life, and that the way it was done might well need to be different from the approach found elsewhere. The disagreement came to a climax when the man was named in a document that recorded some of the issues, events and highlights in the recent life of the church. Those who had favored confidentiality were shocked, and some sought a public apology. None was given. But shortly after, the man was overheard commenting to friends how much he had appreciated being mentioned in the report, because people had been so kind, and it made him feel he was an important part of the church. He was a gift through whom that congregation learned the difference between being a caring profession and being a church.

A further kind of burden-bearing, subtly different again, is care of the bereaved and despairing. Such distress may seem like the care of the sick and dying – that is, it may seem time-bound ("after three years or so you begin to get over it"); but to the sufferer, it invariably seems more like the care of the confused and dependent – an open-ended chasm. The whole panoply of human distress – of loss, of hurt, of estrangement, of loneliness, of unassailable obstacles and impossible odds – are woven into the weft of common life. And the Church's guides are the companions of Job, who "sat with him on the ground seven days and seven nights, and no one spoke a word to him, for they saw that his suffering was very great" (Job 2.13). This, for many, is where the abundance of the gifts God gives the Church seems hardest to perceive. It is, for many, the moment of greatest strain in their friendship with God. In the face of scarcity, the role of caregivers is to embody abundance: to remind and embody all the other gifts of God – to provide a wider context for those gifts that seem to be lacking – using words if they have to. It may be a long, dark night with no sign of dawn. Yet all the more is it vital to recall God's call to persistent, stubborn worship ("the Lord gave, and the Lord has taken away; blessed be the name of the Lord"), enduring friendship ("Who will separate us from the love of Christ?") and undeterred shared meals ("You prepare a table before me in the presence of my enemies").

And this is the ground on which the Church's engagement with many of the contentious issues of medicine lies. For technology is more frequently the result of moral confusion than the cause of it. So often technology seeks to make a better world without us needing to become better people. Technology can never answer questions like what constitutes a good death, why society does not give up on someone just because they are sick or dying, and what kinds of circumstance make suffering worthy and dignified. The efforts of the Christian community are to bind the sick and the dying, the confused and the dependent, the bereaved and the despairing, into one body with those whose troubles are more intermittent or less visible. Such a body constitutes a visible challenge to the imagination of those whose assumptions have been shaped by the possibilities of technology and the limits of care.

Should limitless efforts be expended to give couples children "of their own" when the Church seeks to embody a community where childrearing is such a shared vocation that parents seldom experience a sense that their children are "their own"? Should permission be given for patients to receive assistance in taking their own lives when the Church seeks to practice the care of the dying in such a way that gestures of faithfulness such as worship, friendship, and shared food never cease, even to the end? Should a blind eye be turned to late abortions on the grounds of disability when the Church seeks to display a culture where all children are treasured and nurtured as gifts bringing surprising and unexpected challenges and blessings? Should a door be opened to the cloning of human beings when the Church seeks to live not as a new body improved by genetic modification but as a renewed body transformed by Baptism and engrafted into Christ?

When Christians are invited to join public discussions over such issues as biotechnology they do so as representatives of a body that adopts the unwanted baby, nurtures the unusual child, persists with the manic or addicted teenager, befriends the terminally ill neighbor, remains present to the elderly friend even while her mind dies. If they can point to such a cloud of witnesses they speak with authority: if not, they have perhaps little to say.

Dependence on the Stranger

To speak of the Church's dependence on God may be regarded as uncontroversial: it is after all implicit in the notion of prayer, in the understanding of creation and of providence, and in almost any reading of the lordship of Christ. To speak of the Christian community's dependence on one another is perhaps unfashionable, in an era in which a congregation is commonly understood as an aggregate of individuals, assumptions of personal autonomy go unchallenged in many churches, and much investment has been made in ensuring public authorities provide for citizens' material needs when they are in trouble – but in principle, interdependence is affirmed politely by many as a plausible idea. But to speak of dependence on the stranger is another matter. Responsibility for, perhaps: duty to, quite possibly; but dependence *on*? This would sound to many, perhaps most, as getting matters the wrong way round.

And yet dependence on the stranger rightly takes its place alongside dependence on God and dependence on one another as the third dimension of the life of God's people – the third source of gifts. Israel's life was characterized by its care not only of the orphan and the widow but also of the alien. Over and over again the stranger is a gift to the people of God. It is Melchizedek who brings out bread and wine and blesses Abraham. It is Pharaoh whose "fat cows" sustain Jacob's family in times of hardship. It is Balaam who blesses Israel in the sight of her enemy Balak. It is Ruth who demonstrates the faithfulness and imagination that Israel will need under her descendant David. It is Achish of Gath who gives a safe home to David and his followers when they are pursued by Saul. It is the Queen of Sheba who gives independent testimony to the wisdom and prosperity of Solomon. It is Cyrus who opens the way for the Jews to return from Exile. Israel depends on these strangers. Strangers are not simply a threat. They are not all characterized by the hard-hearted hostility of Moses' Pharaoh, of Goliath of Gath, of Sennacherib of Assyria, and Nebuchadnezzar of Babylon. Time and again strangers are the hands and feet of God, rescuing, restoring, and reminding Israel as elsewhere God does himself.

Likewise Jesus and the early Church discover faith and mercy amongst strangers. On meeting the centurion whose servant he is asked to heal, Jesus says, "In no one in Israel have I found such faith." It is the Samaritan leper who is the only one of the ten healed who turns back to praise God and thank Jesus. Finding the resilience and devotion of the Cannanite woman who seeks healing for her daughter, Jesus similarly says "Woman, great is your faith!" It is Cornelius whose visit from an angel pushes the Church into revising its understanding of Gentile faith. And it is in the Samaritan that Jesus tells his followers that they should see the model of a good neighbor.

Indeed Jesus' parables offer a framework for how the people of God recognize their dependence on the stranger. From the Good Samaritan they learn that they themselves are strangers, dependent on the mercy of those they may well have been taught to hate. From the dishonest manager they learn that those who matter most are those who owe God most. From the rich man and Lazarus they learn that they are to care for the poor not for the poor's sake but for their own (their eternal salvation depends on it), that they are to care for the poor not because the poor are deserving but because they are poor (Lazarus' moral character is not discussed), and that their care for the poor is a testament to their regard for God. And from the parable of the last judgment they learn that the poor are sacraments of Christ, providing perhaps the most immediate opportunity to encounter Christ every day, and that their judgment will focus on what they took for granted, what they did when they assumed no one was looking, rather than on their set-piece moments of piety.

The parable of the last judgment makes explicit what is implicit at several other points in the Gospel narratives: that Christ is the stranger. Christ is the one who is excluded at the moment of his birth ("no room at the inn"), exiled shortly after ("then Joseph . . . took the child and his mother by night, and went to Egypt"), emerges from notoriety ("can anything good come out of Nazareth?"), has no home ("the Son of Man has nowhere to lay his head"), at a vital moment no friends ("all of them deserted him and fled"), and finally a cursed hill on which to die ("they came to a place that is called 'The Skull'") and no secure place to be buried ("so Joseph took the body . . . and laid it in his own new tomb"). Part of what it means for Christ to be savior is that he puts himself in the position of the one who needs to be saved.

What the parable of the last judgment affirms is that the stone that the builders rejected has become the cornerstone. The forgotten stranger is in fact the king. The parable has the same essential structure as the parable of the wicked tenants: both affirm that many people are blind to the way God reveals himself and that their salvation is in peril as a consequence. What the parable of the last judgment enjoins is the simple, ingenuous practice of mercy.

> I was hungry and you gave me food, I was thirsty and you gave me something to drink, I was a stranger and you welcomed me, I was naked and you gave me clothing, I was sick and you took care of me, I was in prison and you visited me.
>
> (Matthew 25.35–6)

These six acts of mercy embody God's call to his people to worship him, be his friends, and eat with him. For they begin with food and drink; they constitute the hand of friendship extended across the bounds of shame, impurity, fear, and need; and they are revealed to be encounters with Christ, and thus appropriately described as worship. They extend to the world the good practices of the body. They define friendship in the context of conversation and food. They are integral to the practices of the Church.

But an ethic that lapses into responsibility for or duty to the stranger is inadequate. It misses the crucial dimension, that the stranger is a gift to the Church. By missing this dimension it creates a tension that should not exist. That tension is between the inner and outer life of the Church – the love expressed among its members and the love they show for outsiders. This may be experienced as the tension between comfort and responsibility. But it is premised on a misunderstanding of the stranger. The stranger is a gift to the Church, not a burden on it. As all the scriptural examples demonstrate, the stranger represents the hand of God, becoming present in the Church to rescue, restore, and remind. The stranger is not the harbinger of scarcity but the sacrament of abundance – not the drainer of resources but the bringer of gifts. Caring for the stranger, sharing food, and offering friendship, are not matters of altruism: they are done in the simple trust that this person has something precious that will sustain or build up the life of the community, even if that gift is slow to be revealed or hard to receive. This is the stone that the builders rejected: but it is destined to become the cornerstone. This is the crucified one: but it will be the one gloriously resurrected.

One local congregation came across a young man in trouble. He was due in court on 117 counts of burglary. The church leaders said to him, "Come and paint our hall." It turned out the young man had a talent for it. He had learned decorating while at a young offenders' institution. He struck up a friendship with the church secretary. The secretary only worked part-time, but hung around and chatted in odd moments. They shared a sandwich a few times. When it came to the boy's trial for burglary, the church secretary went along and said "Give this lad another chance: let him work for us." The judge said "Well, you're certainly cheaper than prison: but I don't rate your chances with him." The young man finished the painting project. He then got together with a couple of friends and started up a painting business. The time came for the ceremony to dedicate the restored church hall. The young man's mother turned up. There was only one person she wanted to speak to. That person was the church secretary. She looked him in the eye, and spoke slowly to him. Each word counted. "When you went to court to plead for my son to keep his job, you saved his life."

Even amongst Christian communities that come to realize their dependence on those who might be seen as vulnerable or "needy," it is generally hard to recognize dependence on two particular kinds of stranger – the member of another faith, and the enemy. The conventional typology of relationships between members of different faiths has been the threefold paradigm of exclusivism, inclusivism, and pluralism. But once it is accepted that all faith is inter-faith – that is, that all faith is practiced in a context of seeking peace and reconciliation amongst friends and strangers – and once one is prepared to consider not just theoretical issues but practices also, then the true nature of the issue emerges. And the true contrast in relation to the member of another faith as a stranger is the choice between tolerance and hospitality (Barnes 2002, 4, 8, 254).

Tolerance assumes conflict: it is an armistice postponing hostilities (Bretherton 2004, 80–103). Tolerance offers no identifiable social practice, and certainly no cohesive model for the setting-right of unjust social relations; when acceptance of differences translates into social policy it unravels into disputes over those who find this kind of tolerance does not tolerate them. Indeed tolerance tends to dismantle communities and silence public discourse, because it becomes increasingly difficult to challenge the ideas of others or to relate to movements broader than the individual conscience. By contrast hospitality is inherently communal: it assumes that in the sharing of food and in the first steps of friendship lies the appropriate context in which to discern the sources of value (and thus the different directions, purposes, content, practices and implications of worship). Christian hospitality assumes the stranger has come to bring a gift – because Christ came to bring unlimited gifts, and Christ was a stranger – and that that gift may turn out to be crucial for the maintenance and flourishing of the Christian community.

Once again the heart of the issue is scarcity and abundance. Tolerance assumes there are realistic limits to acceptance and that each difference needs to be kept in check lest it overwhelm the other. Hospitality assumes that generosity leads to replenishment from unexpected sources: there is no anxiety over diminution of resources or pollution of pure doctrine. Jesus transforms the relationship between hospitality and holiness.

> Instead of having to be set apart from or exclude pagans in order to maintain holiness, it is in Jesus' hospitality of pagans, the unclean, and sinners that his own holiness is shown forth. Instead of sin and impurity infecting him, it seems Jesus' purity and righteousness somehow "infects" the impure, sinners and the Gentiles. As Marcus Borg puts it: "In the teaching [and practice] of Jesus, holiness, not uncleanness, was understood to be contagious." For example, the hemorrhaging woman has only to touch Jesus and she is healed and made clean.
>
> (Bretherton 2004, 94)

In one local church there was a couple who went on holiday together and, at one point, sought a lift to a scenic viewpoint. Their guide was a Muslim man. When they reached the viewpoint they got out their cameras and posed in front of the scene from various angles. Just as they began to think about moving on they realized that their guide had not been visible for some time. Walking around a corner they spotted him, semi-prostrate, making his prayerful oblation to God. They were humbled, realizing how they and he had respectively spent the previous 15 minutes. When they returned home they shared with their congregation a prayer that they had found helpful, which went "If I love thee for hope of heaven, then deny me heaven; if I love thee for fear of hell, then deny me hell; but if I love thee for thyself alone, then give me thyself alone." The congregation took readily to the prayer, and some asked its origin. When they discovered it was a Muslim prayer, there was some confusion. But the couple who had been on the holiday pointed out that just as their guide had been a gift to them in jolting their own spiritual complacency, so this prayer could similarly be a gift, perhaps dispelling some ignorance and prejudice about Islam.

This chapter concludes with dependence on the enemy. Dependence on the enemy is the climax of the Church's performance, because it most appositely imitates Christ, it most provocatively displays the practice of the Church, it requires every dimension of the gifts received through all the forms of dependence described in this chapter, and it ultimately displays abundance in a context that assumes scarcity.

To depend on the enemy seems to be an absurdity: for does not the enemy embody everything that undermines and pollutes the body of Christ, and is not dependence on the enemy a pernicious cocktail of idolatry, naïveté, and collusion with evil? How then can it be the climax of the Church's performance? To respond to this requires reviewing the claims of this chapter, building an argument by steps, and finally seeing the practices outlined in this chapter as circular. Thus, in the first place is the notion of dependence. Dependence in itself – as the characteristic of every aspect of Christian performance – is an affront to the widespread notion of autonomy. Fears about depending on the enemy begin with fears about depending on anybody. They let you down, they exploit, abuse, mistreat, manipulate, and eventually toss you away. It is true, they do. But autonomy is not the answer.

Dependence begins with dependence on God: Jesus says "Father, forgive them; for they do not know what they are doing." In the face of the enemy, he looks to his Father. The regular habits of prayer, and the embodiment of those habits in the relationships of household and community, shape disciples in a self-understanding based around dependence rather than autonomy. God is not a mechanism for securing autonomy; on the contrary, in discovering their dependence on God disciples realize the liberation that lies in transformed notions of dependence. And this is where dependence on one another – interdependence – begins to emerge. Disciples depend on one another for the ordinary aspects of life, they discover ways in which these ordinary rhythms are interlaced with dependence on God, and from those ordinary habits emerge the practices that sustain the community when its members get into trouble. But because the community depends on God, and not just on itself, it knows that its maintenance and flourishing depend on gifts coming from outside. And thus it rediscovers the ways in which God brings gifts through strangers – that the poor and the vulnerable and the very different may be offering the community things it can scarce live without. But some of these strangers bring "gifts" that seem extremely threatening, gifts that are very hard to incorporate within the community's life, not least because they may be specifically designed to damage or destroy that life.

And at this point three moves are required. The first is to complete the circle, and to realize that dependence on one another and dependence on the stranger lead back to dependence on God. "Love your enemies, do good to those who hate you, bless those who curse you, pray for those who abuse you" (Luke 6.27–8): Jesus takes the issue back to dependence on God.

> If you love those who love you, what credit is that to you? For even sinners love those who love them. If you do good to those who do good to you, what credit is that to you? For even sinners do the same . . . But love your enemies, do good, and lend, expecting nothing in return. Your reward will be great, and you will be children of the Most High; for he is kind to the ungrateful and the wicked.
>
> (Luke 6.32–3, 35)

Jesus points out that dependence on one another is not enough: one must depend on the stranger and at the extremes of that dependence one realizes that depending on the stranger means depending on God. The second move is to separate the stranger from the evil that may be in their heart. It is not the enemy that is evil, but the intention in the heart of the enemy: obliterating the enemy may temporarily alleviate the danger to the community, but it is unlikely to discredit the evil intention – and may have the opposite effect. To speak of dependence on the enemy is to draw renewed attention to the significance of dependence on the stranger, and thus to focus the discernment of the community on what this stranger is bringing that may be given hospitality – even if the community may need all its resources to withstand the threat the enemy appears to pose. And this mention of all the community's resources leads to the third move – when the community turns its attention to withstanding the threats coming from enemies, it considers what its resources really are. And what it finds is that its resources are the very practices of dependence on God, one another, and the stranger. Where in these resources lies a violent or aggressive response to a threat? Such practices come from elsewhere. They are the practices of communities that have found that the practices of threefold dependence have not given Christians everything they need to worship God, be his friends, and eat with him. They are the practices of disciples who have found the gifts of God scarce in time of need. The Church depends on the enemy, in the end, because the enemy provides the final test of whether Christians truly depend on the abundant gifts to be had through God, one another, and the stranger – or whether, finding them insufficient, they will look elsewhere.

Chapter Seven

RESTORING

My whole argument is a plea to recognize the plenteous gifts God has given his people to enable them to answer his call to follow him and live a reconciled life. But I recognize that the Church has not only disregarded these gifts but positively failed to embody God's redeeming grace in clumsy and sometimes hideous ways. This chapter is given over to acknowledging the Church's sin, while also outlining the gifts God gives the Church to address even the grossest breaches of its calling. The Church's ability to embody forgiveness constitutes perhaps its most significant witness to the world: for it is where priestly and prophetic ministry most poignantly meet.

Speaking the Truth

There are three great mysteries at the heart of the Christian faith. The first is, why did God bother to create in the first place? The second mystery is why, given the mess his people made of things, did God continue to bother? Why did he not give up humans when they turned out the way they did? The third mystery is perhaps the greatest mystery of all. Why do his people not bother – why can they not be bothered? The horror is deeper than simply not "being bothered," of course. Christians have not just ignored God's playground, they have damaged and abused their fellow players, and even dismantled the playground itself. Perhaps four levels of disorder may be identified: sin, evil, collusion, and poverty of imagination. These expand the categories I offered in Chapter One. The first two expand the idea of sin as "perversity"; the last two expand the description of sin as "lack of imagination."

Sin is the sheer perversity by which people mishandle the gifts of God, turning a gift of grace into a weapon of harm, transforming an opportunity for the worship of God into a moment of idolatry. In her novel *Still Life*, A.S. Byatt narrates how the popular and charismatic new parish priest Gideon Farrar takes the young people of the parish away for a weekend and encourages them to explore their feelings. The boys in the group relish a leader who makes them feel it *matters* what they do. One shy member, Ruth, talks for the first time about her mother's illness and death, about her father's remarriage, and about her desire to be a nurse. Stephanie, the curate's wife, had felt uncomfortable with Gideon since his first, rather flirtatious, conversation with her. Some weeks after the youth weekend, she goes up one evening to the church hall unexpectedly to find Gideon alone in the small office with one of the teenage girls, with his hands inside her blouse. "It was the pale plaited girl who said little and looked quiet, the one who was training to be a nurse" (Byatt 1986, 329–30). This is a story of the perversity of sin: a man who is surrounded by grace – the gift of ministry, the faithfulness of a colleague, the lively enthusiasm and eagerness of a youth group, a place in the story to be enjoyed and shared, all the practices of the Church in generosity and hopefulness and trust available to him. And yet the story is forgotten, the gifts neglected, the moment disgraced, and power turned to violation. Like David sending Uriah to his death and taking Bathsheba to himself, it is God-given power turned to willful harm. It is the mystery – and the horror – of sin.

Evil is the sinister process by which the perversity of sin becomes the active program of a people or institution. To say "evil" is not just to say "sin" with a loud voice: it is to recognize that in every generation there are agonizing examples of how Christians have become fixated on a cause that has blinded their eyes to grace. Perhaps most ghastly in recent times has been the participation of many congregations in the genocide practiced in Rwanda in 1994. Hugh McCullum tells of one Fr Wenceslas Munyeshyaka, the parish priest of a huge Roman Catholic church in the center of the capital Kigali (McCullum 1995, 44–9). Up to 8,000 Tutsis sought sanctuary there in ghastly conditions. Yet almost daily people were abducted and killed by the machete-wielding militia, known as the *interahamwe*. Frequently Fr Wenceslas took Tutsis around to the back of the church and killed them himself. On one occasion a hundred Tutsi boys were massacred outside the church. Those inside the church had become hostages, part of an elaborate scheme to prevent the church being attacked by the Tutsi army. Elsewhere McCullum tells of meeting a Presbyterian minister who watched as members of his congregation, people he had baptized, butchered his entire family. Like the spirit in the crowd in Jerusalem on Good Friday, spreading like a bush fire and inducing them to call for the release of Barabbas and the

crucifixion of Jesus, there is no explanation for it. Evil, like sin, is fundamentally inexplicable, a horrifying mystery.

Collusion names the more passive participation of Christians and their
churches in patterns of perversity, or the way people hasten to profit from
the sins of others. Over a whole host of issues it is constantly pointed out
that for the triumph of evil all that is required is that the good do nothing.
The conditions of world trade, which keep so many in developing countries
in poverty, and the depredation of the planet resulting in climate change are
among the most obvious areas in which Christians are often as much as
anyone a part of processes in which almost everyone claims to be powerless.
In one local church a prayer and action group was set up with great enthusiasm and met two or three times with plenty to discover and do: but
gradually almost every member found the music group, or the working
men's club, or the difficulty in getting a babysitter, or the need to keep up
with marking and preparation for the classroom, too much; and the issues of
justice and trade and those falsely imprisoned fell off the church's agenda
altogether. Like the disciples scattering from Gethsemane and thus letting
the injustice of Jesus' arrest and trial continue unchallenged, even those best
placed to see the contrast between grace and disorder persuade themselves
there is nothing they can do. Collusion is often a matter of neglect – and
thus of passive participation in oppression and disorder.

Hugh McCullum tells of a remarkable meeting in Rwanda in August
1994 of 20 members of the Presbyterian Committee for Rehabilitation –
later known as the Surviving Church and later again as the Repentant
Church. They recalled soberly that every Tutsi in their churches was dead,
together with those Hutus who had refused to cooperate with the militias.
They wondered why practically none of the bishops or leaders from any
denomination had condemned the genocide. They realized "the church
didn't change people: instead the church was changed and became weak."
The pastor whose family had been butchered said slowly "We lost our lives.
We lost our credibility. We are ashamed. We are weak. But most of all, we
lost our prophetic mission. We could not go to the President and tell him
the truth because we became sycophants to the authorities" (McCullum
1995, 75).

Finally poverty of imagination refers to the clumsy ways within communities in which insecurity can become jealousy, fear can become cruelty,
self-pity can become laziness, powerlessness can become despair: in short,
the ways in which the local church seems a very long way from the
kingdom. It sometimes seems that every grouping of people, a congregation
included, becomes a power struggle, a location for playing out family
dysfunctions, an opportunity for rehearsing and displaying the banal and

underhand vices of life without grace. In one local congregation a bitter argument broke out between two members. One had taken in a local teenager and given her lodging for several months, the other doubted the teenager's integrity and offered plenty of unsolicited counsels of caution, many deriving from the textbooks of a newly-begun profession. When the teenager reported that she had fallen down the stairs and induced a miscarriage, the differences of view spilled over into loud dispute. Had she ever been pregnant? Had she in fact had a secret abortion? Was this simply attention-seeking? Nothing was clear. Was this a disagreement in love? Was it one insecure person trying out their new-found socio-psychological skills and patronizingly questioning the motives of an honest person trying their best? Or was it another person feeling guilty about their level of education and opportunity and perhaps deceiving themselves by arrogantly refusing to listen to advice when it could save them from the naïve folly of superficially trying to help? Or was it two conflicting methods of facing despair? Like the disciples squabbling about who will get the best seats in the kingdom, local churches are often places where, in Edwin Muir's phrase, "the word made flesh is here made word again" – and a harsh word, at that (from "The Incarnate One", Muir 1991).

These four dimensions of disorder are not exclusive. They feed each other. But the reason for listing them here is that the practices of forgiveness and reconciliation may differ significantly from one kind of disorder to another. Yet together they set a context for what it means to speak the truth.

Speaking the truth sometimes seems physically impossible. In one local church there was a family who had experienced a deep tragedy. A young, effervescent, life-giving woman died leaving a husband and four children, all entering adulthood. Her only son was determined to speak at her funeral. Everything else was carefully planned and managed, but at 10 o'clock on the night before her funeral, her son had nothing prepared for his address. A priest sat down beside him. "Tell me, what would be the worst thing that could happen tomorrow? That you would burst into tears, or would offend someone?" There was a long pause, after which the young man said, "That I wouldn't speak the truth." "And what is the truth?" said the priest. "That the last week of her life was pure hell," he said. "Well," said the priest, "why not say that?" "I somehow can't," said the young man. "Everyone's so determined to be positive and happy." The priest took a risk. "Maybe that's because everyone in this family has found truth difficult for about 60 years – since your great-aunt died after having a child when her doctor had predicted she would, and then your grandfather died very young and your father was never told why . . . [and on and on, listing several more examples]. Maybe if you stood up tomorrow and said it was hell you'd being doing a favor to more people than you realize." The young man did exactly that. And the congregation was transfixed by his courage. And every generation of his family began to grieve as if for the first time. For at last there was a truthful story around which their anger and sadness could gather.

Thus the gifts of reconciliation begin with the telling of a truthful story. Only on the base of a truthful story can disciples practice admonition. "If another member of the church sins against you, go and point out the fault when the two of you are alone. If the member listens to you, you have regained that one" (Matthew 18.15). Admonition contrasts two stories: the story of grace, of creation, calling, Christ, the Church, and consummation; and the story of sin, the story of self-justification, self-deception and self-pity – of sin, evil, collusion, and failure of moral imagination. Admonition involves judgment, because judgment names the difference between the two stories. Admonition depends on being able to render both accounts as truthful stories. On the one hand the Gospel of grace must be told as living, urgent narrative in which the logic of cross and resurrection is transparent and thrilling. On the other hand the narrative of disorder must be told in such a way that the protagonist recognizes himself or herself, sees that their own perspective is acknowledged and understood, but can then see how agonizing is the contrast between this narrative and the Gospel of grace. These are two different kinds of truth, of course. The one is a claim about the nature, orientation, and purpose of the universe; the other an aggregation of significant elements into a plausible sequence. But to set them side by side makes clear that within the practice of admonition lie not only the reality of judgment but the hope of conversion. The second story says "Yes, you may be in great pain – but look at the pain you have caused. Christ was profoundly sinned against, but did not sin in return: if your pain is too great to bear, plead with Christ to bear it. Do not transfer it onto others. Yes, you may have been a victim, but this is not the whole story about you. See how your behavior has made a victim of others, and see how the Gospel of grace can take you and them out of this cycle of victimization." Thus does the truthful story of the Gospel enable disciples to begin to tell truthful stories about themselves and one another.

It is important to dispel notions of self-righteous judgmentalism from the practice of admonition. Thomas Aquinas helpfully regards fraternal correction as a "kind of alms" (Aquinas 1948, IIa IIae q. 31, volume 3, 1314). John Howard Yoder summarizes the teaching of Matthew 18.15–18 as follows:

a The initiative is personal, not a clergy function. The one who is to address the offender is the person who knows about the offence, not a clergy person.

b   The intention is restorative, not punitive.

c   There is no distinction between major offences and minor ones: Any offence is forgivable, but none is trivial.

d   The intention is not to protect the church's reputation or to teach onlookers the seriousness of sin, but only to serve the offender's own well-being by restoring him or her to the community.

(Yoder 2001, 2–3)

Thus does God give his people gifts to enable them to worship him, be his friends, and eat with him, even in the face of sin and evil.

Discovering Goodness

So if anyone is in Christ, there is a new creation: everything old has passed away; see, everything has become new! All this is from God, who reconciled us to himself through Christ, and has given us the ministry of reconciliation; that is, in Christ God was reconciling the world to himself, not counting their trespasses against them, and entrusting the message of reconciliation to us. So we are ambassadors for Christ, since God is making his appeal through us; we entreat you on behalf of Christ, be reconciled to God. For our sake he made him to be sin who knew no sin, so that in him we might become the righteousness of God.

(2 Corinthians 5.17–21)

An exploration of the practices of repentance, forgiveness, reconciliation, and restoration must begin with a frank admission: sometimes they work and sometimes they do not; or at least, sometimes their work is very slow. So while this section first highlights the gifts God gives for restoration, it also points to gifts that may come into play when full reconciliation seems highly unlikely or out of reach. When it works, there is indeed a new creation, and the ministry of reconciliation is indeed a dimension of how the Church embodies Christ. But Paul's words are a self-acknowledged "entreaty": in other words, he himself is pleading with his readers to follow a path of reconciliation with God and thus become reconciling presences in the life of their neighbors. Even for Paul, reconciliation was clearly sometimes a matter of unfulfilled hope.

If the first practice in relation to disorder is telling a truthful story, and the second is admonition, the third is repentance. In one local church there was young woman who went away to university and, while there, formed a long-standing relationship with a man some years older than her. When she became pregnant she looked to her partner for support and strength, but found that he had no desire to become a father. She came home and turned to her parents in bewilderment and desperation; her mother took it upon herself to decide that there was only one course of action. Soon she had an abortion. Grieving the loss of the child and mourning the way that those around her had been both controlling and lacking in the compassion for which she yearned, she tried to put the event behind her, resume her studies, and even seek to re-establish the relationship with the man whose love she still longed for. She struggled to break out of a cycle of powerlessness. Finally one day, university over and her career about to begin, she went back to her local church to make her confession to the priest. In preparing what she was going to say she realized that, despite her awareness of the wrongs done to her and her sense of being in a significant way abused, she felt a sense of personal guilt. She had consented to go through with something she had always – before, during, and after – believed to be wrong. In articulating her story, she took out of it all references to those who had betrayed or pressured her, and spoke simply of what she had done, without excuse or denial. On hearing the declaration that her sins were absolved, she felt a surge of unprecedented joy. She leapt up, walked as discreetly as she could to the door of the priest's house, and then gleefully ran around the church next door not once but twice. It was not that the powerful forces in her life were in no sense to blame; it was not that the past was wiped away. But in discovering herself as a sinner she had finally named the degree to which she was a prisoner: and repentance led to the possibility of being forgiven. Forgiveness had enabled her to distinguish between sin, evil, collusion, and poverty of moral imagination. She was not just a victim: she was a sinner too. And now she was free. Free from her sin, she could now for the first time address the ways she had given others power over her life, and begin to speak the truth to them. For the first time she began to see how choices she had made as an adult had been influenced and shaped by ways she had been treated as a child. Locked into a profound sense of powerlessness from damaging childhood experiences, she began to perceive how these experiences related to the way she had responded as an adult. At last she started to feel empowered to address the hurts and pain of her childhood: but she did so in the strength of discovering that she too was a sinner, and, even more important, a forgiven sinner.

John Milbank describes this process in these terms:

> Inevitably and unavoidably, victims pass through a moment of hatred for those who have offended them . . . [Later] The victim comes to remember and revise his past hatred more objectively as a correct refusal of the negative, and the impairment of his own power; but at the same time through renarration he is able to situate and qualify this hatred in relation to a renewed understand-

ing of the deluded motives of his violator. Most crucially, his offering of forgiveness involves not simply a cancellation of his earlier hatred, but a kind of
dispossession of his own hatred, as he comes to understand . . . how his negative reaction belonged to a whole sequence of . . . events mostly outside his
control.

(Milbank 2003, 52, 54)

Huge controversies have raged over the correct sequence of repentance,
forgiveness, and penance. And yet surely what matters is that they all be
treasured and practiced as gifts of God to the Church. Since the abandon-
ment of public confession, penance has become more complex, but
remains a vital practice. In one local church two students became friends.
One was from a tradition that carefully emphasized the uniqueness of
Christ's sacrifice, the necessity of repentance, and the finality of forgiveness. The other was longing to feel the kind of freedom discovered in the
foregoing story. The two friends went together to the cinema to see the
film *The Mission*. They watched the graphic opening of the film as it
depicted a crucified Jesuit being thrown into the torrential waters heading
for – and over – the colossal Iguacu Falls: a vivid portrayal of the cost of the
ministry of reconciliation. They watched as the Jesuit Fr Gabriel set about
an idyllic ministry with children in the heart of the primeval forest. They
watched as the slave-trader Mendoza was told by the woman he loved that
she loved not him but his brother Felipe. They watched Mendoza murder
Felipe. They watched Fr Gabriel return to the town and confront Mendoza
with his crimes (the sin of murder and the evil of slavery) and invite him to
choose his penance. They watched Mendoza, burdened with a great weight
of armor, climbing the arduous ascent of the waterfall, heading in peni-
tential pilgrimage for the idyllic villages far upstream. And as Mendoza
strained at the weight of his burden, the first friend cried out – in a packed
cinema – "He doesn't need to do it! He is forgiven!" Mystified heads
turned to request silence, but also to discover, perhaps, how the Reforma-
tion debates came to be alive and well in a provincial late twentieth-century
cinema. They turned back to the film to see the ropes that tied together
Mendoza's burden slashed by the native peoples he had come to serve, the
armor topple far to the foot of the waterfall, and his forgiveness made
manifest. And the second friend, along with the whole audience, discovered that the correct sequence was less important than the praise of the one
who made such forgiveness possible.

Again, John Howard Yoder sums up the way God restores abundance
amid the scarcity of conflict – in words that epitomize my whole argument.

To be human is to be in conflict, to offend and to be offended. To be human in the light of the gospel is to face conflict in redemptive dialogue. When we do that, it is God who does it. When we do that, we demonstrate that to process conflict is not merely a palliative strategy for tolerable survival or psychic hygiene, but a mode of truth-finding and community-building. That is true in the gospel; it is also true, mutatis mutandis, in the world.

(Yoder 2001, 13)

Yoder compares the "rule of Christ" with contemporary practices of conflict resolution, and finds numerous common features – a template of the gifts God gives through the practices of reconciliation and restoration:

a   The process begins at the point of concrete offence, with a real problem.
b   The intention is not punishment but resolution.
c   The frame of reference is a value communally posited as binding the parties.
d   We should assume the process is not a zero-sum game. The mediator trusts that a solution is available whereby both parties will win; each party affirms the other's rights.
e   The first efforts are made in ways that minimize publicity and threat, and maximize flexibility without risk of shame.
f   The process makes use of a variety of roles and perspectives carried out by competent, caring, yet objective intervenors.
g   The skills and the credibility of intervenors can be validated by experience and accredited by colleagues and clients.
h   The ultimate sanction if negotiations fail is public disavowal of the party refusing reconciliation; what is left is either to let the injustice stand or to see the civil powers intervene in their ordinary way.

(Yoder 2001, 12)

To explore why reconciliation and restoration are often so difficult, it may be helpful to refer back to my distinction between sin, evil, collusion, and poverty of moral imagination. Forgiveness of the first, sin, still leaves the remaining three waiting to be addressed. And even forgiveness of sin notoriously leaves a host of questions unanswered: Who is to forgive, the victim, or a sovereign representative of a community of sinner and victim? What is to be done about what cannot be repaid, "the years that the swarming locust has eaten" (Joel 2.25)? How is the victim to relate to the impenitent offender? What happens when the offender is dead? Is forgiveness blindness to abiding antipathy, and a foolish gesture that makes future offence only more likely? These are among the reasons why forgiveness often seems out of reach.

Meanwhile forgiveness of the other three – evil, collusion, and poverty of imagination – seems impossible because of the way each resists being resolved into a straightforward instance of the first, sin. For example, for the Presbyterian minister in Rwanda to forgive those who murdered his whole family is a process possible to articulate, if not wholly to comprehend; but to forgive the genocide as a whole seems beyond possibility – almost a category mistake. Hence the significance in reconciliation of the painstaking business of breaking evil down into concrete acts of sin – as the Truth and Reconciliation Commission in South Africa set about doing. As one observer put it, "the function of truth commissions, like the function of honest historians, is simply to purify the argument, to narrow the range of permissible lies" (Ignatieff 1996, 110–22). Even this tends to leave the third dimension, collusion, largely unrepented and unforgiven. As for the fourth, poverty of imagination, it is always in danger of seeming trivial when unfinished business remains in the other three areas. People who try to be "nice" and yet have deep reserves of anger inside have often pretended that what was in fact sin was instead poverty of imagination – that the cruel criticism was simply careless, that the habitual lateness was simply poor timekeeping. The trouble with trying to make all disorder into lack of imagination rather than naming instances of sin is that only when it is named as sin can it be forgiven. Only when a truthful story is told can it lead to admonition, repentance, and reconciliation.

Thus forgiveness and reconciliation often remain out of reach. But that does not mean that these four dimensions of disorder constitute a fundamental scarcity that drains away the abundance of God. God gives his people everything they need to be his friends. That they do not always become friends of one another does not mean God has not, in the practices of reconciliation and restoration, given them sufficient gifts. It simply shows how desperately those gifts are needed, how rigorously they must be rehearsed, how conscientiously they must be practiced, how sensitively they must be made available beyond the membership of the Church.

When reconciliation fails, all is not lost. There is a variety of courses of action still available. Persuasion is the first: the unjust judge says to himself, "Though I have no fear of God and no respect for anyone, yet because this widow keeps bothering me, I will grant her justice, so that she may not wear me out by continually coming" (Luke 18.4–5). Persuasion constitutes a consistent, repeated reminding of the costs of alienation and the possibility and benefits of reconciliation. Some are brought to repentance and reconciliation through simply being worn down by those seeking it. Warning and anger are other resorts that in different ways make explicit the consequences of withdrawing from reconciliation. And then there is constraint and punishment. Here is the context for a theological account of punishment. It is part of a process of restoring the offender to friendship with the victim, the community, and God. The three go together. Imprisonment has its roots in the restriction of a wayward monk to his cell and thus his solitary "peniten-tiary" period for preparing to be reconciled with his community. The purpose of imprisonment is eventual reconciliation. The reason capital pun-ishment is wrong is not just that it is the taking of a life, or just that it is a sentence that cannot be reversed if the conviction is later overturned, or that its role as a deterrent is unproven: it is because capital punishment makes impossible the fundamental purpose of punishment, which is restora-tion to community.

When persuasion, warning, and anger have failed, and constraint or pun-ishment are ineffective or inappropriate, there are perhaps two other courses of action, both provisional. One is to do nothing. This is sometimes a wise pastoral response in situations where a face-to-face meeting between one or more injured parties and the offender promises to be counterproductive – particularly when two individuals have hurt each other more or less equally. There are times when it is better to wait than to orchestrate. Another is to do nothing positively in relation to the offender or the victim, but to encourage each to do something beautiful – to make, set aside, enact, or otherwise create something that they could not have perceived without the regrettable circumstances of the unresolved sin, but which yet transcends those circum-stances by pointing toward a truth greater than that sin. Beauty is, after all, a way of speaking the truth. This points in the direction of liturgy.

Thus talk of reconciliation must acknowledge that sometimes it is at the very least a very slow road, and sometimes so slow that it is at a standstill. But it must never take these painful incompletenesses as normative. What must not happen, as John Milbank articulates carefully, is that undoubted evil (he is referring to the Holocaust) becomes the one given, beyond the reach of God's gifts, and is excluded from the process of reconciliation altogether.

> Talk of radical evil, an absolutely corrupted will, a motiveless crime that can never be atoned, and so forth, falsely *glamourizes* this (perhaps) most terrible of events, by rendering it outside all comprehension whatsoever, and thereby absolutizes it, granting it a demonic status equivalent to divinity, and finally perpetuates its terror, since what is redeemed remains in force. The argument which runs "*This* evil was so terrible that we belittle its horror if we describe it as negative" effectively means that this evil was really so impressive that we had better accord it a status in being equivalent to the Good.
>
> (Milbank 2003, 54–5)

Thus reconciliation sometimes fails. But this is not because some evils are so awesome that they overshadow God's glory. Neither is it because God has not given his people the gifts of reconciliation. It is sometimes because evil, collusion, and poverty of imagination are not easily resolved into sinful acts that can be identified, acknowledged, repented of, and forgiven. It is sometimes because even when this can be done, repentance or forgiveness is withheld. And it is sometimes because even if the will to repent and/or forgive is there, the sheer pain of the irreparable damage done is so deep that the pain needs time – lots of time – before reconciliation can take place. And that brings us to healing.

Embodying Beauty

Healing gets a bad name in Christian circles only when it becomes separated from the other practices of the Church. The practices of healing belong in relation to all the gifts of God explored in the foregoing chapters: healing takes its appropriate place as part of answering the call to be God's companions, to join the ministry of reconciliation. It is part of the transformation one can expect to grow out of justification and sanctification. Healing means exhibiting more of the fruits of the spirit – becoming a witness to abundance rather than a herald of scarcity.

Jesus seems in no doubt that forgiveness and healing belong together.

> Then some people came, bringing to him a paralyzed man, carried by four of them. And when they could not bring him to Jesus because of the crowd, they removed the roof above him; and after having dug through it, they let down the mat on which the paralytic lay. When Jesus saw their faith, he said to the paralytic, "Son, your sins are forgiven." . . . "Which is easier, to say to the paralytic, 'Your sins are forgiven,' or to say, 'Stand up and take your mat and walk'? . . . I say to you, stand up, take your mat and go to your home." And he stood up, and immediately took the mat and went out before all of them.
>
> (Mark 2.3–12)

The paralyzed man would have been regarded as a sinner: either, if he had been incapacitated from birth, a bearer of his parents' sin, or, if he had been paralyzed later, his own. But aside from forgiving his sin, Jesus heals him in three further ways. He restores him to community, by sending him home. He transforms him from a burden into a carrier, from a person carried on a mat to a person who carries a mat, who is thus, by implication, now in a position to carry others on it. And he delivers him from the withering control of the scribes, for whom he remains a sinner: his friends have symbolically removed the "roof" – that which stands between earth and heaven;

now Jesus, the heavenly "Son of Man" takes away all that might paralyze him in every other way. The whole scene is a paradigm of Jesus' mission to Israel.

This becomes clearer when one realizes the identity of salvation and health. "Health" is a different term for all the associations that come with the word "salvation." Thus salvation is the goal of all the practices of the Church. Salvation is the name given for healthy life in the kingdom. Salvation is the inspiration behind repentance, the consolation of penance, the purpose of forgiveness, the paradigm of reconciliation, the aim of restoration. And the connection between salvation and forgiveness is transparent: "For if you forgive others their trespasses, your heavenly Father will also forgive you; but if you do not forgive others, neither will your Father forgive your trespasses" (Matthew 6.14–15); "Whatever you bind on earth will be bound in heaven, and whatever you loose on earth will be loosed in heaven" (Matthew 18.18). The practices of forgiveness and reconciliation truly are the keys of the kingdom, the path of salvation. Health is a way of talking about anticipating kingdom life. And healing refers to a moment or a process by which the kingdom is made present in the experience of a person or community. Healing is an eschatological fruit.

Robert Jenson perfectly summarizes the reasons why the link between forgiveness and healing concludes not only this chapter but also this section of the book.

> Both sin and sickness alienate from the Eucharist. In a proper practice of penance, the sinner is welcome in the service but not given the elements; the sick person may be brought the elements but cannot take his or her part in the celebration to which they belong. "When a person is in either situation . . . the pastoral care of the church is called for. The sick person or the sinner needs to be reconciled to the community" and to the future kingdom which the eucharistic celebration anticipates.
>
> (Jenson 1999, 264–5, quoting Preston 1997, 172–3)

God thus gives his people everything they need to worship him and to be his friends: we now discover what it means to worship him and to be his friends by eating with him. This is the gift of the Eucharist.

Part Three

THE BODY OF CHRIST
AS THE EUCHARIST

Chapter Eight

MEETING

Gathering

The beginning of the Eucharist is like an orchestra warming up. Before a concert, there are shuffles of furniture, rustles of musical scores, and tentative sounds as each instrument is tuned and harmonized. Likewise the audience clamber toward appropriate seating, rummage amongst outer clothing, and murmur expectations. Meanwhile a host of intermediaries have prepared the way – selling tickets, cleaning the concert hall, organizing rehearsals. And long before, a composer has written the score, a publisher has circulated it, and a tradition of its performance has emerged. In just the same way, the Eucharist starts slowly.

The word "congregation" (*grex* = crowd + *con* = together) testifies to the significance of gathering for defining the Church. The people of God mass together like streams trickling into a flowing river. Like the nations going up to the mountain of the Lord's house (Isaiah 2.2–4), people leave aside their daily tasks and come together to form a congregation. For some, the Eucharist begins the moment they enter the doors of the church or meeting-place. Everything that takes place from then until they leave that building has a special significance. For others, it begins as soon as they leave their house. Everything they encounter, from then on, is part of the Eucharist. For others again, it begins the moment they rise in the morning. The ordered liturgy of their daily discipline is shaped by the need to come to the Eucharist with heart, mind, stomach, and strength pert and ready for the wonder to be revealed. For others again the Eucharist is not a habit – they begin the day perhaps not knowing if they will join the assembly or not. For them, the Eucharist begins in the moment of invitation, or in whatever constitutes the providential coincidence that leads them to come to the meeting-place on that day. And then there are those for whom the

Eucharist has begun long before. Their vocation is to begin each liturgy as soon as the last one is over – or even earlier.

It takes all these kinds of people to make a Eucharist. Their gathering into an assembly is seldom an ordered, tidy process. Some will be early and others late, some will be noisy and others silent. But this gathering, more than anything else besides Baptism, gives the Church its identity. That identity is constituted by three gifts: time, space and action.

First of all, the Eucharist gives the Church time. On one day of the week, the day of the Lord's resurrection, Christians gather to share a meal. The other days of the week find their significance in relation to this day – whether they are the three days after this celebration or the three days before the next one. Particular days of the year have special importance. On those days, Christians mark and celebrate key events in the story of salvation – notably the birth, death, resurrection, and ascension of Jesus and the sending of the Holy Spirit. The weeks of the year find their significance in relation to the celebrations of these key events. Thus they may be five weeks after the feast of the resurrection or three weeks before the celebration of the birth. And, in turn, each year finds its ultimate significance by its relation to the year when the Son of God came into the world.

The Eucharist is, fundamentally, a regular shared meal. As a regular shared meal it gives Christians a way of binding time. Because it is a meal, it requires preparation. Food and drink, if only in the form of wafers and wine, need to be procured ahead of the day. Those charged with the setting of the context of the meal, in word and action, and of distributing it to the assembled company, all need preparation. So the meal needs to take place at a stated time and in a stated place. Food is one of the principal human needs that prevent Christian faith becoming an otherworldly, timeless ideal. Because the Eucharist is a shared, corporate activity, requiring preparation, it makes the Church find a regular rhythm of celebration. It cannot take place privately, simply whenever is convenient for an individual. And because it is regular, its rhythm comes to order the shapelessness of time. The Eucharistic gathering becomes one element, albeit the key one, in a pattern of shared action, reflection, planning and experimentation. Life is no longer a linear sequence of one thing after another, but a rhythmic ebb and flow, a constant sending out to love and serve and share, a constant return and gathering to praise and repent and ask. What is not done by the beginning of the next celebration can wait; and all that has been done is transformed. Each celebration looks back to the last, and forward to the next; and meanwhile recalls the heritage of Passover and Exodus, the Lord's supper, crucifixion, and resurrection, and anticipates the destiny of the final banquet. Each Eucharist locates the local congregation in time, in relation to these great moments in the story of God and his people. Thus gathering gives the Church time.

Likewise gathering gives the Church space. Because Christians need each other if they are to be able to experience the gift of the body of Christ in the food of the Eucharist, they cannot be just anywhere when they worship. Because the Eucharist is an embodied, corporate practice, God's people need to come together in one place. They become for that period, if for no other, a visible community. Thus the Eucharist makes the Church visible. The Church is not, for that period, a vague idea, a marvelous principle, an invisible influence. By becoming a particular gathering in a particular location the Church locates itself in space, and is made visible. It becomes incarnate, a body gathered to receive the Body. It opens itself to scrutiny, judgment, criticism. Stimulated by such exposure, it seeks to ensure that every aspect of its gathering embodies and communicates its gospel – the unending blessing of God, the catastrophe of sin, the faithfulness of God's vocation to Abraham, his redeeming purpose in Moses, the pouring out of love in Jesus, the empowerment of the Holy Spirit, the hope of a new heaven and earth. In seeking to make their worship faithful to this gospel, Christians seek to make their whole lives follow the same pattern. In this way the Eucharist makes the Church; and inseparable from the way it does so is the way gathering makes the Church visible.

The need to make time and space to eat is essential to sustaining the body. It is the key to locating the Church in relation to the whole of creation. For, like the whole of the animal world, the body of Christ needs food. But unlike most of that world, it perceives that the definitive way to eat food is as God's companions. And the way to do that is to gather at a stated place and time and to share food together. In other words the central purpose of food is to enable people to meet God in the Eucharist. All other purposes of food – survival, enjoyment, celebration, indulgence – are secondary to this purpose. Food is given to human beings primarily so that they may discover what it means to be God's companions. Like other bodies, the body of Christ needs food, but, being a special body with a special purpose on behalf of all other bodies, it is given special food. So essential is this link between the food eaten together, being the Church, and God's central purpose expressed in Jesus, that each is given the same name – the body of Christ.

The third gift of gathering is action. Christians gather to do a specific thing together. This specific action, eating together, bestows on the Church its identity, because it gives it a definitive practice. Learning to perform this action well informs and educates Christians in their performance of all other actions. If the Eucharist is the definitive practice of the Church, it is the first place Christians should look to guide their own practice. To give an example, if a married couple wonder how they will find the grace to stay together, they may be shaped by the practice of Eucharist to discern where the key may lie. On the night before He died, Jesus gave instructions for how the Church was to stay together and remember him. His instructions were to eat together. In learning to eat together, the early Christians discovered they had to learn most of the other skills of common life. They had to greet one another, be honest with one another about their faults, celebrate and give thanks for what they had been given, remember the truth, pray and in praying discern the difference between what they needed and what they wanted. And today in the Eucharist it is just the same. In eating together Christians rediscover what it means to be the Church.

Likewise it may be that a newly married couple resolve to find the same way of staying together that the Church finds. When a couple eat together, they learn almost everything they need about being together. One person has to anticipate and buy the food. One person has to give the time to prepare it. One person has to give the time to clear the meal away and wash the dishes. If someone is feeling romantic they can put music on, light a candle, and soften the lights. Even if not, and they are just feeling like a cup of tea, they can remember they are married by asking their partner if they would like one too. When people of the current generation talk about keeping in touch, what they usually mean is email, mobile phones, landlines, or even perhaps a letter. The irony is that none of these involve touching anybody. Eating together is one way, perhaps the most important way, in which people learn to touch one another. In eating together, they become one another's companions – bread-sharers. The prayer for married couples is that by eating together they will become one another's true companions and in so doing will rediscover what it means to be companions of God.

Thus in gathering to eat together, the Church discovers its need to incorporate into its worship a wide range of other practices, at least in elemental form.

Greeting

The presence of God

There is a moment when the assembly discovers that it is a church. The gathering is largely complete, most of the people are present, and they are transformed from an array of diverse gatherers into the body of Christ. This is what may be called the greeting. One person emerges from the assembly and greets the whole company. At this point, a number of things take place.

First, the congregation become aware that they have entered the presence of God. God's presence is overwhelming and beyond the capacity of any one person's imagination. But the instruments through which that presence can be approached are all around: a Bible may be visible, likewise bread and wine and a table on which they may be placed, and perhaps water and an area where Baptisms might be conducted. All that is needed is a recognition that the Holy Spirit is present to animate these signs and symbols. The congregation carry the promise that "where two or three are gathered in my name, I am there among them" (Matthew 18.20). They share with St Paul the experience that "the Spirit helps us in our weakness; for we do not know how to pray as we ought, but that very Spirit intercedes with sighs too deep for words. And God, who searches the heart, knows what is the mind of the Spirit, because the Spirit intercedes for the saints according to the will of God" (Romans 8.26–7).

A great cloud of witnesses in the scriptural narrative become aware of God only after the intensity of his presence is over. Jacob, for example, wakes from sleep and says, "Surely the Lord is in this place – and I did not know it! . . . How awesome is this place! This is none other than the house of God, and this is the gate of heaven" (Genesis 28.16–17). Perhaps the most significant of these stories is that of the disciples on the road to Emmaus. They reflect with one another, "Were not our hearts burning within us while he was talking to us on the road, while he was opening the scriptures to us?" and with the other disciples they "told what had happened on the road, and how he had been made known to them in the breaking of the bread" (Luke 24.32, 35). Everything that happens in the opening part of the Eucharist is intended to ensure that the congregation become aware of the presence of God *before* the intensity of that presence has passed.

The two characteristic moods of the greeting are fear and joy. Fear, because the consistent witness of the scriptural narrative is that the presence of God is an awesome thing. As Isaiah vividly discovers, the imagination cannot take in the enormity of what it means to be overwhelmed by God. "Woe is me! I am lost, for I am a man of unclean lips, and I live among a people of unclean lips; yet my eyes have seen the King, the LORD of hosts!" (Isaiah 6.5). Joy, because of the discovery that despite the infinite qualitative difference between God and his people, God nonetheless longs for his people to worship him, be his friends, and eat with him. Perhaps the definitive description of the attitude suitable to the beginning of the Eucharist is in the account of Jesus' resurrection. The angel says to Mary Magdalene and the other Mary, "'Do not be afraid; I know that you are looking for Jesus who was crucified. He is not here . . . He has been raised from the dead, and indeed he is going ahead of you to Galilee; there you will see him.' . . . So they left the tomb quickly with fear and great joy" (Matthew 28.5–6, 8).

Fear and joy are both forms of expectation. Essential to the transition from gathering to greeting is the sparking of an atmosphere of expectation. Immediately the congregation become part of the great heritage of what God has done among his people. He has revealed his purpose, called a people, turned the world upside down; he has shared suffering, demanded mercy, come among his own people in visible form; he has given instruction, raised the dead, fed the hungry: will he not do such things today, now, within the next hour? Expectation is shared faith brought into the present tense. God has acted; he has promised; he longs to make himself known and to deliver his people from slavery: will he not fulfill these hopes today?

The regular experience of being in the presence of God trains the congregation to wonder. This is where the imagination discovers what it was designed for – to gasp in awe at the limitless scope of the creative and redeeming purpose of God. This is the beginning of all wisdom. It is the measure of all knowledge. It is the definition of humility. For the story of creation and salvation, in which Christians make the extraordinary discovery that they have a part to play, is a story not about them but about God. So the first requirement of Christians is not that they learn to perform their role in the story, but that they learn to wonder that there is a story at all, and that they have been miraculously included in it.

In one congregation it became a frequent practice for the person presiding at the Eucharist to say a formal greeting and then to ask the congregation to discuss, briefly and honestly, in what way each member was expecting God to make himself known today. In twos and threes, members of the congregation would point to the part of the service where they were particularly anticipating that God's presence would be very clear. In doing so, they heightened one another's awareness of the wealth of understanding and experience gathered in that place of meeting on that day.

The presence of one another

Second, the members of the congregation become aware that they are in the presence of one another. If God gives his people everything they need to worship him, this truth is seldom more tested than it is at this moment. How many congregations notice the empty seats more than the full ones? How many communities gathered for worship experience that gathering as one of collective scarcity rather than mutual abundance? "If

only we had a person who could . . . " is a widespread cry, and a host of aspirations follow concerning music, formation of child or youth discipleship,
preaching and teaching, transport, and so on. At the greeting, the congregation realize again that the body of Christ has many members, and that all its
gifts are given for the building up of the body. The gifts are everything that
the Church needs – but seldom everything that the congregation want. And
so the congregation recognize at the greeting, as the members look around
to see who is present, that this Eucharist is to be shaped by enjoying the gifts
God has given, not by grieving for some wished-for gifts (held to be preva-
lent in "real" churches) that God has bewilderingly chosen to withhold. As
Jesus took loaves and fish and made an abundant supper out of humble
resources, so God makes the worship he requires out of the gifts he has
given to each humble congregation.

One small congregation, meeting in a modern building, decided to change
the way they arranged the chairs for the Eucharist. After several years of
looking at a largely blank white wall, they moved the rows of chairs into a
sequence of horseshoes and started looking at each other. They came to
realize that conventional churches arranged pews so the most one could see
of one's fellow members was the back of their heads. In other words, other
members were seen as an obstacle to worship. But this congregation had so
little that was beautiful to look at, they could think of nothing better than to
meditate on the human forms that each member possessed. On one occasion they were challenged to discern the gifts God had given to them as a
body. After a period of silence, each person was asked to identify a particular
gift that had been given to the person next to them. After years of regretting
what they could not do because they were small, some members began to
articulate the virtues of what they had been given. Referring to the intimacy of worship and the way each member had come to discover that God
could speak through their own stumbling words, one said, "You know,
some of the things we do, we could not do if we were bigger." It was the
first time someone had articulated a sense that that church was not a failure,
but could be something that no other church could be.

At almost every celebration of the Eucharist, there will be those present
who are not expected. They may blend in as if they were among the regu-
lars. But they may not. The greeting is the moment when the regular
members discover that today's congregation is not necessarily the one they
wanted, hoped for, or chose – but is nonetheless a gift. If they receive it as a
gift, they will meet the abundance of God; if they scorn it as a distraction,
they will continue to experience worship as scarcity. Part of the atmosphere
of expectation that awaits the manifestation of God is an alertness to the
way his coming may be in the form of a surprise guest – an expectant

mother, constantly needing the loo, a noisy toddler, needing a warm place to play, a recalcitrant young person, jumping the railings of respectable behavior, a bewildered man, seeking a safe harbor from a roaring ocean of mental unease, a visitor or refugee from an unfashionable country, seeking in common symbol to bypass the shortcomings of language, an alcoholic older woman, already under the influence though the day is yet young. Will these strangers experience a greeting from a congregation that regards them as a blessing? Ramps for wheelchair users, loop systems for those whose hearing is impaired, larger print service sheets for the visually impaired – in a host of ways a congregation demonstrates its faith that those who were closest to Jesus in his earthly ministry are closest to him today, and shows itself alert to the coming of God in the form of a stranger. This is one way in which the Eucharist becomes a form of judgment.

Absence

Third, the members of the congregation become aware of who is missing. There is a host of reasons why people may not be present. The reasons may be as final as death. They may be as circumstantial as sickness or travel. They may belong on a spectrum of estrangement, beginning with a failed alarm clock, continuing with shame or anger toward members or other parties, and on to outright rejection of God, the Church in general, or the local congregation in an attitude of hurt, pity, indifference, or blame. They may simply have never been invited – or have never heard the story.

Sometimes the absences speak so loudly that they dominate the greeting. If for example there has been a serious breakdown of ministerial or pastoral relationships, empty seats may signal distress, horror, grief. More commonly the empty spaces train the congregation to remember those whose faithfulness shaped the community, to be ready to care for those experiencing sickness or hardship, to share a little of the good shepherd's love for the lost, and to develop a broader notion of the communion of saints. For a sense of the saints in constant worship of God brings the members of the congregation to a humble recognition of how alienated every person is from the vocation of friendship and eating together that God intends universally.

One local congregation chose to embody this notion, the communion of saints, through a photography project. They sought to surround the area used for worship with photographs of notable characters, all of whom lived in the area around the church, but none of whom came to worship on a Sunday. A group of single mothers, who used the church for a weekly art class, identified the people concerned, shot, developed and mounted the photographs, and displayed them around the church. Thus the worshiping congregation were surrounded on a Sunday with those for whom they prayed. When a bid went from the neighborhood to the government for large sums of urban regeneration funding, there was a sudden search for photographs that expressed what was good about the community. The photographs on the church walls were ideal for the purpose, and were duly used. Thus had the local church's faithful notion of gathering to worship helped a neighborhood realize its human worth.

Authority

Fourth and finally the congregation become aware that one person has been set aside to preside over the service. This is the person who has emerged from among them and now faces them, greeting them with time-honored words. This is the moment in the life of the Church when it defines the notion of authority. For the person who stands in the center of the assembly bears five roles that constitute authority in the Church.

One of these roles is to bring to the fore all the gifts given to the congregation. "Every scribe who has been trained for the kingdom of heaven is like the master of a household who brings out of his treasure what is new and what is old" (Matthew 13.52). If God has given his people everything they need to follow him, perhaps the most vital role in the community is that of the person whose responsibility it is to ensure that everything God has given to a congregation is used in worshiping him. Authority lies with the person who has listened to and engaged deeply with the community, who knows the joys and sorrows of its people, and who perceives the difference between technical ability and a gift that builds up the Church. Such a person is able to take risks and demand people's courage, because the members of the community know that they are being treated as people bearing gifts for the building up of the body, rather than as individuals developing powers for any one person's self-advancement.

In the language of contemporary culture this is the role of the facilitator. The facilitator takes responsibility for setting the mood of the assembly, for creating an engaging environment, establishing common rules of conduct, giving participants permission to express thoughts and feelings, bringing out the best in everyone present, always keeping the purpose of the gathering at the center of attention, attending to time, ensuring a healthy shape and an appropriate ending. A facilitator does not do all the work alone, but seeks to animate a flourishing culture of expression, sharing, perception, insight, and transformation. This is authority in interrogative mode – asking questions, stirring the imagination, unsettling groundless assumptions, overturning unnecessary hierarchies, teasing self-important life-draining customs. It is a servant role. The characteristic emblem of this kind of authority is the table-waiter. "For who is greater, the one who is at the table or the one who serves? Is it not the one at the table? But I am among you as one who serves" says Jesus (Luke 22.27). Authority in the Eucharist is defined as that which enables all the gifts of the people to be brought to the table, and so waits on the table that everyone who eats at it has enough.

In one local congregation there was a considerable number of children, many of whom were full of largely untrammeled energy, and most of whom had chosen that morning not so much to be in church as to be any-where other than home. The Eucharist was always an event for all ages, so there was always a task to be performed in turning a chaotic scene of chasing children and exasperated adults into a congregation who were self-consciously worshiping as the body of Christ. The custom became for the person presiding to stand, centrally, near the back of the place of meeting, and begin by inviting the congregation to dwell on what they were looking forward to bringing to the altar that morning, and what they were hoping to receive. Then, after a pause, and sometimes a little sharing of expecta-tions, there would be a formal greeting and the Eucharist would begin. This was facilitative, interrogative authority at work.

A second role of authority is to say and do what it needs one person to say and do. It requires one person to gather the assembly and identify begin-nings and transitions; one person to focus the congregation's attention on the central moments, by word, posture or gesture; one person to recognize when a period of silence, an opportunity for open prayer, or a series of repeated songs has come to an end and to register conclusions of other kinds. This is a different, but complementary, kind of authority: if the first kind is that of the facilitator of a group, this second kind is that of the chair of a meeting. Because the chair looks after due order, the agenda, normal process, necessary decisions and agreements, members of a meeting are free to pursue their equally important offices and roles. But if there is no recog-nized chair, the meeting has no way of beginning, no way of making progress, no way of achieving change, and no way of ending.

This is authority in imperative mode. It is the simple ordering of the way things are going to be for today. Its gift to the Church is to prevent the assembly endlessly deliberating over preliminaries. Instead of anxiously debating "How does God speak?," "What is he saying today?," "Who has the right to declare what God is saying today?," "What if someone says God is saying something different?" and so on, the person presiding expresses their authority and simply greets the congregation with "The Lord be with you," or similar, and the service begins. Likewise the words "Go in peace" announce that the service ends. Such is the gift of authority. The characteristic action of this kind of authority is the breaking of the bread. The broken bread is at one and the same moment an embodiment of the death of Christ and an enactment of the way that death gives sustenance – everything they need – to his people. The one who breaks bread has in hand the vital transforming elements that no amount of facilitating of the congregation's gifts and thoughts and feelings could provide. "Take this, and eat it": these are words that point the Church in a direction it could not find for itself. They are words of authority.

In one local church the person presiding became concerned that a rather large proportion of the congregation was in the habit of gathering very shortly before the start of the service or often of appearing some minutes into the service. In other words the gathering was still going on while the greeting and reconciling was taking place. He responded to this by making it known that he would in future be in his stall, praying silently, ten minutes before the stated service start time – and thus that the gathering would become a more studied event of ten minutes' duration. Thus when it came to the greeting, a much larger proportion of the congregation was ready to begin. By intervening in the process, the "chair" had restored due order.

A third role of authority is to speak to the congregation on God's behalf. Some things simply need to be said – not as a recollection of events of the past, nor as anticipation of things to come, but as declarations of what is happening now. Sins are forgiven here, now, and in the sight of all. Somebody needs to say so. The word of God communicated in the Scripture is proclaimed afresh among the congregation, in the form of a sermon or equivalent from someone recognized as being called and equipped to do so. It is not delivered as one opinion among others, but as God's word for today. The peace of God is declared before it is shared. The bread and wine are announced as bearing the gift of eternal life. The blessing is pronounced. This is authority in indicative mode. Such moments in the service are not requests or invitations or instructions or prayers. They are statements of the way things are, in the kingdom enacted in worship. The language of announcing "the way things are" is the language of prophecy.

This is the most significant form of authority embodied in the Eucharist. It is the most significant because it is the one least found elsewhere. The questioning, teasing, encouraging role of the facilitator is widespread. Every sports coach seeks to harness all the skills of the team in order to maximise its potential and get an edge on the opposition. Every conductor strives to encourage and cajole the orchestra to use every faculty to create a sound that surpasses all previous performances. Countless management courses offer to reproduce such models in the complexities of industry, commerce, and business of all kinds (although not all are explicitly directed to the understanding of gifts and flourishing that the New Testament proposes). Meanwhile the functional leadership of the chair is equally generally understood. Imperative authority is always likely to provoke passive mistrust, visible truculence, or outright opposition and even aggression, for lurking behind its resonant tones is always a hint of force. But there are still plenty of roles in society that require the exercise of this kind of power: a police officer, a doctor, an elected politician, a schoolteacher, and a parent of young children all know what it means to say "this is the way it is going to be today if any of us is going to get anywhere."

But to say "this is the way things *are*" is something quite different. Underlying the appeal of the facilitator is the flattering sense that in complete self-expression the individual or group will find all the resources needed for the task in hand. Underlying the appeal of the chair is the more sober constraint of necessity or coercion. But this third kind of authority has nothing to appeal to besides its own rhetorical power. Can it describe the new reality, the kingdom, in ways that inspire confidence, transform perception, motivate obedience, and encourage witness? The key to this rhetorical power lies in the fact that it is not a matter of words alone. The words are always in the context of a definitive pattern of practices that exemplify, embody, and offer the new reality of the kingdom. And that pattern of practices is the Eucharist. When the person presiding at the Eucharist says, in whatever way, "this is the new reality," that new reality is not just a story of salvation or a promise of glory: it is always also the new reality being enacted, performed, enfleshed in the corporate action of the Eucharist. The authority of the indicative mode lies in the integrity of the actions that surround it. When it comes to authority, actions speak louder than words. The Eucharist is not just the context in which the sermon is preached authoritatively to the congregation. The Eucharist *is* the sermon that embodies the authority with which the Church speaks to the world.

A fourth role of authority grounded in the greeting is to speak to God on the people's behalf. There are three moments in the liturgy when this is particularly evident. One is the collect. Another is the period of intercession. The third, and by far the most prominent, is the great prayer of thanksgiving. (Sometimes the absolution is a prayer of this kind.). In many churches the collect is said by the whole assembly together, and the intercessions are led by a member of the congregation. This focuses attention on what kind of authority is constituted by one person saying the Great Thanksgiving. Is this simply a legacy of a time when the congregation was largely illiterate, and texts in any case hard to come by, and thus it made perfect sense for one person to take on the speaking role? In other words is this fourth kind of authority no more than and no different from the second kind of authority, that of the functional chair of the meeting? Or is there a priestly authority here, authority in imprecatory mode, echoing Moses going into the cloud to speak with Yhwh (Exodus 19.20), or Zechariah entering the sanctuary of the Lord in the Jerusalem Temple to offer incense (Luke 1.9)?

Whether or not the role of speaking the Great Thanksgiving before God must only be done by a person set aside and authorized by episcopal seal is a controversial issue. It is vital that the role of speaking on behalf of the people does not become speaking instead of the people. What is much less controversial is that training and experience enable certain people to perform this ministry well. And for our purposes at this stage, that is the important point, for it discloses a fourth understanding of authority. It is the authority of a person set aside to care for the most significant aspects of the Church's life, formed and trained to carry out those offices well, and sufficiently experienced in the role to be able to exercise it without inhibition or self-consciousness. The characteristic embodiment of this authority comes in the funneling or focusing of the congregation's prayer in the central words of the Great Thanksgiving: "Father, by your Holy Spirit let these gifts of your creation be to us the body and blood of our Lord Jesus Christ; form us into the likeness of Christ and make us a perfect offering in your sight" (Archbishops' Council 2000, 199). It is this authority that most clearly connects one congregation to another. These persons charged with channeling the prayers of the people to God at this central moment are united in a shared understanding of formation, discipline, and purpose, embodied in some traditions in the person of the bishop.

Thus the person who emerges from the congregation to say the greeting, and so constitutes the Church and turns an assembly into a Eucharist, incorporates four kinds of authority. There is the facilitative, *interrogative* authority, with its somewhat subversive quality, that is grounded in the gifts the Holy Spirit gives to the congregation, and the need to give them permission, encouragement, and release. There is the *imperative* authority of the meeting chair, with its almost kingly authority, grounded in the functional need for a certain person to set and apply rules of conduct for the sake of common order. There is the *indicative* authority of the prophetic word, the performative utterance that speaks the truth of God into the emerging pattern of practices that exhibit the kingdom, the unique gift of naming and describing the reality of a moment suffused with the presence and transforming activity of God. And there is the *imprecatory* authority of the word addressed to God on behalf of others, the role of the priestly representative, loaded with a mystical heritage, but emphasizing the need for the formation and authorization of the person bearing that authority.

Each of these kinds of authority has its corresponding kind of obedience. The first, interrogative, kind, requires of the members of the congregation wholehearted participation, a thoroughgoing openness to bringing every gift – mental, material, physical, spiritual – into the activity of worship, a readiness for receiving every gift brought by others, and an expectation of discovering new gifts in themselves and others in the course of this vulnerable exposure. The second, imperative, kind, requires the congregation to behave as one body rather than as a loose assembly of unconnected individuals. The third, indicative, authority expects the congregation to be the transformed people they have been called to be – to share faith, to share insight, to share needs, to share peace, to share food, to share vision. The fourth, imprecatory authority demands, like the second, a deep humility, a recognition of and respect and gratitude for the calling and role of others that release, rather than constrain, one's own calling and role, and an understanding of the importance of preparation, training, and collegiality in relation to the good conduct of worship.

Each of these kinds of authority rests on a notion of abundance. The facilitator assumes that God has given the congregation everything it needs to worship, to be God's friends and to eat with him: the facilitator's role is just to give these gifts permission to play. The chair again assumes there is more than enough, and recognizes that for a limited period sufficiency should take precedence over abundance. Prophetic authority assumes that God will speak to every situation – that there is no human condition outside the compass of God. And prayerful authority likewise assumes that every aspect of the congregation's life is open to being transformed by the grace of God.

This leaves one other significant form of authority, about which something positive and something negative may be said. It is the authority of sanctity, the authority gained by those who have led lives of evident goodness, wisdom and faithfulness. It is the proper respect for those in almost every community who stand out by the quality of their lives – people of character who have the law of the Lord inscribed on their hearts (Psalm 37.31). The words of greeting do not assume this kind of authority. It is, of course, to be hoped that the formation, training and experience of the person presiding have carved a supple well of holiness in the heart; just as it is to be hoped that the regular practice of joining in the Eucharist has similarly shaped the character of the members of the congregation. But Church history and present experience are littered with people who have held such roles but whose lives and characters have soured others and damaged the body. And so it is vital to remember that the character of the one presiding does not determine the validity of the sacrament, as Augustine insisted in the face of the Donatists. There is an authority that lies in the sacrament itself, in God's decision to work through the liturgy however deep the shortcomings of its participants: and this authority is characteristically made visible in the vestments worn by the one presiding. The purpose of these vestments is to divert attention away from the fragile character of the one wearing them, and toward the authority of the sacrament itself, and the glorious mystery of how God in Christ through the Spirit is present in it and acts through it. But if the sacrament is all that it promises to be – if the congregation participate in it as wholeheartedly as it calls them to – then it should foster lives of holiness, and these lives are part of what it means to say the Church as a body has authority.

Being Reconciled

The practice of confessing sin as part of the Eucharist includes four elements, which are not always entirely distinguished in the liturgy: invitation, personal repentance, corporate confession and absolution.

Invitation

First, the invitation recognizes that when friends meet again after a breakdown in a relationship, great or small, the appropriate word to begin the conversation is "sorry." The word may seem inadequate – particularly so if the breakdown has been very great or the word does not yet seem to be accompanied by a commitment to learn, to change, and to make reparation. But until the word is uttered, its loud absence will cloud all interaction. In just the same way, if the Eucharist is truly to be a celebration, the breakdown in relationship between God and his people, known as sin, must be left at the door. The invitation reminds the congregation of this relationship and of the way to restore it. In the process it offers a model for the restoration of all broken relationships.

In the first place the person inviting the congregation to confess their sins affirms the goodness of God and the original blessing of human beings to be his friends. The Christian story does not begin with sin but with God's decision to be in relationship with humanity and the whole creation. Thus when the breakdown of that relationship is introduced it is not as something that simply had to be but as a catastrophe in which they themselves have participated.

Of course sin must be introduced. But the way it is introduced is highly significant. The fact that a declaration of God's overarching purpose precedes it means that it does not have the first word – it is not a given, it is not something that must be accepted with resignation, as the tragedy of the human condition. It is a later, secondary interruption of an original, possible, restorable relationship. The fact that it is introduced in a corporate setting means that no one can deceive themselves and deny that they are part of it. Self-deception is wrapped up in sin. It is the narrative form sin takes in the mind of the disciple. It is the weaving together of plausible and groundless reasoning and pleading to tell a false story. When the congregation are invited to confess together their sin, they are being confronted with the falseness of the stories they each tell themselves. They are given an opportunity to allow the truth of the Gospel to dismantle the falseness of their stories. There may be many reasons why members of the congregation feel moved to confess their sin: out of love for God, guilt about transgression, unhappiness with the consequences of actions, or anger at their own foolishness or insensitivity; or out of recognition of their participation in the great social shortcomings of the world – inadequate distribution of resources, prevalence of curable disease, environmental depredation, oppression of minority groups, and many more. These anxieties may well be appropriate, but the emphasis of the invitation is not on regrettable circumstances, but on whether or not the story that underlies them, justifies them, accompanies them or brings them about, is true. Sin is not that which makes people unhappy or that which causes pain: it is life that is based on a false story, a story that leads to worshiping something other than the God of Jesus Christ.

So the invitation is a call to the congregation to renarrate their lives according to a true story. Telling the true story of God provides the setting, the necessary context, in which members of the congregation can tell a true story about themselves. And vital to that true story of God is his steadfast love, his constant longing to restore the broken relationship. The invitation recalls the original purpose of God, and the way sin sours that shared life of plenteous blessing. But most importantly, the invitation rehearses the limitless grace of God, the awesome journey on which he goes to heal the breach and find the lost, his unrelenting mercy to those who stop running away from him, and his longing to sit and eat once more with his friends. This is the truth that the invitation proclaims; this is the truth that sets disciples free. And confession is about becoming realigned with this truth, and seeing all one's actions in the light of this truth. The third slave is living according to a different narrative, with a different view of God: "I knew that you were a harsh man, reaping where you did not sow, and gathering where you did not scatter seed; so I was afraid, and I went and hid your talent in the ground" (Matthew 25.24–5). The scribes and Pharisees are living a different narrative, with a different view of themselves: when Jesus says "Let anyone among you who is without sin be the first to throw a stone at her," they leave the woman they took to be a sinner, and slowly disperse (John 8.7–9).

Thus the invitation does not portray certain activities as inherently bad and requiring immediate repentance. Instead it portrays a true story, and pleads with the members of the congregation to consider whether their lives reflect this story truthfully. It is not that some sins are greater than others on some kind of objective scale; it is more that some kinds of life are grounded in stories that distort the true story more violently or drastically than others. The invitation is a plea to the congregation to return to or be conformed to that true story, and in doing so to retell, or begin for the first time to tell, a truthful story about themselves. But this plea is grounded in a promise, that because it is God, not humanity, who achieves the work of salvation, members of the congregation stand before God in the strength of their honest repentance, not their unblemished innocence. What matters is not the prodigal's stumbling apology but the father's outstretched arms, running feet, and heartfelt kiss, the ring, robe and sandals, the banquet, and the household of rejoicing. If they will worship him, he will be their friend and will eat with them.

Repentance

After the invitation comes a pause for repentance. Though corporate, this is primarily a time for personal reflection. It is not so much an opportunity for cataloging particular sins as a moment to contrast the glory of the true story with the meagerness of the false ones. Repentance means naming and stripping away the fear that distances the disciple from the Gospel. This stripping away is an experience of nakedness. In contemporary Western culture nakedness has a number of associations. In a statement of power it connects with the health club, the place where the capacity of the body is celebrated in the music of self-belief. In an aspiration of beauty it is found in the cinema of sexual desire, a longing to transcend the constraints of the body. And in one of the most dreaded places of today's culture, the nursing home, it is associated with frailty and loss of dignity. But the significance of the figurative stripping away in the context of repentance concerns a different kind of nakedness: the nakedness of birth and of death. The moment of truth that reveals that we brought nothing into the world and we take nothing out (1 Timothy 6.7), is accompanied in confession by the grace of the recognition that "nothing in my hands I bring, simply to thy cross I cling." What is stripped away by recollecting the nakedness of birth and death is any presumption that a human being could have a single claim on God, any reason to suppose that the condition of the creature before the creator is anything other than utter nakedness.

But the nakedness that matters most of all, the nakedness that comes between birth and death and to which the disciple returns in every act of repentance, is the nakedness of Baptism. The penitence of corporate confession is a return to the naked humility of Baptism and an anticipation of the naked fragility of death. Baptism is the definitive moment when new disciples renounce the stories that place them at the center of the universe, the false stories that rampage around searching for fulfillment, satisfaction, comfort, stimulation, security or glory, and treat the rest of creation as a mere means to that end. At Baptism, disciples are clothed with the grace of God's story, and find their vocation as they discover that they too have a place in that story.

In touch once more with the transformation of Baptism, the congregation are empowered to explore the logic of repentance. Once stories of misguided fulfillment have been exposed for what they are, the disciple seeks strength to dismantle the rhetoric that first ingratiated them to the imagination. This is not the hurried search for words that will soften an inevitable fury, but the careful exposure of darkest thoughts to the transforming light of benevolent day. Dismantling the rhetoric of false stories leads to perceiving the embellishments of empty promises and deceptive allure, and recognizing the maze of lies that arises from and supports such a story. Whether the pause for repentance highlights apparently petty addictions, largely hidden jealousies, clumsy minor thefts, or small instances of global failures, each has been furnished by a pattern of self-deceptive stories, the promises they offer, and the lies they require. Baptism is the offer of freedom in place of slavery, and it is this offer that the congregation seek to accept in the pause between the invitation to confess and the confession itself.

In one local congregation there was an elderly woman who had lived all her life in the neighborhood. She had attended the church longer than anyone could remember – perhaps 50 years. Everyone in the church, from the wildest child to the oldest salt, loved and revered her. One day, during worship, she was asked why she attended church so faithfully. She was a person of action rather than words, and her life had been devoted to care rather than cleverness. Without pause, she simply responded, "For my sins." There was silence. If she, who was holy, came for her sins, where did that place everyone else? Clearly her joy came from knowing God's forgiveness, and her faithfulness came from knowing that that grace could be found nowhere else. When she died, the congregation realized that she had symbolized everything they believed in. In her gentle way she expressed that she had been formed by the worship in which she had shared.

Confession

From personal repentance the congregation begin to articulate corporate confession. The fact that specific, often familiar, words are used is highly significant. It recognizes that naming sin is a skill developed by the Church over centuries. These are not just painful or petty personal shortcomings. This is a recognition that this congregation has participated, even during this last week, in the catastrophe of discarding God's everlasting invitation to worship him, be his friends, and eat with him. A scandal, a waste of shame has taken place, and these people have been a party to it, and yet again they fall on the grace of God, learning as they speak these words of confession that they have no claim to stand outside the crowd and claim a righteousness of their own. These crafted words give voice to silent grief – the grief of Sarah, when she realizes the force of her laugh; the grief of Judah, when he realizes he has slept with his daughter-in-law Tamar; the grief of Aaron, when he realizes the sin of the golden calf; the grief of Jephthah, when he perceives the foolishness of his vow; the grief of the prodigal son, when he sees his father; the grief of Peter, when he hears the cock crow. Such grief is overwhelming and isolating, and part of the gift of confession at the Eucharist is that it offers words to those who are silent in shame and company to those who are alone in their sin.

The renarration of the world's story has already been implied in the invitation to confession. The dismantling of false stories has been begun in the pause for repentance. What is new in the confession, and carries awesome weight, is the promise to sin no more. Jesus offered two sentences to the woman dragged into the Temple. One was "I do not condemn you." The second was, "Do not sin again" (John 8.11). A gift and a task. But in promising to sin no more, to cease from the thoughts, words, and deeds that have been unworthy of God's company, the congregation take on a burden whose weight they will not be able to bear. There can be no repentance without a resolve to stop sinning; but there can be no self-knowledge without the recognition that temptation, in some form, will be too much. Thus confession is the moment when the congregation discover the meaning of freedom. Freedom does not mean dependence on the resources and capacities of the self. That is what has been exposed and renounced in repentance. Freedom means dependence on the grace of God. Only in God's strength can any resolution to sin no more be founded. The service of God is perfect freedom. The truth – that no effort of will or purchase of favor but only God's grace and forgiveness can enable a person to stand before God – sets disciples free.

Once again it is important that this is a corporate act. If the whole of humanity's estrangement from God were to rest on the shoulders of one individual, the burden really would be intolerable. So intolerable, in fact, that it would make kneeling to confess impossibly daunting, and would make imputing personal blame for global fault absurd. If every Christian's repentance was simply a personal matter, who would address the great scandals of the world, the countless children dying for lack of clean water, the enormous investment in weapons, and the unjust terms of global trade, the depredation of the earth, the pollution of the air, and the denuding of the sea? By confessing sin together each congregation can recognize that while their own role may be invisible, their role as one body, in sinning and resolving to sin no more, is significant.

The members of the congregation are recognizing that it is not just their own sin that is separating them from God, it is everybody's. Slavery afflicts not just individuals, but the people of God as a whole. So the members of congregation confess not just their own sins, but the sins of the body. This is an extension of what has been established at the greeting: that this is no longer an assembly of individuals, it is now the Church, the body of Christ. It is also an anticipation of what will take place at the sharing of the peace. For the reality is very often that the sins that separate the congregation from God are sins committed with or against others in the congregation itself.

The regular practice of corporate confession is one way in which the Church learns what it means to be one body. If, for example, a member of the congregation arrives late to the Eucharist, and has missed the corporate confession, they discover that they need not make a private confession, disengaging from the rest of the body as the liturgy continues; for the rest of the congregation have already said their confession for them, and received absolution on their behalf. The rest of the congregation have acted in their stead, rather like godparents do at the Baptism of an infant. Thus again the practice of corporate confession becomes an embodiment of grace.

One local congregation reconsidered the practice of corporate confession in a culture of social deprivation. It was recognized that few people in the neighborhood needed reminding of their failure. Many, however, needed to recall that they were neither uniquely guilty nor uniquely innocent, that they were loved unreservedly, and that they were not written out of the story. It became a frequent practice in the liturgy of that congregation to invite two members to form a human sculpture. There would often be quite a long pause before two members came forward. It was generally understood that coming forward indicated that one had something in particular to confess. But details were never sought or explained. The gesture was done on behalf of all. There was only one rule: one could not volunteer anyone except oneself. The two penitents would kneel upright, facing one another, heads resting on each other's shoulder, hands on one another's upper arms. The statue proclaimed that there is no reconciliation with God without reconciliation with neighbor, and that each neighbor is as broken and needy as the other. For the person on the left, God lay beyond the person on the right. For the person on the right, God lay beyond the person on the left. Few words needed to be said, but adults and children could walk around and touch the statue if they so wished. The ritual was a performance of the Gospel of grace, a call to repentance, an assurance of sins forgiven, a demonstration of the liberating power of a truthful story, and an offering of hope to the community.

Absolution

The last of the four elements of being reconciled is absolution. Absolution is first of all a confirmation of the mercy of God declared in the invitation to confession. This requires of the congregation an exercise of great meekness, and becomes indeed an occasion for formation in the virtue of humility. For having been confronted with the horror of sin, the way it perverts the truth, the urgency of the need to confess and an opportunity to do so, the members of the congregation then discover that they do not have the power to ruin the story – any more than they have the power to restore it. The ever-rolling stream of providence rolls all of them away. However mortifying their sin, it cannot alter their fundamental identity as God's beloved child; it cannot revoke God's everlasting purpose to be their friend and eat with them; nor can it define for ever the destiny of those they have hurt. If even crucifying God's Son could be incorporated in God's unfolding story, its perpetrators and idle witnesses forgiven, and its unspeakable results turned upside down within three days, then the congregation must learn that none of its sins is greater than the extent of God's mercy.

In Anne Tyler's novel *Saint Maybe* (1992), the central character Ian is heavy-hearted with guilt for passing on information that might have caused his brother to commit suicide. His brother left behind a widow for whom the burden of three small children is too heavy. Some time after her death,

Ian walks into a place of worship that calls itself the "Church of the Second Chance," and expresses to the pastor a desire to be forgiven. "You are not forgiven," says the pastor – much to Ian's dismay. Before finding forgiveness Ian has to discover on the one hand whether his part in the events was as decisive as he had always assumed, and on the other hand whether there is something practical he could be doing to make the situation better. It quickly turns out that to house and care for the three orphaned children, which he had previously regarded as unthinkable, is a real possibility. The book tells the story of the rich life he is given, all arising from the experience of not, initially, being forgiven.

Absolution is a reminder of Baptism, because in pardoning from sin, God refreshes the baptismal grace of adoption. The members of the congregation discover the rest of the service – the rest of their lives – can be enjoyed and cherished because their adoption by the Father, "from whom every family in heaven and on earth takes its name" (Ephesians 3.15) has been reaffirmed. This is also where Christians re-encounter the resurrection of the body. For just as in Baptism the body goes down into the water as if it were buried (Romans 6.4), before being raised out of water as out of the ground, so in absolution the bowed head and bent knee of confession are transformed into the joyful recognition and restored stature of adoption.

Adoption by the Father is reflected in justification by the Son. If confession and absolution are a reminder of Baptism, and the death and resurrection of the body, they are also an embodiment of the death and resurrection of Christ. Just as freedom is a discovery rather than a possession, so salvation is a gift not a reward. It is in the power of the crucified Christ, in the faith that the crucifixion is a moment that transforms the meaning of glory and of weakness, and in the conviction that the death and resurrection of Christ secures and epitomizes the offer of reconciliation between God and creation, that justification lies. The nature and manner of that justification are amplified in the sharing of food that follows later in the liturgy. But the fact of justification is already here in the absolution. Absolution declares that members of the congregation are pardoned and delivered from all their sins. All that was embodied and achieved on the cross is brought to this moment, when believers are forgiven for what they have been a party to and delivered from the consequences of their transgression.

The action of the absolution is a Trinitarian one. Indeed, the congregation meets God as Trinity through the action of the absolution. Adopted by the Father and justified by the Son, Christians are sanctified by the Holy Spirit. Through the absolution, the Spirit confirms and strengthens them in all goodness. This empowerment underlies all that follows in the liturgy – praise, thanksgiving, intercession, peacemaking, sharing, blessing.

It anticipates the dismissal, because in the dismissal the members of the congregation realize their vocation to love and serve. The restoration of forgiveness is suitably accompanied by the opportunity to make things better, to transfer from being part of the problem to being aligned with the solution. It is this furnishing with the gifts of the Spirit, this reclothing with the robes of Baptism, that the absolution begins and the dismissal completes.

All of these Trinitarian elements lie in the absolution, and anticipate other parts of the liturgy. But they are all to some extent in the background, because the most important feature of the absolution is its finality. These sins are forgiven. They are expunged. They are not forgotten, but their power to ruin and destroy, their power to affect eternally, is taken away. They do not need to be confessed again. They do not need to overshadow the rest of the service. Indeed they must not. Thus the absolution makes the rest of the service possible. The assembly has gathered; and in greeting it has been transformed into a Church. All that stands between it and God has been taken away.

Being Silent

Quite properly, the first action to which the congregation now turns is praise. (I shall consider praise in the next chapter.) Once praise has subsided, there is only one appropriate mood to follow it, and that is silence.

There is a story of a group of sherpas in the Himalayas who walked and climbed with a group of Western mountaineers for several days and nights. After a long period of almost continuous journeying, they rather abruptly halted, put down the equipment, and rested, not to sleep, but apparently to wait for something or someone. On enquiry from the Westerners, the sherpas explained, simply: "We have traveled a long way; we are waiting for our souls to catch up with our bodies."

This is the role of the silence that follows the offering of praise. A long way has indeed been traveled. An assembly of people has become a congregation, the Body of Christ. In doing so they have become aware of God, of one another, of authority, and of all in God's creation that is not sharing in the opportunity to worship. They have been reminded of their true place in God's story, and have been horrified to realize how they have acted as if living out a rival story; they have acknowledged this bewilderment, and promised to live God's story again, and been restored to God's companionship. They have risen from penitence to share in glory, praising the God who creates, saves, and empowers and discovering in song the mercy of providence and the possibilities of faith. From the breadth of gathering to the depth of repentance to the height of glory: in silence the members of the congregation allow their bodies to catch up with their souls. They have been trained in silence by what they have already done together.

The period of corporate silence that follows the outbreak of praise is perhaps the most significant act of witness in the whole of the liturgy. It is perhaps the only moment when every person in the assembly is consciously still. The point is not so much the absence of sound as the common purpose of those who seek to be still and know who is God. Unlike every other action in the service, there is no ancillary purpose or benefit other than pure worship. There is no community-building song, no relationship-restoring handshake, no joint movement or shared consumption or appropriate education or careful performance. There is simply prayer, a demonstration of corporate life in the presence of God and the proper condition of God's people in that presence. The congregation have been united in authority, in confession, and in praise: now they are united in prayer. In this pause they do nothing, materially, to advance the well-being of any creature on earth; neither do they get to know each other better. But they do proclaim their faith that the Holy Spirit's work is not dependent on human cooperation; they do embody their discovery that all prayer is rooted in the common prayer of the communion of saints; and they do practice the tradition that all prayer is fundamentally waiting on the will of God, and an invitation to God to mold the character into the shape of his Son.

In some celebrations the period of corporate silence is concluded with prayer that gathers up the diverse meanings and purposes of the silence into one "collect." The collect gathers both the people and their prayers. It is an exemplary prayer, addressed to the first person of the Trinity, making a simple petition that incorporates and focuses the prayers of the preceding silence, and concluding with appeal to the mediation of Christ. There is often also reference to some divine act or attribute, and to the purpose for which the petition is made (Jasper and Bradshaw 1986, 265–7). The collect gives a fitting end to the corporate silence, but also trains the congregation in significant aspects of prayer. The congregation is placed in relation to each member of the Trinity. The special role of Christ as mediator is reaffirmed. The importance of each and every prayer in relation to God's saving acts in history is displayed. And the constant encounter with the unfailing character of God is recalled.

But attention to the details of the collect should not distract from the silence that precedes it. This is an icon of the Church. The congregation, often standing at this point, called, restored, and full of praise, are "of one heart and soul" (Acts 4.32). They are lost in wonder, love, and praise. They are experiencing what it means to worship God and be his friends.

There is of course no such thing as silence. There is instead a choice or discernment of which sounds, movements, and sensations to regard as significant and a commitment either not to respond to any such sounds, movements and sensations for a given period or to embrace such distractions without being disturbed by them. In this sense the silence before the collect epitomizes the issues of description that pervade Christian ethics. What defines this silence is its context. The composer John Cage published a work of "sound organisation" called *4'33"*, which is a work of silence, the performer not playing a single note. The performance of the work points to many of the things the silence before the collect addresses. The audience become extremely attentive to background and inner sounds, movements and gestures that would otherwise be ignored. They develop a heightened awareness, ultra-conscious of the significance of absence, mindful perhaps for the first time of the silence as more than the gap between sounds (Giles 2003, 59–62). In much the same way the silence before the collect heightens the congregation's awareness of the nature of the Church. Apparently nothing is happening: but in that "nothing" is so much: assimilation of forgiveness, experience of being a member of the body of Christ, rest after extended praise, expectation of God's voice speaking through the Scripture readings to come, and experience of hunger and thirst for God to fill the gap opened up by forgiven sin. This silence epitomizes the Church's condition before God. And it is preceded and followed by praise and prayer, just as the Church should be.

Chapter Nine

HEARING

In this chapter I explore four ways in which God's people hear his word and discover that word to be everything they need to follow him. I begin with the Psalms, which I see as the definitive form of praise and lament – ways in which the members of the congregation find God's song in their hearts. I then explore the practice of listening to Scripture. This is followed by the practice of hearing the preached word: the sermon is a continuation of the embodiment of the Scripture. Finally I suggest that the politics of the Church and the way it reorders time are made explicit in the period of discernment after the sermon, a moment when the congregation actively receives what God has carefully and abundantly given.

Joining in the Psalms

Of all the patterns of activity embodied in the Eucharist, one is more important than all the others: praise. The chief end of all human beings, indeed all creation, is to glorify God and enjoy him forever. A significant role of the person presiding, as we have noted, is to unleash the energies of the congregation and to channel them into glorifying God: to foster the gifts that have been given and to cajole them into a harmony of praise.

The definitive forms of praise are the moments when the narrative of Scripture is set aside for a peroration of adulation. These are the Psalms, hymns, and canticles. The congregation are on their knees for the confession. By leaving their sins at the door, disposing of them at the outset of the service, they are taught that their shortcomings cannot dam the ever-rolling stream of God's love. Their sins do not determine the shape of the Christian story, but instead are outnarrated, absorbed into a more pulsating narrative. The congregation then stand to glorify the God who has found a place for them in his story, and they remain standing to experience the feeling of being part of that story. That is what the Psalms and hymns give them. The Psalms explore the height and breadth and length and depth of the life of faith. They are passionate, confident, mystified, wondrous, brutal, proud, grieved, and desperate. But never sentimental. The Psalms paint a world in which no Christian thought is too terrible to name, no Christian feeling too fearful to express. Confession and absolution have reunited believers with the heaven prepared for them; now in the Psalms the human heart expands to fill the moral universe.

The Psalm is both a continuation of the confession and an anticipation of the Scripture readings. For it reiterates what the confession affirms, that fitful human striving is but a parody of God's abiding love. And it looks forward to what the Scripture proclaims, that the overwhelming arms of God nonetheless embrace the clumsy falterings of human discipleship. "If we want to pray for the unemployed, the sick, or those in intellectual doubt, we find all that we need in the Psalms" (Hebert 1935, 219). The congregation sings the hymnbook of ancient Israel over and over again, not just to learn and learn from the story the Psalms tell, but gradually to become what they sing, a human psalm themselves. A human psalm has the courage to do what the Psalms do – to lament, to catalog the grief of the hurt and betrayed, to pause in the bewilderment and sadness of the oppressed. Sometimes one must say "God has forsaken me"; sometimes, before one has finished a long lament, one yet finds oneself saying "he has saved my life" (Psalm 22). The Psalms find words for grief, just as they do for joy. They are proclamations of abundance, of too much joy, and of enough grace even in despair.

> The Psalter is therefore an epitome of the whole religious history of humanity: its struggle to worship God; its struggle with the powers of evil, as something anti-human and de-humanizing; its recognition that evil is yet something in men: its consequent despair over its own sin and inadequacy, and over the apparent indifference of things, perhaps even of God . . . A meditation upon every phase of man's history, the Psalms are a meditation upon Christ and His Passion, since in Christ and His Passion humanity and the history of man are summed up. But the Psalms are no less applicable in different ways to any individual, in so far and in such wise as he enters into and partakes of that life of humanity which is in Christ.
>
> (Hebert 1935, 219–20)

In one local church there was a woman who worshiped faithfully over 30 years, and let the Psalms enfold her experience into their music. After years of allowing her life to become a psalm, a psalm that sang of the joy and despair on both sides of faith's coin, she went a step further. Blending the rhythms of the laundry where she worked with the rhythms of the Psalms that she sang, she found the words to compose her own psalms, her own songs of praise and protest and longing and love. She had become a psalm, and had shown others how to go and do likewise.

The moment after the absolution is suitably an occasion for a Psalm, canticle (often the "Gloria in excelsis"), hymn or song of unambiguous joy. Augustine famously claimed that the one who sings prays twice, in word and in song. The heart of song is praise – at the goodness of life, of life restored, of glorious creation, and creation renewed. Perhaps the epitome of all the Church's song is the "Exsultet", the great hymn of joy traditionally sung at the Easter Vigil, perceiving the story of salvation written through God's creative purpose, seeing even the Fall as a happy setback because it led to so great a restoration. The "Exsultet" places on a cosmic level the transformation marked on a personal and communal level every time a congregation rise from their knees after the absolution to sing a hymn of joy. Singing after being forgiven is a uniting practice, for even if the sins confessed have been largely personal ones, the restoration that is pronounced is corporate. The assembly has been united as a congregation at the greeting, and are now reunited with God in confession and absolution. It is therefore with the whole company of heaven that they rise and join an eternal hymn of praise.

> Singing is a model of the way praise can take up ordinary life and transpose it to a higher level without losing what is good in other levels. . . . It can also combine discipline and precision with great liberation of body, feeling and imagination, beautifully exemplifying the "sober drunkenness" which the early Church saw as a true mark of being "in the Spirit."
>
> (Hardy and Ford 1985, 15)

This is the moment when those who have "stood still, looking sad" (Luke 24.17) are rejuvenated, and eyes that have been downcast are raised on high. In one congregation on Easter morning the first phrase of the Gloria was the prelude to an explosion of bells, streamers, whistles, and shouts, as the pent-up inhibitions of Lent finally found their voice in the joy of the resurrection. This may be a time for dance, for a physical release of ordered exuberance. It is certainly a moment in which the eye of the congregation can take in such wonders as the architecture of the meeting-place has to give. If it is an ancient church or cathedral, the soaring of arch or the subtlety of form express the way that even if the people do not shout "Hosanna," the stones themselves cry out (Luke 19.40). If it is a building of no such evident praise, a great wealth of visual art – banners, windows, hangings, sculpture, and painting – may express the same joy. In one modern church building in a neighborhood of significant social and economic deprivation, windows had been so frequently broken, and the porch had for so long been used as a meeting place for a "posse" of disenchanted young people, that the congregation decided to use a legacy to erect two large iron gates, protecting the windows and excluding the posse from the porch. Seven years later the young people had grown up, relations were much improved, and the members of the congregation reflected on whether the gates truly communicated to the neighborhood the joy that was in their hearts. After discussions with the original donor, local residents, and artists, the congregation decided to transform the iron gates that hung outside into a vast wing suspended inside, hovering over them as they worshiped under its shadow. One kind of protection had been substituted for another: a sword had been turned into a ploughshare; and the building at last cried "Hosanna" to the glory of God.

If joy, praise, and thanksgiving really are the true expression of human fulfillment – if humans truly were made to glorify and enjoy God forever – then this moment in the liturgy should be the foundation of Christian anthropology.

> The keynote is one of constantly astonished joy, with expectation of more than enough being given to meet our problems, even if they are not all solved . . . Our whole life is continually thrown into the air in praise in the trust that it will be caught, blessed, and returned renewed.
>
> (Hardy and Ford 1985, 76)

The definition of human being, made in the image of God, is a forgiven sinner, praising God for life renewed. This is not just a maximal definition of life – a definition that can encompass the everlasting joy of the saints and angels: it is also a minimal definition.

Minimal definitions become important when the conditions of human life are contested. This is especially the case at the beginning and end of life. At what point does human life begin? It may be that praise and joy are significant here. A baby can smile and laugh long before it can speak, and it can kick even in the womb. All these attributes could be taken as forms of joy and praise. Similarly euthanasia is sometimes advocated in the context of a person experiencing great pain. But a minimal definition of humanity that rests on being created to glorify God is bound to question whether killing a person out of compassion for their pain can ever be an expression of praise for God's glory.

In one local congregation there was a woman who was missing from the Ash Wednesday service. Since this was almost unknown, enquiries ensued and she was found to have collapsed at home. Rushed to hospital, she spent the next three days in intensive care, having developed septicemia. Few efforts to communicate had any effect, until one person decided to sing some of the hymns she had missed at the service. When the words "Dear Lord and Father of mankind, Forgive our foolish ways" were sung, her eyelids flickered a last acknowledgement. On the Saturday her struggle ended, the words of the twenty-third Psalm enfolding the family as they passed through the valley of the shadow of death. The hymnbook and psalter had given her and those around her a language through which to express the last stumbling gestures of love – and that language was the language of praise, learned in the liturgy.

Listening to Scripture

At the moment when they are read in the context of worship, the books of the Bible become the Scripture of the Church. In just the same way as the greeting turns an assembly into a church, so the proclamation of Old and New Testament passages turns their words into the Word. This is the action of the Holy Spirit (as discussed in Chapter Three): bringing the Bible to life, in the single word, "Today!"

Diversity

The diversity of genre and witness in Scripture shapes the way the Church thinks about diversity in other spheres. For example, it offers a model of how a congregation may understand diversity amongst its members. Scripture does not confine itself to one book, but communicates one truth in many ways. In some of the books the perception of the incarnation is explicit; in others it is less clear, and in others again it is hard to discern. Some of the books have a confident overarching narrative; others have condensed wisdom; others again have more disparate collections of traditions and stories. Though no single book tells the whole story of God, each has been understood as indispensable for a complete rendering of his character. If any one book were taken away, the ability of the Church to meet the true God in the reading of Scripture would be weakened. In a congregation it is just the same. In some members, faith burns brightly: in others it is less vibrant. Some members can draw on long experience of faithful discipleship; others on a dramatic moment of transformation; others again stumble from insight to bewilderment to fragile trust to renewed vision. No single person could stand for the whole congregation, but each person brings a vital perception of the shape and significance of the Scriptural witness. What would happen to the Church if one of these members were taken away?

Likewise the disunity of the Church internationally is a cause of much grief and regret. And yet each of its diverse strands has a part to play in embodying the story of God. No single church or denomination can claim to incorporate every aspect of God's purposes. Each has a different blend of faithfulness, discipline, suffering, courage, and wisdom. But diversity and disunity are not the same thing. Diversity is a sign of health in the Church, so long as it mirrors the diversity of Scripture. Once the Church believes it can read the Bible without the eyes and ears of some of these diverse elements, that diversity has become disunity. And then the Church's ability to hear God's word is seriously impoverished.

This is the heart of the Church's understanding of issues of equality and inclusivity. One way of addressing such issues is to locate them at the gathering point in the liturgy. One might refer to Paul's much-quoted words that "There is no longer Jew or Greek, there is no longer slave or free, there is no longer male and female; for all of you are one in Christ Jesus" (Galatians 3.28). One might then say that all are made in the image of God and are equally loved by God. Alternatively one might ground that same inclusivity in Baptism. One might say that in becoming part of Christ's body in Baptism, each member has an equal role in God's drama. Again, one might look to Paul's admonitions of the Corinthians for the way that they allowed people at the same communion service to eat strikingly different amounts (1 Corinthians 11.21), and thus ground a notion of equality in the sharing of food.

Each of these approaches has much to commend it. But none of them quite conveys what is conveyed by the moment of listening to the Scripture. What this practice conveys is that the Church needs a myriad diversity of people if it is to be able to read the Scripture well. It is not that a diversity of people have a "right" to be there. Such a right would convey nothing substantial about how they should conduct themselves once they were there. What it means is that a diverse Bible requires – almost creates – a diverse people to be able to read it.

Exodus tells the story of how an oppressed people were led to freedom. If a church has no members who have any experience of that depth of oppression, can it hear the story fully? Daniel and Esther recount tales of the Jewish experience of exile. If there is no foreigner, no resident alien among the congregation, will the stories be heard in the same way? Is the assembly not enriched by reading stories of David misusing his power or Solomon executing judgment if those stories are read in the company of political leaders and judges? Is the church not therefore equally enriched by reading stories of lepers and of the woman with hemorrhages by hearing those accounts in the company of those whose diseases make them social outcasts? The meeting of Mary and Elizabeth is a celebration of pregnancy, and it is hard to read it so well if a pregnant person is not present. The joy of Simeon and Anna is a celebration of old age, and likewise it is hard to hear the story fully if there is no elderly person there. The story of Jacob and Esau is a story about twins; the story of Hannah is a story about childlessness; the story of Jairus' daughter is a story about a parent's bereavement. These are common but not universal experiences, which take on a new meaning when embedded in the life of a congregation. How therefore can a church manage to read the story of Peter and Cornelius or Jesus and the Syrophoenician woman if it does not know in its common life the reality of racial distinction? How can Christians hear the parable of Dives and Lazarus if they do not know in their fellowship with one another the pain of class difference and economic inequality? How can a congregation engage with the relationship between Sarah and Hagar if it has none of the pain of gender discrimination and the subjection of women? And in the remarkable exchange made possible by global travel, it is increasingly possible for congregations the world over to discover from one or more of their number what it means to read Exodus as an Egyptian Christian, Esther as an Iraqi Christian, and Joshua as a Palestinian Christian.

It is not that the Church has a duty to unjustly oppressed or ignored social groups. This would put the Church in an unduly high position of status, ministering unto the needy out of its bounty. It is instead that if the Church is not made up of the full diversity of human existence and experience, it cannot hear all that the Scripture has to say – because it does not mirror the extraordinary diversity that is in Scripture. One might have thought that from reading Scripture the Church is moved to minister to the poor and needy. But one might first think that if the Church does not include the poor and needy it cannot properly hear the Scripture. This is why equality does not convey the same depth of meaning in the Church that terms like ministry or vocation do. Equality may still convey a minimal understanding that the Church in its life should never fall beneath. But a notion of ministry rests on an understanding that when a member brings to the body a perception of the Scripture rooted in identification with its context, such a perception builds up the Church. Such a gift makes the Church something it could not otherwise be. God has given the Church everything it needs to read the Scripture: but often these priceless voices and resources lie neglected, even subjugated, within congregations, or even outside the fellowship altogether.

In one congregation, at a quiet evening celebration of the Eucharist, a member of the leadership team was reading the Gospel when she came to the passage that said that when Joseph heard that Mary was pregnant, he resolved to "dismiss her quietly." The person reading dropped the Bible onto her lap, and stared straight ahead. After a few moments, she quietly said, "I was pregnant at 14. I was made to have an abortion. I wonder every day who that person would have been." The Gospel reading, sermon, and Creed abandoned, the congregation continued the service in intercession. In another congregation, dominated in leadership and membership by men, a woman member rose to read the Old Testament lesson. It described how hard it was to find a good wife, and what her attributes were. The person reading the lesson visibly shook as she read, her voice quavered, a hint of tears lay near the surface. Everything in her spoke of the tension of hearing those words in a contemporary context. But she completed the lesson and sat down before the tears flowed. No one in that community ever saw that passage as a quaint pastoral sermon again.

Reading

The way the Scripture is read is an important factor in shaping how the Scripture is heard. In one congregation a large Bible was carried into the assembly in a formal manner at the start of the service, and placed at the center of the gathering-place where everyone could see it. The Bible was then carefully opened and a period of silence kept. The formal opening symbolized the opening of the congregation's heart to receive the Scripture, and the location of the Bible indicated the desire to place the Scripture at the center of the community's life. In another congregation the Gospel reading was read from a small balcony. The members of the congregation turned round to hear the Gospel, and had to look up, for the balcony was some distance above their heads. Over time they came to perceive that *understanding* the Gospel was less a matter of intellectual grasp than of *standing under* its authority. Another congregation placed the lectern toward the back of their building. Not only did this mean that they had to turn round to hear the Scripture readings – but, since the entrance door was mostly made of glass, it meant that they could see outside at the same time as they heard the Bible being read. They began to offer a particular welcome to any strangers who came into the assembly at the moment when the Scripture was being read – and there were many, because there were often people milling around outside the building. The congregation learned to receive the Gospel as a stranger – making demands, requiring hospitality, needing to be understood, and assuming that the life of the community would change as a result. And meanwhile the congregation learned to receive each stranger as a gospel – even when, as with some of the more mischievous young people, they were texts of terror.

An important aspect of the way a Church reads Scripture is the lectionary. The careful distribution of passages of Scripture across a three-year or similar cycle keeps the Bible large, and a congregation's perception of it broad. Any congregation will be tempted to focus on the parts it likes – parts that suit its preferred lifestyle or history of interpretation or approach to worship. A lectionary limits the longing of the preacher to communicate the whole Gospel every week. Over three years, or whatever constitutes the whole cycle of the lectionary, the whole Gospel should emerge, amplified by, or even in spite of, the qualities of the preacher. The rhythms and cadences of the Church year emerge from and to some extent shape the sequences of the lectionary. These rhythms and cadences influence the color and texture of worship, the flowers and trimmings and vestments that indicate the mood of the season. Candles at Advent and Easter, incense at Epiphany, a donkey and palms on Palm Sunday, flames and streamers at Pentecost, loaves and produce at Harvest – all these embody the liturgical shape of the Church's life. While the last chapter examined the way gathering gives the Church time, here it is worth pausing to consider the related issue of the way the calendar and lectionary give the Church timing.

Timing reflects the rhythm of the liturgical year. Advent and Lent, for example, are seasons of penitence and reflection. They have traditionally been times of refraining from ostentatious celebration, in both liturgy and communal practice. Alleluias are omitted from the liturgy. Meanwhile those considering marriage are encouraged to wait until a more celebratory time of year. As Ecclesiastes notes, "For everything there is a season, and a time for every matter under heaven: . . . a time to weep, and a time to laugh; a time to mourn, and a time to dance; . . . a time to embrace, and a time to refrain from embracing." Easter, by contrast, is a 50-day extravaganza of rejoicing. Rejoicing is, for some, as much of a discipline as the hardships of Lent. The timing of the lectionary and calendar are ways in which the Church learns to discern timing in other aspects of its life. For example, the relationship between the Church and the Jewish people has always been a highly significant one. It highlights questions of God's faithfulness to his promises, the significance of Jesus, the relationship of Christianity to its historic sources, and, more recently the response to the existence of the state of Israel. Should the Church actively evangelize the Jews? For many, in the century after the Holocaust, this is a matter of timing. There is a time to evangelize, and a time to refrain from evangelizing. There is a time for the joyful and urgent sharing of the Easter faith, and there is a time for the penitent and reflective recognition of sins committed and terrible damage done. Similar issues are raised over a host of urgent, controversial, or pressing issues of the day, whether they concern the balance of world trade, the role of gay people in the Church, or the rate of climate change, the damage to earth, air, and sea, and the decline of animal biodiversity. For some of these the moment may be in Advent, waiting for the coming of the kingdom; for others, the timing may be Good Friday, suffering divine things; for others again it may indeed be Pentecost, the energetic *kairos* of change in the power of the Spirit.

Narrative

As the pattern of the Scripture readings establishes itself over the cycle of the lectionary, the congregation comes to appreciate the broadly narrative character of the Bible. Here is a story that begins with creation, acknowledges the poison of sin, traces the calling of the patriarchs, the journey to Egypt, slavery and exodus, the giving of the law, and the entry into the Promised Land, notes the establishment of the monarchy, the building of Jerusalem and the Temple, the split in the kingdom, the Exile in Babylon, the return, and the Second Temple, announces the coming of Jesus, his ministry, his death, and resurrection, portrays the sending of the Spirit, the mission to the Gentiles, and the contours and crises of the first churches, and concludes with the expectation of the full realization of God's reign in the climax of history. It is by no means entirely narrative – there is a great deal of law, poetry, prophecy, and epigram. But most of the non-narrative elements find or assume their context in the company of the underlying narrative, and many explicitly refer to significant events in the thread of Israel's history.

The perception that God's blessing and salvation come in the form of a narrative develops in the congregation a range of narrative skills. Just as a publisher adopts or develops a house style, so the members of the congregation perceive a house style in the Scriptures. They learn to see the author at work. They note characteristic features of the narrative. There is the mysterious pattern of revelation, evoking fear and great joy: "Surely the Lord is in this place – and I did not know it!" (Genesis 28.16); "Were not our hearts burning within us while he was talking to us on the road, while he was opening the scriptures to us?" (Luke 24.32). There is hidden providence, and God's determination not to let human intransigence have the last word: "You intended to do harm to me, God intended it for good" (Genesis 50.20); "The vessel he was making of clay was spoiled in the potter's hand, and he reworked it into another vessel, as seemed good to him" (Jeremiah 18.4); "They put him to death by hanging him on a tree; but God raised him on the third day" (Acts 10.39–40). There is the upside-down kingdom and God's way of bringing it about: "Those who were full have hired themselves out for bread, but those who were hungry are fat with spoil" (1 Samuel 2.5); "He has anointed me to bring good news to the poor. He has sent me to proclaim release to the captives and recovery of sight to the blind, to let the oppressed go free, to proclaim the year of the Lord's favor" (Luke 4.18–19). There is God's compassion and mercy, and his longing to embed these virtues in his people: "I know [my people's] sufferings, and I have come down to deliver them from the Egyptians, and to bring them to a good and broad land, a land flowing with milk and honey" (Exodus 3.7–8); "You shall also love the stranger, for you were strangers in the land of Egypt" (Deuteronomy 10.19); "What does the Lord require of you but to do justice, and to love kindness, and to walk humbly with your God?" (Micah 6.8). These are the house style of the author of Scripture. By listening to God speak in Scripture, the congregation learns to discern God's voice in other conversations. By tracing the author's characteristic moves in Scripture, the congregation learns to trace God's characteristic acts in the theater of his glory today.

Another narrative skill the congregation learns in listening to Scripture is the ability to recognize beginnings and endings. Stories begin in obscurity – Abraham in Haran, David in Bethlehem, Nehemiah in Susa, Mary in Nazareth, John on Patmos. They begin with the overwhelming, often unsought, dazzling grace of God: "Go from your country"; "Before I formed you in the womb I knew you"; "Do not be afraid, Zechariah"; "Saul, Saul, why do you persecute me?" "He said to him, 'Follow me.'" God then gives those whom he calls everything they need to follow him, even if they only falteringly realize it: in a pillar of cloud by day and night for direction, in manna that offered food for daily bread, in laws to guide each detail of life, in his promise of deliverance, in the knowledge that "I am with you always," in the sending of the Spirit, who "will guide you into all truth." These are the ways stories begin. And if stories begin with grace, they end with blessing and promise. God tells Noah, "I will never again destroy every living creature as I have done. As long as the earth endures, seedtime and harvest, cold and heat, summer and winter, day and night, shall not cease" (Genesis 8.21–2). Moses dies, the Promised Land in sight. Paul reaches Rome, and "lived there two whole years at his own expense and welcomed all who came to him, proclaiming the kingdom of God and teaching about the Lord Jesus Christ with all boldness and without hindrance" (Acts 28.30–1). John concludes his vision with Jesus' assurance "Surely I am coming soon!" (Revelation 22.20). By witnessing how God's stories begin and end, the congregation learns to discern the action of God's Spirit in the world, to perceive how God sows his seed and reaps his harvest, to see when God is doing a new thing, and to trust that he has not yet finished with every recalcitrant soul or disheartened missionary.

Listening

Listening to Scripture is the way the Church comes to understand the meaning and authority of revelation. Christians are always likely to think that the Scripture is something that they read – but in fact the Scripture reads them. It searches them out and knows them, and reads their thoughts from afar. It subverts all the habits of detached scholarship. The careful scholar is the disinterested observer, noting how Napoleon lost the battle of Waterloo, or what happens when salt dissolves in water. In this spirit the careful scholar addresses the Scripture reading, and wonders how this strange story can have any bearing on her own story, or on the overarching story of modernity. But the Scripture claims, commands, and questions, and in the process dismantles detachment and invites, even requires, engagement. "I am with you always"; "Wash one another's feet"; "Who do you say that I am?" – these are, on one level, statements, commands, questions. "Know that I am God"; "Love your enemies"; "Can you not stay awake one hour?": these are indicatives, imperatives, interrogatives – but on another level they are headlights, and Christians are rabbits caught in them, and they gradually cease to ask what relevance this story has to them and their time, and begin to wonder, fearfully, if their lives and their generation are exposed as meaningless in the light of the truth of this story.

In one congregation there was a woman who, privately, had always seen Jesus as something of a hero, epitomizing most of the values her organization stood for – he talked about justice, probably believed in equal opportunities, admittedly was not strong on health and safety, but certainly stood up for the individual, especially minorities, against the system. She could even be persuaded to read the Bible, because it advocated values, and she believed in values. But it was not until the pressure of life took its toll on her mental health, and she found support and strength in a community of faith, that she began to realize that reading the Bible brought no liberation, and would not do so until she allowed the Bible to read her. She found courage to do that by hearing the Bible read in the context of the Eucharist, in the company of others like her.

The practice of attending to and sitting under Scripture is the definitive way that Christians learn to listen. Listening in its simplest sense means attending to the spoken word. But listening in a broader sense, in the way the term is used, for example, in the practice of counseling, means taking in the whole communication of the speaker. Taking in the whole communication of God means more than hearing the spoken words. It means being aware of the manner of speech, the messages contained in posture, urgency, silence, and breathing, the resonance with previous conversations and the degree of interaction with the listener and the environment. Listening also means blocking out some impressions in order to focus on others. It means delaying judgment, withholding observation, reducing distraction, and sometimes ignoring interruption. It means being sufficiently relaxed to allow the speaker to shape the conversation, yet sufficiently alert to take in every message the speaker is giving. All of these habits apply to and derive from listening to Scripture. In a sense the first part of the service is principally designed to make the assembly into a church that can hear God's word in Scripture. The greeting, confession, celebration, and silence comprise the appropriate preparation to converse with God – to be his friends. Now they are ready to take in the whole of God. This means hearing accounts of his action – his shaping of the universe, his delivering the Israelites, his calling David, his sending the Son. It means discovering how those actions have been interpreted in other places in Scripture – in song, in prophecy, in imitation, in worship. It means attending to the wider narrative context of every reading – in relation to the Scriptural story as a whole. It means being aware of the liturgical context in which the Scripture is being read, and its specific relation to any other readings read at the same service. And it means perceiving God's will even through the faltering responses of those whom he has called – when Nathan declares to David "You are the man!"; when the third slave says "I knew that you were a harsh man"; when those on the left hand say "When was it that we saw you hungry or thirsty?"; when Peter hears the cock crow. But it must also mean listening in a similar way to the person speaking the words: seeking in their demeanor, tone, wonder and awe the transformation that the Scripture offers.

In one congregation the reader of the Old Testament passage spoke the words of the Scripture while kneeling on the floor. The listeners, about 60 in number, were arranged in a semi-circle around the altar, and the reader knelt facing them in front of the altar, offering material symbols derived from the passage to illustrate the story as it proceeded. As the reading began, one member of the congregation, seated a little further away than some of the others, requested that the reader speak rather louder, to be more clearly heard. The reader said that the nature of the passage and the sensitivity of the symbols required a subtler voice, and that it might mean that the listeners had to work a little harder than usual. The member of the congregation was angry, and expressed a conviction that everything must always be done to assist those whose hearing was impaired in any way. But the reader insisted that the Scripture requires the congregation to work hard in order to listen – that it is not a consumer package for instant digestion but a strange voice to be wrestled with, and it might require listeners to move physically if they were to be able to hear it well.

Hearing the Preached Word

The Scripture readings form an arrow – the Old and New Testament readings forming the two angles of the arrow and the Gospel reading forming the shaft. If the readings together form the arrow, the sermon, the point where all three readings meet, must form the point of the arrow. When there are regularly three readings, the congregation learn how to hear and read the Gospel: that is, that Christians read the story of Jesus in the context, on the one hand, of the story of Israel, and on the other hand, of the experience of the early Church. The Gospel is always news that emerged from the Jews and was discovered to be the truth by the people who came to be called the Church. To return to the image of the arrow, the story of Israel and the experience of the early Church clarify the point of the Gospel.

The sermon proclaims that the God who acted in the story of Israel, came in Jesus, and was alive in the early Church, is living and active today. It therefore trains the congregation not just to be part of a tradition, but at the same time to be alert to the ways in which that tradition is taking flesh in front of their own eyes. The sermon is an event, not a report. It is not an account of the truths that were made known to the preacher some days (or years) earlier when surrounded by scriptural commentaries and compilations of timely anecdotes. It is not an aggregation of insights on a scriptural passage presented by a diligent researcher to a pencil-sucking congregation. It is a moment when heaven comes to earth, when the truth of the way God acts in history, his longing for the restoration of friendship with his people, comes face to face with the reality of human intransigence and fragile striving. It is a moment when Christians rediscover who they are by seeing, face to face, who God is. It is a moment when earth comes to heaven, when the truth of what humanity is in sin is redescribed by the glory of what humanity is in Christ. It is an incarnational moment, when

God's divinity meets our humanity in the spoken word, and the congregation discover that he became what we are, so that we might become what he is. It is a resurrection moment, when the apparent givens of sin, death, and evil are stripped away and the possibilities of humanity in the new creation are transformed. The congregation who begin the service wondering what God is going to do today should find in the sermon some discovery that honors their expectation. The encounter between the preacher and the congregation should mirror, in its intensity, the encounter between God and his people. God gives his people everything they need. The purpose of the sermon is not to scratch around searching for faint traces of God's ways. It is to recall and portray the overwhelming tidal wave of God's blessing and redeeming purpose, and, lest the congregation drown in the abundance of grace, to focus and funnel the tidal wave down onto a specific moment, now, and to a particular aspect of God's being and action that transforms an identified dimension of contemporary existence.

The sermon is a moment of revelation. It is about meeting God face to face. Here is the God who has acted before to save his people and here is the God who will act again to set them free. This is not a secret knowledge. It is not a cryptic code that unlocks a door to direct the initiated down a labyrinthine path that saves them from a mysterious catastrophe. It is a prophetic conviction that, when the Church is formed, sins confessed, glory celebrated, and Scriptures read, God speaks through the interpreting word of the authorized preacher. And the revelation that comes is true to the character of the God revealed in Scripture, but nonetheless full of surprise and wonder and mercy anew. If the heart of human alienation from God were ignorance, the sermon would be a time for education. Ignorance, foolishness, and misunderstandings are dimensions of alienation, no doubt, and education has its place in shaping the character of disciples. But that place is not primarily the sermon at the Eucharist. For the heart of human alienation is sin, and what is required is not simply education and edification, but revelation and repentance.

If the sermon is to be shaped by the Gospel it must be "good news of great joy for all the people" (Luke 2.10). In other words, to the extent that it is information, it must be information that is not available elsewhere. In retelling the story of God's action in the past, the preacher redescribes present reality. By portraying how God's activity, hidden or plain, is the key to understanding history, the preacher makes plain that God's activity is the key to understanding the present and the future. It is thus information that shapes the character and understanding of the congregation. The sermon is revelation not education, good news not knowledge, formation not just information, saving truth not just wisdom.

To return to the picture of the arrow, if the sermon is the sharp point of the arrow, the direction of that point may vary. On most occasions it will point deep into the heart of God – a revelation of an aspect of God's character revealed in Christ. But sometimes it will be directed to the life of the community of faith, and the sharp edge of the arrow will be felt by the congregation as one aspect of its life is revealed by the Gospel in spirit and truth. Sometimes the point will be directed to wider society more generally, toward the myths that captivate the national or international imagination. On other occasions the arrow points deep into the self, and the sharp point of revelation touches on deceptions and transformations written into the habit and fiber of every member of the congregation.

Perhaps the most important role of the preacher is to locate the congregation in time. God has opened the drama in creation, has declared his purpose in Israel, and has revealed himself fully in Christ. He will finally draw the whole story to a close at the eschaton. The role of the preacher is to locate the congregation between these givens, to retell the story in such a way that the gifts of creation, Israel, and Christ are fully received and the gift of the eschaton is appropriately understood. The name of the time between Jesus and the eschaton is Church. This is a great part of what it means to say the world needs the Church if it is to understand what it is to be the world. For the Church, as described by the preacher, is that body of people who know the space and time of their lives to be defined by the boundaries of Jesus' ascension and return. And the preacher reminds the congregation of the nature of this time, the way it has been characterized by creation, Israel and Jesus, and the habits and practices that equip Christians to live in the time known as Church. Thus the members of the congregation practice fitting their own small stories into the larger story of God.

Inhabiting the space and time revealed by the Gospel, the preacher sets about describing the reality of the world seen through the lens of the kingdom. The power of preaching is not just that it can make vivid the new relationship of God and his creation made possible by Christ; it is also that, in the strength of that new relationship, the preacher can redescribe the apparent givens of human existence in such as way as to portray them anew as gifts. This is the power of moral description. "Neither this man nor his parents sinned" says Jesus; "he was born blind so that God's works might be revealed in him" (John 9.3). In saying this, Jesus makes possible a whole new pattern of moral description. The given of disability is transformed into the potential temple of God's glory – and in the broken and crippled Christ, the separation between the mighty God and the vulnerable experience of disability is removed. Through narrative, irony and reversal, the preacher may upset conventional notions of "ability" and "disability" and transform the perception of disability through the surprises of the Gospel. "Which is easier," asks Jesus, "to say to the paralytic, 'Your sins are forgiven,' or to say, 'Stand up and take your mat and walk'?" (Mark 2.9) – and in so putting this question, Jesus dismantles conventional givens concerning disease and sin. Through stories of healing and reconciliation the preacher may point out that many shortcomings which had been assumed to be sin may in fact be disease, whereas some sufferings that had been taken to be disease may in fact need repentance. "Love your enemies," says Jesus, "and pray for those who persecute you" (Matthew 5.44). In saying this, the given of war and violence is transformed into a moment of worship. Through a portrayal of wisdom and foolishness, of the abiding attraction of Barabbas and the true power of the cross and resurrection of Jesus, the preacher may question the necessity of war and renarrate the apparent inevitability of violence. Jesus says to Martha, "Did I not tell you that if you believed, you would see the glory of God?" (John 11.40), and in so challenging her he challenges the given of death. Through analogy, exposition, and courageous honesty, the preacher may set the horror of death in the context of Jesus' resurrection and the kingdom of heaven, and so redescribe even the most abiding given as a gift. Thus the sermon defines moral description by shaping the moral imagination.

Discerning God's Voice

Like the first part of the Eucharist, the second part concludes with a period of silence. But it is a different kind of silence. The silence that precedes the collect ponders the great events that precede it – becoming a church, being forgiven, lifting hearts in praise. The silence that follows the sermon senses the point of the arrow, the witness of Scripture, and its sharp edge in contemporary life. The role of the sermon is to ensure that the congregation discover that through the Scripture and reflection on its experience they have come face to face with God. During the silence that follows the congregation have an opportunity to discern the shape of life that that encounter now requires. While the whole of the liturgy portrays a new politics, this is a moment when the Church may discover the difference between a politics that is about discernment in the context of abundance and a politics that is about distribution in the face of scarcity.

The prevailing ethos of the richer contemporary democracies is that the goods of life are those that one secures for oneself, and that the role of the state is to guarantee the ability of the individual to maximize their own security, possessions, abilities, and experience. The result is that the nation

lives increasingly in a perpetual present tense, with fewer links to a significant shared past and even fewer projections of a meaningful corporate
future. Meanwhile the culture that prizes the acquisitive individual has
eroded the kinds of intermediate forms of social interaction that foster
shared goods and practices. The body of common language and common
goals and practices on which to found corporate aspirations is diminishing.
The churches that flourish in this culture tend to be the ones that mirror it
uncritically. The challenge for the churches is to embody an alternative
culture based on an increasing common language of shared goods and
shared practices while remaining in the present tense – that is, not lapsing
entirely into the past (nostalgia) or the future (utopia).

There is another notion of politics. Politics is not just a tiresome consequence of human shortcomings, it is an ongoing conversation about how
to bring out and empower the ocean of different gifts and talents in a community. It is not about the limited money in people's pockets, it is about the
limitless potential in their hearts and minds and souls and bodies. It is about
how to engage all the energy that is about, and how to discern and embody
that which constitutes the good life. It may not always be happy, beautiful,
or rich, but if a community can express such a notion of politics, it can
experience a goodness that other communities, with their impoverished
politics, can only envy.

What the congregation has had the opportunity to rediscover in the
Scripture readings, is that God makes this second kind of politics possible by
giving his people everything they need to follow him. Discernment is not
primarily a matter of moral effort. It is not so much that there is a shortage
of goods, of knowledge, of wisdom, of information, of revelation, of God –
such that the Gospel moves Christians to overcome these shortcomings
through renewed exertion and the straining of every sinew for good. Discernment is instead principally a matter of moral imagination. It takes
imagination to realize that God has given the Church far too much, rather
than not enough. It takes imagination to open the heart to receive the
abundant gifts of God, rather than to assume those gifts are scarce and look
elsewhere. It takes imagination to allow oneself to be overwhelmed by
God's gifts, and not to develop such formidable resistances to those gifts that
one has become almost unaware of them.

If God overwhelms the Church by the abundance of the gifts he gives it,
he also gives the Church every means it needs to engage these gifts. That is
what the practices of the Church, in particular the Eucharist, are about.
These practices provide the form of the politics of the Church; deliberation
over the best use of the abundant gifts of God provides its content.

The silence after the sermon is a neglected part of the liturgy amongst most congregations. In one local congregation a custom developed when the Eucharist took place in the evening. After the second reading the priest habitually invited the congregation to reflect on their experience in a specific way that linked with the Scripture passages. The opportunity did not seek a right or wrong answer but simply invited members to set their experience alongside the scriptural portrayal. The invitation might be "I wonder if you have known someone with a disability" or "I wonder who you think really runs the country." The sermon that followed usually wove some of those responses into a presentation of the word and an insight into the character of God and the practice of the Church. Sometimes members of the congregation added observations at the end. On one occasion the priest was particularly pleased with what she had in mind to say and forgot to invite the congregation to share their experience. The following morning an outraged member of the congregation sought her out. "Last night," he said, "you simply talked at us for fully 15 minutes, and then just stopped. There was no opportunity for discussion whatsoever." The priest, somewhat defensively and ironically, pointed out that this would have been his experience of worship every Sunday if he attended almost any other church both in that city and quite possibly throughout the world. Yet here was a man, living in a deprived community, who had through the repeated practice of listening and discerning, come to take for granted that his experience was an important part of the proclamation of God's word, that he had a place in God's story. This was an assumption, a form of his faith, that liturgical habit had taught him. It helped him to see the unique opportunity his church was offering to its community – to find their story in God's story.

One congregation always celebrated the Eucharist with every member present throughout – infants, children, young people, and adults. The custom was for the person presiding to kneel on the floor and present a scriptural passage using wooden figures, a felt underlay, and assorted other artifacts. By keeping the storyteller's eyes on the figures, rather than the congregation, by speaking gently and by handling the materials deliberately and tenderly, the presentations came to take the form more of a meditation than a performance. On one occasion the presentation concerned the Good Shepherd. Bringing together themes from Psalm 23, Luke 15 and John 10, the presentation displayed the safe sheepfold, the good pasture, the refreshing water, and the places of danger where a sheep could get lost. The members of the congregation shared their experience of the church and the neighborhood, and whether each felt safe, good, refreshing, or dangerous. One child said for him the church was like the refreshing water, because home was a place of danger. One adult said church was a place of danger, because once she and others had been pelted with stones as they left the service. Finally attention fell upon the sheep themselves, which were made out of different kinds of wood. "I wonder if it makes any difference that the sheep are different colors," said the storyteller. Immediately one of the older children responded adamantly "It makes no difference at all – we should treat them all the same." Not content, the storyteller pressed a little further: "I wonder what makes them all the same." There was a long pause. No response was forthcoming from the 30 or so members present. At last there was a quiet voice from a six-year-old child near the back. Pointing at the wooden figure with a sheep across his shoulders, she said, "Because they all have the same shepherd."

This episode displays the politics of the Church at work. The presentation on the theme of the Good Shepherd was a sermon because it was an event that portrayed the heritage of Scripture as saving truth for today. And yet it did not see the end of the sermon as the conclusion of what God had to say to his people today. It trusted that God was communicating through the experience of the congregation, prior to this moment but also, definitively, in the dialogue between this presentation and the congregation's prior experience of God. It offered plenty of time – perhaps 10 or 15 minutes – for that dialogue to take place, and allowed silence to be part of that dialogue. And the genre of the dialogue was wonder. The statements made were seldom indicative statements of undisputable fact – except when a contributor named their own experience, and even then the experience was offered to the assembly as a gift, rather than delivered as a given. Responses were never sought through direct questions, to which there might be expected to be right or wrong answers, thus creating a conventional hierarchy of knowledge and information. (A sentence that begins "I wonder" does not end with a question mark.) Instead, contributions were invited through an initiative of genuinely open-ended wondering, in which the person speaking ensures that they never offer an invitation into an area where they already know there is a "right" answer: "I wonder what it was like for the 99 sheep when the shepherd left them on their own"; "I wonder whether the shepherd ever gets bored of looking after the sheep." Such wonderings give the congregation permission to explore revelation without fear of "getting it wrong." In that context, the insight of a six-year-old is as valuable as the wisdom of the ancients or the learning of the educated.

And this is not just a matter of theological reflection: "I wonder whether all the sheep realize what the shepherd does for them"; "I wonder whether it is somehow good for the sheep to go through places of danger sometimes"; "I wonder if there is anything the shepherd can do to make the 'valley of the shadow' less dangerous." It is also a matter of politics. "I wonder what the shepherd would do if more sheep arrived"; "I wonder whether there is enough good pasture for all the sheep"; "I wonder how the water stays fresh"; "I wonder what the sheep talk to each other about." This is a genuine politics that involves every member of a congregation deliberating over the goods of their common life in the light of the abundant gifts of God and grace of the Gospel.

A comparable process sometimes takes place in neighborhood social and economic regeneration. A room-sized model of the neighborhood is constructed in a local public building. Groups of local people are invited to wander around the model, talking with one another and sharing memories, dreams and reflections. They are encouraged to interact with members of the community they would not usually talk with or even meet. By speaking to the model, rather than to one another, residents forge a common vision of a shared future, relating not just to the physical environment but to the forms of life that will inhabit it. The process is called "Planning for Real." This is a dynamic form of local politics. It is a genuine deliberation over shared goods. The "wondering" that I have described incorporates many of the advantages of a process like Planning for Real. But its unique dimension is that its subject is a story that the participants accept as revelation. They sit under the story, "standing under" its authority, but in the spirit of the slaves who traded with the talents, they wrestle together with its import, significance, and shaping power for their shared existence today.

The political dimension of this kind of dialogue is made explicit in the practice of communal discernment described by Ernesto Cardenal. Cardenal founded the Christian commune Solentiname on an island in an archipelago in Lake Nicaragua near the Costa Rican border in 1966. He used dialogue as the principal form of engaging with the Gospel, setting aside a conventional sermon and preferring to interject exegetical and other observations into a corporate commentary that took place either after the Gospel reading or in a thatched hut after the communal lunch after Mass.

On one occasion the Gospel came from Matthew 6.24–34, and the dialogue turned to "Therefore do not worry, saying, 'What are we going to eat . . . '." One member, Marcelino, responded, "It doesn't mean don't work, but don't worry about it." Francisco added "There's a lot of selfishness among the poor. I think we're poor because we're selfish." But Jose Espinosa countered, "No, those who exploit us are the selfish ones . . . I sowed a rice field and it came up fine and the price is awful." Others agreed. But Felix was with Francisco: "You have to accept the will of God. It's the will of God that we stay poor." Jose Espinosa was adamant: "No, the will of God is that we fight, and he's going to fight at our side." An artist Samuel wondered about whether Christ meant to eliminate progress: "Would we return to the economy of primitive people? They were perhaps happy, but economic concerns, competition, ambition rightly understood (I call it initiative instead) have all been necessary for progress . . . We could ruin the economy." But Coronel, seeing Marxist and Gospel economic systems as "more modern than capitalism," says that "These very fine words would produce a very fine economy." Marcelino concludes, "The kingdom of God is love. And justice, it's the same. Let's try to bring about this society of love and justice, and then there will be no more exploitation. And therefore there will be abundance for everybody. We'll all have not only food and clothing but also schools, clinics, hospitals, adequate housing, all we need" (Cardenal 1977, 221–37).

Cardenal starts by saying that the authors of his books are the people who participate in these dialogues, and talk and say important things – and he lists some of their names, Pancho, a conservative, Julio Mairena, a great defender of equality, Tomas Pena, who cannot read, but talks with great wisdom, and so on. But then Cardenal corrects himself, and recognizes that

> The true author is the Spirit that has inspired these commentaries (the Solentiname *campesinos* know very well that it is the Spirit who makes them speak) and that it was the Spirit who inspired the Gospels. The Holy Spirit, who is the Spirit of God instilled in the community, and whom Oscar would call the spirit of community unity, and Alejandro the spirit of service to others, and Elvis the spirit of the society of the future, and Felipe the spirit of proletarian struggle, and Julio the spirit of equality and the community of wealth, and Laureano the spirit of the Revolution, and Rebeca the spirit of Love.
>
> (Cardenal 1977, ix–x)

Chapter Ten

RESPONDING

The congregation responds to God's word in a host of ways. But here I examine three liturgical responses, which in many churches follow carefully in sequence. And the reason that Creed, intercessions and peace follow revelation may be that they represent faith, hope, and love. The abundance of God gives his people not only all the revelation they need but also a pattern of faithful response.

Confessing Faith

After encountering God's word in Scripture and sermon, the congregation responds with a long "Amen," in the form of a declaration of faith. The Creed is a description of the God embodied in the Scripture and extolled in the canticles, a God who makes a playground for his friends to inhabit, enters the story himself, undergoes excruciating pain and secures limitless glory, enfolds humanity in the reach of his everlasting arms and is destined to share his life with us for ever. And the congregation speaks these words with their eyes on the cross, the form that discloses the cost of love and the character of God's kingdom. Saying the Nicene Creed together in the context of the Eucharist shapes Christians in a number of ways.

Earlier we saw how the Eucharist gives Christians space, by requiring them to meet together in a specified place and at a specified time in order to carry out together embodied practices such as sharing food that could not be enacted alone or apart. The Creed gives Christians a comparable sense of verbal space, by setting a series of boundaries within which conceptual practices may take place. The Creed is a document that witnesses to the contested nature of truth in the history of the Church. The story of the Council of Nicaea in 325, the circumstances in which it was called, the

arguments of Arius and his supporters, the swings of the theological barom-
eter in the course of the fourth century, the turbulent career of Athanasius,
and the conclusive finale at Constantinople in 381, all testify to the Church's
struggle to discern divine truth amid teeming human debate. It is a significant warning against sentimentality. There is no pious legend concerning
the writing of the Creed. It is said that the 70 translators all arrived at the
identical translation of the Septuagint, having worked hard for 70 days.
There is no such story about Nicaea. Doctrinal truth has always been political, and with politics come passion, power games, and intrigue. In pro-
nouncing the Creed together, Christians acknowledge that this was the best
effort of the Church in the early centuries to articulate how God was in
Christ yet God is one. This inspires them in their turn to make their own
best efforts to articulate how incarnation and Trinity are at the heart of
contemporary faith. Standing to say the Creed places Christians in the his-
torical tradition of those who continue to wrestle with these questions
while accepting the formulation of Nicaea as definitive. To the extent that
the Creed is seen as a summary of revelation, it becomes like the Scripture,
the subject of preaching – and likewise needs the action of the Holy Spirit
thus to bring it to life, and write it on the hearts of the congregation.

Perhaps more significantly, saying the Nicene Creed together maps out
some theological boundaries within which the Eucharist takes place. The
God encountered in the Eucharist is the Holy Trinity. The Holy Trinity is
named as Father, Son and Holy Spirit. The Father is the creator of all that is;
the Son is of one being with the Father, and all things were made through
him. He was incarnate, crucified, and raised; he ascended, reigns, and will
return. The Holy Spirit is equal in status to the Father and the Son, and
spoke through the prophets. The Church, Baptism, and resurrection are also
articles of faith. These are therefore the theological boundaries that hedge
the Eucharistic table: a Scriptural faith in the Holy Trinity revealed definitively in Jesus Christ, fully God and fully human, believed in by the
universal Church, embodied in the sacraments, and located in the time after
this revelation but before the eschatological consummation.

Saying the Creed together week after week establishes for Christians a
number of rules that guide the way they talk about God. The first rule
emerges from the form of the Creed. The Creed is almost entirely made up
of statements about God, rather than claims about human existence. By
describing God as a Trinity, the Creed implies that all conversation is a
reflection of the fundamental conversation – the inner-Trinitarian conversation. The significance of this is that it suggests that theological discourse
is a conversation in which more than one voice may be truthful and one
may continue to dialogue without implying that earlier formulations were

inadequate. Another rule that derives from this one is that theological conversation must open dialogue not close it down. The Creed does not come
at the end of the service. It is not the last word. It comes after the period of
revelation through Scripture, and before the embodiment of companionship in the sharing of food. It is like the mast of a ship that keeps these two
sails in harmony. If it does not make the sharing of food possible it has not
kept the Church in the unity of peace. In this sense it stands for all other
rules in the Church. Rules are intended so that the faith that is given
through the Scriptural revelation shall be embodied in the sharing of food.
If those rules make the sharing of food less, rather than more, possible, then
it brings into question whether they are good rules.

A rule that has become more evident in the era of liturgical renewal is the
recognition that the Creed is the faith of the Church, rather than necessarily
the experience or testimony of any one individual. Truth and falsity, faith
and doubt, do not lie principally in the conscience of the individual but in
the gathered assembly and the Church as a whole. On any one occasion, the
faith of one member of the congregation may be strong and vivid, the faith
of another faint and fragile. The latter does not miss out parts of the Creed
simply because they are felt to be more difficult, but the former recognizes
their responsibility to carry the faith of the latter until such time as it shall
return clear and lucid. Faith is learned by a people saying the Creed
together: there is no integrity to be gained by individual silence in the midst
of corporate witness. All this is expressed in the opening word, "We."
Whenever an assembly of people make a corporate statement of conviction
beginning with the word "We," there will always be some who feel the force
of that conviction more powerfully than others. But that is a matter of
strength, rather than weakness, because the use of "We" commits the
members of the congregation to foster the well-being of one another's faith,
through listening, sharing, teaching, encouragement, and example. Likewise
saying the Creed is a rehearsal for speaking of faith to those who do not
believe – at work, at home, or on demand. The Creed is reason for the hope
in one's heart – but the faith being shared is always "ours" not "mine."

The location of the Creed in the liturgy is thus significant in two respects.
On the one hand, as has been mentioned, the Creed comes after the Scripture and before the sharing of food. This ensures that theological truth is
always pondered with an awareness of its social context. There can be no
adequate confession of faith in circumstances where the just distribution of
food is not taking place. On the other hand, the Creed's more precise location is that it comes after the sermon and before the intercessions. In other
words the Creed is anchored in revelation and in prayer. The Creed looks
like a series of propositions – a mountain of theological bricks piled one on

top of another: but in fact it turns out to be a prayer, concluded by the word, Amen. It is a challenge to all forms of truth that do not present themselves in the form of a prayer.

In many congregations the custom is to stand to say the Creed. Standing for the Creed echoes standing for the Gloria. For the Gloria gives voice to the joy of reconciliation that follows the absolution; and the Creed gives voice to the wonder of revelation that follows the sermon. And just as the joy of the Gloria leads to the prayerful silence before the collect, so the wonder of the Creed leads to the prayerful litany of the intercessions. The former is the solidarity of a people standing together as forgiven sinners; the latter is the communion of a people standing together to recognize their incorporation in God's story. Later the congregation will stand to share peace and be prayerful for the Great Thanksgiving – again, their standing is an embodiment of the unity of a people entering the heart of God's life. The people who have stood to worship, stand to be God's friends, and will stand as they prepare to eat with him.

The Creed is a vital link between the Eucharist and Baptism. Just as the confession of sin and the absolution echo the decisions, commitments and liberation of Baptism, so the confession of faith echoes the putting-on of Christ, the clothing of the new Christian in the robes of faith, hope, and love. When the members of the congregation say the Creed together, they stand for a moment again before the waters of Baptism, with all the intensity of sin behind them and the kingdom ahead of them. The Creed identifies the God who alone can redeem them, and demonstrates the myriad of implications that derive from God's decision never to be except to be for us in Christ.

In one congregation there was a woman who faced up to the reality of the Creed as she prepared for Baptism. The sheer force of the words stared at her as the awesome nature of the sacrament reared above her, like a wave about to crash over her head. Noticing her pensiveness, the person preparing her for Baptism asked her how she felt about saying these uncompromising sentences. With measured tones, looking back over 50 years of a life lived escaping the shadow of God, she said: "I have come to see that this thing is really all about obedience."

If the Creed is the point in the liturgy where the congregation learns to reason theologically, it is also the place where Christians learn the virtue of courage. Over and over again in the Gospels, when people are challenged to declare whether they believe, the issue is not whether they have enough knowledge or understanding, but whether they have the courage to face the consequences. When Martha goes to meet Jesus on the road outside Bethany, and Jesus says "I am the resurrection and the life. Those who believe in me, even though they die, will live, and everyone who lives and believes in me will never die. Do you believe this?," Martha's subsequent confession of faith heralds almost immediate transformation in her brother's life (John 11.25–6). When Jesus asks the disciples on the road to Caesarea Philippi who they say he is, Peter's confession of faith triggers Jesus' disclosure of the true nature of his Messiahship, and a major crisis in Peter's identity as a disciple (Mark 8.27–33). When Peter claims, "Even though I must die with you, I will not deny you" (Mark 14.31), he sets himself up for the time of trial concluded by the twofold cock crow. When the thief on the cross says, "Jesus, remember me when you come into your kingdom" (Luke 23.42), the moment is a decisive break with the values of the other thief, and a definitive statement of faith in the face of death – not just his own, but Jesus' too.

So the question the members of the congregation ask themselves when they are invited to stand and confess their faith is, "Do I dare to say the Creed?" If the scriptural witness points so clearly to the link between declarations of faith and personal crisis and cost, can the congregation face the consequences of reciting these words? There are many examples in the history of the Church where saying the Creed constituted a political act of this kind. In the twentieth century the Barmen Declaration was an explicit statement of the lordship of Christ in the face of the competing claims of the Nazis. And William Cavanaugh points out how torturers in Pinochet's Chile invariably already knew the information they were extracting from their prisoners. The point of the torture was to extract a litany of conformity to the Pinochet regime and its view of the world – a kind of alternative creed to the Creed of Nicaea. Cavanaugh describes how Christians in Chile created opportunities for the spontaneous performance of a truthful litany and liturgy, naming torturers and identifying places of torture, and creating a climate in which the claims of the Creed of Nicaea could once more be heard in all their political significance. These were acts of extraordinary courage (Cavanaugh 1998).

Interceding

If God gives his people everything they need to follow him, the practice of intercession is both a recognition of that need and a plea for that need to be met. Intercession balances the honesty and humility of need with the faith and hope of expectation. Expectation is at the heart of hope. If the congregation constitutes a hopeful people, it will be pervaded by a consistent air of expectation. The intercessions represent hope in the way that the Creed represents faith and the peace represents love. Each is a valid response to the manifestation of God's action and character through Scripture, sermon, and period of discernment. But expectation is the way a congregation embodies its confidence that the God who has acted in history will act today.

Intercession teaches Christians that they are needy people. But yet again the location of the intercessions in the liturgy is highly significant. The needs of the people are not identical to the needs they were aware of when they entered the place of meeting. They have been altered in four important ways by what has happened since the service began. Each of these ways demonstrates how worship shapes character.

First, they have confessed their sins before God, and, in doing so, have learnt the difference between pain and sin. Confession has not named everything that is amiss. There are hurts received, disappointments endured, honest mistakes regretted, misunderstandings undergone, loves lost; there are earthquakes and floods, congenital disorders and birth injuries, mystery viruses and misadventure; meanwhile there are the perennial struggles of the workplace, the family, and the mirror of mortality. Confession has stripped away the sin of greed, of selfishness, of laziness, of lust, envy, and pride – but it has left behind a great catalog of pain for which there is no one to blame: and that is the stuff of intercession. Learning the difference between pain and sin teaches Christians compassion – that quality that recognizes in others a common human experience of need and pain.

Second, they have received absolution for their sins, and in doing so have begun to distinguish between healing and forgiveness. Forgiveness removes the weight of blame and punishment and fear from the sinner; but healing names those aspects and consequences of sin that take longer to repair, and those dimensions of creation's fallenness that continue to inhibit the well-being of the community of believers. Forgiveness requires confession, but healing needs intercession. Forgiveness removes the poison, but healing restores the body. Forgiveness ends the war, but healing makes the peace. Reconciliation with God is something that only God can offer, and it is appropriately situated at the beginning of the service. But the often slow process of repair, restoration, relocation, and eventual flourishing in community is something in which a whole range of people – friends, family, medical staff, legal officers, professional caregivers, fellow disciples, teachers, colleagues – may participate, and it is appropriate to locate this appeal close to the sharing of the peace, that emblem of restored community.

Third, the members of the congregation have heard the proclamation of the Gospel in Scripture and sermon, and in doing so have begun to separate suffering from evil. Just as not all pain is sin, so not all suffering is evil. The plea for God's mercy is a longing that God will intervene to end suffering.

But the plea for God's justice is slightly different: it is a longing that God will intervene to overturn evil and oppression. When Jesus is approached by some people who compare the death of some Galileans at the hand of Pilate with those 18 who were killed when the Tower of Siloam fell upon them, the same distinction is clear, between oppressive evil in the first case and undeserved suffering in the second. And when the thief on the cross takes issue with his fellow criminal on his attitude to Jesus, it is over just this same distinction between suffering and evil: accordingly he says "We indeed have been condemned justly, for we are getting what we deserve for our deeds, but this man has done nothing wrong." The whole of the liturgy embodies a process by which God addresses, transforms, outnarrates, and overturns evil; the intercessions are the moment when the congregation brings to God particular and general instances of suffering, not unaware of his justice but seeking his mercy.

Fourth, those coming to intercession have paused to discern God's voice in the sermon and in the life and witness of their fellow worshipers, and in doing so have begun to note a difference between what they need and what they want. Throughout the Old Testament Israel is discovering what it means to be God's beloved, and how that relationship should shape all other desires. As God's beloved, Israel need only collect enough manna for the day (Exodus 16), for God gives his people everything they need. As God's intimate companion, Israel does not need a king (1 Samuel 8) like other nations, for God is Israel's king. In the Gospels that deep covenantal dependence is focused on the aspirations of the disciples: "You know that among the Gentiles those whom they recognize as their rulers lord it over them, and their great ones are tyrants over them. But it is not so among you; but whoever wishes to become great among you must be your servant" (Mark 10.42–3). And their needs are their heavenly Father's closest concern: "Therefore do not worry, saying, 'What will we eat?' or 'What will we drink?' or 'What will we wear?' For it is the Gentiles who strive for all these things; and indeed your heavenly Father knows that you need all these things. But strive first for the kingdom of God and his righteousness, and all these things will be given to you as well" (Matthew 6.31–3). In this spirit, Jesus promises, "Ask, and it will be given you; search, and you will find; knock, and the door will be opened for you" (Matthew 7.7). The issue of what God's people need is invariably a question of identity, because as God's beloved, God's people have already been given everything they need – Jesus, the Holy Spirit, the Kingdom, Scripture, Baptism, Eucharist, all the practices of the Church. In intercession, the naming of need begins to identify what is genuine need and what is, perhaps understandable but nonetheless peripheral, want. The bringing to God of a catalog of wants is honest, transparent, and open; but nonetheless it risks making God an idol, by seeking from him not so much the transformation of reality to imitate him as the alteration of circumstance to suit ourselves. And it is not even the case that the intercessor wants for others what they need; for in the new reality of the kingdom the need of one is the need of all, for all need one another to flourish if they are more fully to be the Church – to read Scripture, to share food, to discover and explore faith, and in all these ways to meet God. The Church discovers the difference between need and want when it realizes that while it strives to be what only it can be, the things it needs are things that everyone can have. The intercessions are the place where God's abundance educates the Church's desire.

Thus the intercessions are shaped as declarations of pain, suffering, and need and a longing for healing, and this shape is largely characterized by their location in the liturgy. But the significance of their location is not limited to what comes before them – it includes what comes after them. Shortly after the intercessions comes the offertory, when bread, wine, and money are placed on the altar. In this context, the intercessions emerge as an act of oblation, an offering of dependence, calling on God to give his people everything they need to follow him. The intercessions are linked to the confession of faith – both acknowledge that all truth, all salvation, and all good things come from God; but they are also linked to the offertory procession, for both witness that the members of the congregation have nothing to offer God but what he has already given them. The offering constituted by the intercession is one that exhibits the concrete practice of faith. It embodies the stubbornness of faith, relentlessly rehearsing the roll call of the needy, the sick, the dying, the bewildered. It embodies the lament of the Psalms, the doleful questioning "How long, O Lord?," the catalog of human misery and creation's groaning. It at least hints at the underlying anger of frustrated hopes and unimpeded injustice, the teeming fury at the dissonance between God's glory and human cruelty – and in naming this anger it underwrites the intimacy of the congregation's dependence on God. In naming every aspect of the world's longing, in exhausting every fragile heartbeat of creation's yearning, the intercessions express Simon Peter's plaintive words, "Lord, to whom can we go? You have the words of eternal life" (John 6.68). Thus the habitual names of institutional leaders, the careful lists of suffering friends, and the urgent locations of periodic crisis figuratively go up to the altar with the bread and the wine, seeking a similar transformation – from the earthy materiality of creation's need to the heavenly wonder of God's merciful abundance.

The intercessions not only educate the Church's desire and constitute its humble offering. They also shape the congregation in particular virtues, of which three stand out. The first is patience. The practice of repeated inter-cession, of relentless knocking on heaven's door, teaches Christians that God's time is different from their own. In God's time, all bad things come to an end. In God's time, there will be no more tears. In God's time, there will be no more death, no more mourning, no more pain. God has prepared for those who love him such things as pass their understanding. As yet Chris-tians do not see this promised glory; "but we do see Jesus" (Hebrews 2.9), and this vision characterizes the hope and the patience Christians discover through regular intercession.

The second virtue is persistence. As members of a congregation look back over years of weekly pleadings, they can see that change did come in South Africa, peace, of a kind, did come in Ireland, and so it must in God's mercy somehow come in Palestine/Israel. Persistence does not imply that as Christians repeatedly offer intercession they get better at it, and thus become more "effective"; it is simply that persistence makes the Church shape its life around the pain, suffering, and need of the world. Persistence changes the shape of the Church: it is not so much that "you will always have the poor with you" (Mark 14.7), it is that, through intercession, even if not through daily experience, you will always be with the poor. This solidarity in the end redefines what the Church means when it says "poor," for the prayers of the Church, and the actions that make those intercessions informed prayers, challenge the isolation that is generally inherent to poverty.

The third virtue is prudence. The story is told of a church whose members were appalled when a nightclub opened up next door to the building used for worship, bringing with it a host of attitudes and habits that stood in tension with the practices and convictions of the regular con-gregation. Questions about the well-being of the nightclub began to make veiled appearances in the regular intercessions: hostility was being dressed up as piety. One night the nightclub burned down. The owner wanted to prosecute the church, for he was aware that many members had prayed for just such a turn of events. But they denied any involvement, and said he should simply claim on his insurance for an "act of God" – which was evi-dently not their responsibility. Prudence emerges as the members of the congregation learn only to request what they can cope with receiving. It helps Christians to see the difference between what God can do and what they believe it is in the character of God to do. Thus if patience teaches Christians about how God works in time, and perseverance shapes Chris-tians to pray more informed prayers and thus get to know the people for whom and the places for which they are praying, prudence encourages Christians to pray better prayers, prayers that more accord with the way God works in the world.

In one local congregation a woman who often attended the Sunday evening service began attending an adult literacy class held in the church on a weekday. It became clear that she had never learned to read well. To help her grow in confidence, she was asked to read a lesson every third Sunday. She was encouraged simply to miss out the longer or unfamiliar words or names, and concentrate on the ones she could read confidently. Gradually her range of words increased. Eventually she was asked to lead prayers. She felt she could not do this spontaneously, as some others did, so she would spend the week asking people to jot down prayers for her to use, which she would then carefully type into her word processor, which she was learning to use on another adult education class, and add in sentences from the prayer book. For her, leading intercessions was the summit of her years of attending church. She realized that this was the moment when she was like Jesus, standing before the Father bringing the people with her. It was also like the anticipated moment of her death, when she would stand face to face with God, and he would ask her, "Where are all the others?" – and she could reply, "Here, in my prayers." One day the person due to lead the intercessions was not present, and there was a silence after the Creed. "I don't mind doing it," she said, after a pregnant pause, and, in stumbling sentences, epitomizing in her own person the needs, the hopes, and the transformation at the heart of intercession, she allowed herself to voice and become the patient, persevering, prudent prayer for the day.

The gift of intercession sums up all that the congregation brings to the altar. Its character is formed by confession and absolution, Scripture and sermon, Creed and offertory. But it is also shaped by the Great Thanksgiving that follows. For the patience, perseverance, and prudence imbued by faithful offering of intercession over weeks and years all educate Christians in the perception of God's providence, his timing, breadth, and openheartedness of action in history, his mercy, loving kindness, and purpose. When Christians have poured out their loves and longings and fears and compassions and pleadings and passions and hopes till they have no more, they are left with thanksgiving. All that they have is what they have been given; there is nowhere else to go for more but to God who has already given so much – who has already given everything. In this spirit, shaped by the practice of intercession and discovering its fundamental grounding in thanksgiving, the congregation is almost ready for the Eucharistic Prayer. But first it must conclude its response to God's word, which is also its offering to God; after the offering of faith in the Creed and the offering of hope in the intercessions comes the offering of love in the sharing of the peace.

Sharing Peace

Christians prepare to hear the Word by being reconciled with God. They make their confession and receive absolution before they share the Scripture. Likewise Christians prepare to share food by being reconciled with one another. Just as Scripture and sacrament are two parts of a liturgical whole, two aspects of the one meeting with God, so being reconciled with God and being reconciled with one another are two dimensions of the one movement of forgiveness.

Like the intercessions, much of the significance of the sharing of the peace may be disclosed by its location in the liturgy. Perhaps most significantly, it comes after the congregation have already confessed their sin and been reconciled with God. In other words those present have been shaped by the virtues of mercy and forbearance, virtues that depend on the knowledge that they too have sinned and been forgiven, that they too have grown through constructive criticism, that they too have moods and quirks and prejudices. They grow in the virtues of humility and honesty, virtues that rest on the realization that the Christian life is not about arriving at perfection, but about making interesting mistakes on the way. Being prefaced by reconciliation with God means that corporate reconciliation is conducted in a spirit of humility. The members of the congregation seek peace with one another in order to embody the peace they have found with God. They do not have a leg (of their own) to stand on; they do not make peace from a vantage point on the moral high ground; they stand only as sinners forgiven by God, and thereby inspired to extend and experience that grace with one another.

One local congregation had a parish away day during which a litany of complaints, anxious frustrations, and a sense of helplessness about one aspect of the church's ministry rained down upon those responsible. That day, when the time came for the Holy Communion, the peace was shared without words – the simple handshake and holding of eye contact were a statement of trust and commitment and reconciliation after perhaps too many words had been said. In being able to share the peace after such a traumatic day, the congregation discovered that it was possible to name the truth without fear.

Sharing the peace also takes place after the hearing of the word in Scripture and sermon. The word proclaims that reconciliation is fundamentally the act of Christ, and that Christ has definitively brought about that reconciliation.

> So if anyone is in Christ, there is a new creation: everything old has passed
> away; see, everything has become new! All this is from God, who reconciled

us to himself through Christ, and has given us the ministry of reconciliation; that is, in Christ God was reconciling the world to himself, not counting their trespasses against them, and entrusting the message of reconciliation to us. So we are ambassadors for Christ, since God is making his appeal through us; we entreat you on behalf of Christ, be reconciled to God. For our sake he made him to be sin who knew no sin, so that in him we might become the righteousness of God.

(2 Corinthians 5.17–21)

The word tells a story that is full of setbacks rooted in human shortcomings and alienation stemming from cruelty, jealousy, and bitterness. But the story teaches Christians that they have nothing to fear from the truth. The worst thing that could happen has already happened, and yet God has nonetheless transformed the worst thing into a source of life and hope: that is what the resurrection means. Knowing this truth sets Christians free (John 8.32).

In speaking the Creed Christians have learned how to live in the light of revealed truth. The sharing of the peace comes after the confession of faith. This enables them to realize that protecting others from the truth is seldom a statement of faith. If the truth sets them free, they may develop the habit of not letting the sun go down on their anger, of seeing the naming of resentment as the first step in the forming of a new relationship based on healing and forgiveness rather than tolerance and turning a blind eye. Perhaps the most vivid recent example of this form of liberation is the work of the Truth and Reconciliation Commission in South Africa. This has been engaged in "the difficult but ultimately rewarding path of destroying enemies by turning them into friends" (Tutu 1999, 138). Healing and rehabilitation, a new sense of a transformed story, are necessary for both victims and perpetrators. The Commission used slogans to attract people to meetings where they would tell their stories and hear others', seek redress for injustices and healing for memories, have lies acknowledged and animosities addressed, and move toward reconciliation. The slogans included "Revealing is Healing," "Truth, the Road to Reconciliation," and "The Truth Hurts, but Silence Kills" (Tutu 1999, 81; Forrester 2003, 64–79).

Sharing the peace comes after the intercessions. This shapes the practice of peacemaking with the character of compassion. Interceding clarifies distinctions between pain and sin, healing and forgiveness, need and want. But in the light of the sharing of the peace, the intercessions also illuminate the distinction between the better (or worse) and the merely different — the wrong and the odd. Is a given problem primarily attributable to alienation from God, a breakdown in forms of communication and relationship between people — or is it primarily a matter of intolerance or of incomprehension of difference? This is the kind of question that is reformulated by the regular practice of confession, intercession, and sharing peace in the liturgy. Proximity to the intercessions sets the sharing of the peace in the context of compassion – of recognition of another's story, of another's pain, of another's "love not knowing how to love well." It helps to distinguish between malice and misunderstanding. And it affirms to the members of the congregation that reconciliation is not in their own strength.

But if the sharing of the peace comes after reconciliation with God, the hearing of the word, the confession of faith, and the intercessions, it comes before the sharing of food. And here are perhaps its deepest resonances.

> So when you are offering your gift at the altar, if you remember that your brother or sister has something against you, leave your gift there before the altar and go; first be reconciled to your brother or sister, and then come and offer your gift.
>
> (Matthew 5.23–4)

This is a significant way in which the Eucharist constitutes the Church. It is not just that in the broken body of Christ the Church finds its peace with God. It is not just that the Eucharist makes the Church one body. It is that the Church cannot eat one body unless it is one body. Otherwise, it eats and drinks judgment against itself (1 Corinthians 11.29). This creates a significant urgency. There is a very limited time to address the points of conflict within the community. Either the sacrament will not continue or the unreconciled parties risk incurring judgment on themselves. Christians discover here that they cannot stand before God's judgment without being called to account for those others who are or should be standing with them.

For sharing peace is principally about becoming one body. This is epitomized in Elias Chacour's account of the early days of his ministry in Ibillin, a village in Galilee, and the day he tried the locked-door trick. In 1966 Fr Chacour became the Melkite priest of this village. What he found was a community racked with divisions and riven by feuds. When he faced the congregation to offer them God's blessing he rediscovered how deeply divided and embittered they were. There was so much spite, hatred, and gossip amongst the people, there seemed nothing he could do. So one day, when the service was concluded, and the large congregation was preparing to leave, he walked down the aisle and locked the church doors, placing the keys in his pocket, and said "You've got three options. You can kill each other – and I'll take your funerals for nothing. You can kill me. Or you can work out how you are going to live together from now on." Ten minutes of silence followed. No one moved. Then the local policeman, who worked for the Israeli police force, stood up, wearing his uniform. He admitted how much he had hated and hurt his three brothers. He begged forgiveness. His brothers embraced him. Then one after another people stood and recalled how they had hurt, cheated, and slandered one another. After an hour the people burst out of the church and started making peace with neighbors, colleagues and old foes. It was Palm Sunday, but Fr Chacour declared that it would be celebrated as Easter Day, because that community had risen from the dead (Chacour 1992, 30–3).

Another celebrated account, that of Vincent Donovan, clarifies why the sharing of the peace takes place at this precise moment in the liturgy. Donovan describes in vivid detail his experience of evangelizing the Masai in Tanzania in the 1960s and 1970s, and of how they rediscovered the significance of the Mass as it shaped their common life. The Mass would begin when the priest drove his Land Rover into the village, as children swarmed for a blessing, elders looked up from their cattle-herding and mothers stirred from their milking. But long before, the consciousness of the coming Mass had begun to permeate the village. It was not confined to a specific building: it started from a spot where some elders had lit a small fire before the priest arrived. Before he entered the village, Donovan would stoop to scoop up a handful of grass, ready to present to the first elders who came to greet him. Grass was sacred to the Masai because their cattle depended on it, and they in turn depended on their cattle. So grass indicated peace and happiness and well-being. If an argument erupted the offer and reception of a tuft of grass would guarantee that no violence would ensue. So Donovan would begin by offering a tuft of grass to the first elder who met him, and this elder would pass it to his family, and they would pass it to neighboring elders and families, and thence all through the village. This was the peace of Christ.

Donovan describes how the Mass would take place all over the village. A woman repairing the mud roof of her house would see this work as part of her offering. A local elder would brief him on the people he was instructing for Baptism. They would then perhaps visit a woman sick with fever, lay hands on her and promise to return with the Eucharistic bread later. The dancing group would be getting going. Donovan would sit down with the core Christian leaders in the village, light a lantern, and teach them from the Bible. By the time they finished it would be getting chilly and the crowd would move near the fire, to be joined by the singers. A woman once gave an account of her faith and, since no one could improve on it, that was their Creed for the day. Another woman might pray for the sick person, and her prayers would incorporate the dry season, herding, and carrying water. One of the leaders would explain the lesson they had received earlier, and everyone would join in the discussion. But it was never certain whether the Eucharist would emerge from all of this. Was it really an offering of their whole lives – family, milking, herding, singing? Had there been selfishness or hatefulness or unforgiveness – had the tuft of grass stopped, had someone refused to receive it? These were the questions that determined whether there would be a Mass. And yet sometimes there was a will to overcome the community's shortcomings, and call on the Holy Spirit to transform it into the Body of Christ, so they could see all of what lay before them – people, flocks, fields, homes, and the whole life of the village as Christ's body (Donovan 1982, 124–8).

Chacour's and Donovan's accounts both display how sharing peace is about being one body. And whenever the language of body is used, the practices of Baptism and marriage become significant. When marriage or Baptism take place in the context of the Eucharist, this is the point where they belong: for sharing peace, marriage and Baptism are each different ways in which the Church is embodied. Baptism and marriage have been discussed in earlier chapters, but they may be highlighted here as key ways in which a Christian community may practice patience and courage. Such virtues not only lead them to perceive all relationships through the lens of death and resurrection, gift rather than possession, but also help them to try once more with challenging relationships and risk rejection by attempting to reconcile.

Sharing peace grounds the practice of reconciliation in a specific moment in the liturgy. But reconciliation is by no means limited to the congregation present. This act of peacemaking is a token of a far more wide-ranging reconciliation. It incorporates not just personal animosities, but corporate enmities. This is the moment when the call to love enemies is rehearsed.

> If you love those who love you, what credit is that to you? For even sinners love those who love them. If you do good to those who do good to you, what credit is that to you? For even sinners do the same. But love your *enemies.*
>
> (Luke 6.32–3, 35, emphasis added)

The practice of sharing peace embodied and learned in the liturgy is to be extended into a whole range of relationships, near and far. Each member of the congregation asks how they can be a reconciling presence in the life of their neighbor, and thus transform the need and lack of the intercessions into the abundance and plenty of the shared meal. And, in the context of the sharing of food to follow, this is also the moment when the love of strangers is embodied.

> When you give a luncheon or a dinner, do not invite your friends or your brothers or your relatives or rich neighbors, in case they may invite you in return, and you would be repaid. But when you give a banquet, invite the

poor, the crippled, the lame, and the blind. And you will be blessed, because
they cannot repay you.

(Luke 14.12–14)

Wider still than that, this is a proclamation of the peaceable kingdom, of
humanity at peace with its environment and the whole of creation. The
sharing of peace, together with the offering of gifts that follows, is a celebration of the right ordering of creation in preparation for participation in
the heavenly banquet. It is the bride prepared to meet her bridegroom.
James Jones (2003, 50) points out that Matthew's Gospel alone tells of 27
animals: the sharing of the peace embodies the harmony prophesied in
Isaiah 11:

> The wolf shall live with the lamb, the leopard shall lie down with the kid, the
> calf and the lion and the fatling together, and a little child shall lead them.
> The cow and the bear shall graze, their young shall lie down together; and the
> lion shall eat straw like the ox. The nursing child shall play over the hole of
> the asp, and the weaned child shall put its hand on the adder's den. They will
> not hurt or destroy on all my holy mountain; for the earth will be full of the
> knowledge of the Lord as the waters cover the sea.

The location of the sharing of the peace directly before the offering of the
gifts makes clear not just that if there is no peace, the offering should be left
until there is. In one local church, the priest was troubled by the degree of
bitterness and unacknowledged grief that festered under the surface of the
worship. It was a church where the person leading was accustomed to wear
a chasuble when presiding. One person suggested that the priest leave the
chasuble on the altar until the peace had been shared, and only put the vest-
ment on and continue with the thanksgiving prayer if the peace was
genuine. Although it was decided that communion was always a gift, and
therefore should not be at the mercy of the moment, the congregation was
moved by the suggestion.

The timing of the peace also demonstrates that the gift that the Church
offers to the world – the distribution of the gift received from God – is its
peace, God's peace. For

> Now in Christ Jesus you who once were far off have been brought near by
> the blood of Christ. For he is our peace; in his flesh he has made both groups
> into one and has broken down the dividing wall, that is, the hostility between
> us. He has abolished the law with its commandments and ordinances, that
> he might create in himself one new humanity in place of the two, thus
> making peace, and might reconcile both groups to God in one body through
> the cross, thus putting to death that hostility through it. So he came and

proclaimed peace to you who were far off and peace to those who were near; for through him both of us have access in one Spirit to the Father. So then you are no longer strangers and aliens, but you are citizens with the saints and also members of the household of God.

(Ephesians 2.13–19)

The peace between members of the congregation and one another, between them and strangers, between them and enemies, and between them and the whole creation, is but an emblem of the overarching peace between God and his people, brought about in Christ. This is God's gift to the Church, and, through the Church, to the world – and it is embodied at this moment in the liturgy.

The kiss of peace is widespread in the New Testament – five of the epistles conclude with it – but in one place it takes the vital, salvific, and almost liturgical dimensions outlined above (Bailey 1976, 158–206). And that place is in the story of the loving father and his two wayward sons. "But while he was still far off, his father saw him and was filled with compassion; he ran and put his arms around him and kissed him" (Luke 15.20). Many features of this story are relevant here – the way the father, like the suffering servant, goes outside the village, and undergoes public humiliation (running was considered indecent) for the sake of the sins of another. But two features stand out for our present purposes about the father and his kiss. One is that a kiss (with arms around, as the story makes clear), like a handshake, is the interaction of two equals. In either case, both must be standing, or at least of equivalent posture. The reconciliation that is the sharing of peace is a restoration to harmony of status – regardless of whether a third party might say that such restoration were deserved. The second, and most germane to the theme of this book, is that throughout this story the father exudes abundance. Despite having his property removed from him at the outset of the story and divided in two so half was lost and gone; despite living through a famine; despite sharing a home with the meanest of sons; despite undergoing not only the private humiliation of one son's demand for the property but also the public humiliation of the other son's refusal to join the party; despite even slaying the fatted calf, and throwing a banquet for hundreds of people – despite, in other words, giving away his property, his pride, and his heart, the father epitomizes abundance from beginning to end. The younger son's profligacy contrasts with his father's abundance, but only in that he spent all those resources on trifles; the story narrates the way his sin is redeemed – and thus redeemable. By contrast the elder son's meanness poisons every relationship he has – in making up a story to explain his refusal to come to the party, he has to fabricate a tale about his brother (that he wasted the money on Gentile harlots), another about himself (that the property does not already belong to him), and a third about his father (that he wants the service of a slave, rather than the love of a son). The story narrates that even this sin is redeemable – but it does not narrate that it is redeemed. The heart of the elder son's sin is that he does not trust that, even in his father's house, there will be enough – even though everything in the story makes it plain that where his father is, there is always more than enough.

The kiss is the symbolic center of the story because it embodies the moment when the father *finds* his lost son, and it is this finding – rather than the son's return – that is the reason for the party. The tension at the end of the story is whether the elder son will be reconciled, will accept the father's kiss – and thus come to the banquet. The kiss is the entrance to the banquet, just as the peace is the entrance to the Eucharistic feast. But the kiss simply displays what the story proclaims throughout – that God abundantly offers everything his people need to follow him: and that offer is never more present than in the sharing of the peace.

Chapter Eleven

SHARING

We come to the part of the liturgy sometimes described as "communion." That designation is apt in that it names that here the congregation shares God's life. But it is distorted if it assumes that communion is not a feature of the whole liturgy. Here I describe seven practices involved in the sharing of food. They begin with offering gifts, a practice that is concerned with reordering creation. There are then three pairs of practices. Giving thanks and lifting hearts summarize the first part of the great prayer. Remembering and inviting describe the second part of that prayer. Finally breaking bread and sharing food bring us to the climax of the whole action of the Eucharist – entering the heart of God through the friendship restored by Christ's passion, and embodying this companionship through the sharing of food.

Offering Gifts

The fourth part of the Eucharist is a microcosm of the service as a whole. The elements of bread and wine are taken, blessed, broken, and shared, just as Jesus was taken, blessed, broken, and shared; and in a similar way the congregation as a whole is taken out of its ordinary pursuits, blessed with the grace and truth of forgiveness and Scripture, broken in the disciplines of intercession, peacemaking, and food-sharing, and shared with the world by being sent out in love and service. In bald terms, at this point in the liturgy the bread and wine are offered, transformed, and received – while in the whole service the congregation, and through them the whole creation, is offered, transformed, and then received.

What begins to take shape at the offertory is a reshaping of human society and a reassembly of the whole creation. The reshaping of society is constituted by the way each member of the congregation offers different things to the table, but each in due course receives back the same thing from the table. Members of the congregation differ in the amount of money they can and do contribute to the alms and oblations, the offerings for ministry and mission of the Church. They differ in their kinds of work and service, epitomized by the money in the collection plate. They differ in the kind of food they are used to eating, and thus the symbolic significance of bread and wine differs for them too. They differ in their of gift of faith, their degree of understanding, their level of commitment. They differ in their social location – their gender, their race, their class, their orientation, their physical health and ability, their mental health and ability, their social and criminal history. All these things differ, but as each stands before the altar, they join a great tradition of those who have offered God something – and in that something have offered everything they have. They join Abel and the first-fruits of his flock, Abraham and his precious son, Hannah and her long-awaited child, David and the offerings of the people for the Temple, Joseph and Mary and the baby they brought to Simeon. This is a reordering of society in which members of the congregation offer all that they uniquely are, and thereby learn to receive back what everyone can have. As they offer to God everything he has given them, God gives them everything they need to follow him.

The offering initiates not only a reordering of society but also a reassembly of creation. If God's people were created to worship him, to be his friends, and to eat with him, then God's creation discovers its purpose when it is incorporated into this transforming process. A conventional understanding of humanity's relationship to creation is to regard human beings as stewards. But this is an inadequate description. A Eucharistic understanding of the relationship is to perceive that the world – like humanity – was made to be the place where God communed with his people. Thus the Eucharist, like the resurrection of Jesus, becomes a defining moment between goodness and glory, source and end, creation and eschaton. It is not an act of control or conquest of creation or "nature," but an act of bringing creation to fulfillment, disclosing creation's purpose. The relationship of humanity to creation is not just to ensure its flourishing, still less simply to prevent its extinction, and even less again to assert dominance over it: instead it is to bring creation into the relationship of praise and thanksgiving toward God epitomized by the Eucharist.

One controversial area is whether it is appropriate to think of the congregation having any gifts that are worthy of offering to God – whether, in fact all the gift-giving at the Eucharist is from God to his people, an act of pure grace. It may be helpful to make a distinction here between a gift and an offer. The notion of gift quickly opens itself into a realm of meanings including exchange, mutuality, expectation of return, and a range of conventional relationships. An offer is different. In the language of theatrical improvization, an "offer" refers to anything an actor does that may be interpreted as keeping the story going – a speech, a facial expression or gesture, an action, even silence. The key is not the quality of the gesture but the genuineness of the permission it gives to respond. There are three kinds of response. One is to "block": this means to deny the premise of the offer, and thus to prevent the story from continuing. Another is to "accept": this means to maintain the premise of the action that constituted the offer, and thus enable the story to continue. The third is to "overaccept": this means to accept the premise but then to fit the offer into a frame of reference, or narrative, much larger than the person offering might have imagined (Wells 2004, 103–42). This is exactly what takes place at the moment of offering in the Eucharist. The members of the congregation do not give God a worthy gift to persuade, entice, or manipulate him to be benevolent toward them. Instead their presentation of bread, wine, and money constitutes an offer – that is, a wholehearted permission for God to overaccept their gift and transform it by placing it within a narrative that transcends the one in which it was offered. The everyday fruit of the earth and the humble work of human hands are about to become the food and drink of companionship with God. It is not that the people pour their life into their offering and that then constitutes an acceptable sacrifice; it is that the offering constitutes the people's active acceptance of what God is about to do amongst them.

Seeing the bread, wine, and money as an offer transforms the way Christians may perceive all their possessions. Everything they have is a gift from God; and at the moment they offer it to God they invite him to transform it so it may become part of a far larger story. The act of offering in the Eucharist becomes the paradigm of the way God is invited not just to make himself known in his creation, but specifically to repeat the pattern disclosed in Jesus. For Jesus, definitively, overaccepted the offer of human flesh and transformed it into a bearer of divine glory. To hold out every gift, every possession, every responsibility, every relationship to God, is to invite God to overaccept every aspect of one's life, to repeat the pattern of Jesus' life, death, and resurrection in every sphere – to incorporate one's whole world into the Eucharist.

One can see the whole of the preceding parts of the liturgy as shaping what the congregation bring to the altar. By confessing sin and being forgiven, the congregation are relieved of the pessimism that every offer is tainted. By offering praise the congregation discover the context for their offering. By hearing God's word the congregation discern the difference between the roles God and his people play in the outworking of his story (and in the drama of the Eucharist), and the significance of each. By interceding the congregation place their offering in the light of their own creaturely need, and by sharing the peace they allow God to remove the last obstacle preventing his full transformation of their common life. Now the question is, what is to prevent their bringing every aspect of their lives to be overaccepted by God in the transcendent glory embodied in the prayer that follows?

The significance of this is brought out by Vincent Donovan in his account of the Mass amongst the Masai in Tanzania. What happens when a people realize that some aspects of their culture are incompatible with the Gospel? The answer emerges at this point in the liturgy. One tribe, the Sonjo, were expert dancers. In their hands the offering became the practice through which the community discerned the good.

> They brought their music directly to the place where the bread and wine were later to be blessed, and performed it there deliberately and carefully. Some of their music was decidedly secular. The elders in that community pointed out to me that the purpose of such a procedure was to make an actual judgement on a very important area of their lives. The time of the Eucharist was the time for that judgement. They were not ashamed of that dance in their own lives, so they wanted that part of their lives to be offered with the Eucharist. There were some dances they were ashamed to bring into the Eucharist. By that very fact, a judgement had been made on them. Such dances should no longer be a part of their lives at all. Eucharist served as judgement for them.
>
> (Donovan 1982, 125)

That which did not belong in the Eucharist belonged nowhere. That which could not be offered to God for his transformation ought not to be retained. Thus the practice of offering gifts at the altar shapes the way Christians think not only about possessions, but about every gift, talent, responsibility, aspiration and relationship.

Lifting Hearts

At the beginning of the Eucharistic Prayer the person leading the service enjoins the congregation to lift their hearts. This has a twofold significance in shaping the life of the Christian community. One dimension is that of feeling, the other is that of the kind of participation being invited.

This is the only point in the liturgy when the members of the congregation are instructed to maintain a particular quality of feeling. To participate in the thanksgiving, celebration, and transformation that is to follow, they *must* lift their hearts. Just as in the offering the congregation discovered that they had to bring every aspect of their lives to the altar, so at the "Sursum Corda" the congregation discovers that it must bring its heart and soul under the same discipline. And the logic is similar. Why must humanity have the correct relationship with the created order? In order that human beings might bring the fruits of creation to their fulfillment at the altar — and thus fully celebrate the Eucharist. Why therefore must God's people learn to discipline their hearts, sculpt their souls, mold their feelings so as not to give in to malevolent moods, malign passions, or maudlin emotions? In order that when they come to the central moment of transformation in the Eucharist, they will be able to lift their hearts without inhibition. Participating in the Eucharist requires heart and soul and mind and strength. It is not simply "going through the motions" — it is "going through the wondering," "going through the pondering," and "going through the passions" as well.

An ethic of the senses is rooted at this moment in the liturgy. The education of desire belongs first of all in lifting hearts together to the Lord. This is a corporate process, and counselors who help other disciples lift their hearts may perceive the purpose of their ministry here. The consumption of toxic substances to excess is wrong in great part because it pollutes the temple of the Spirit that is the human body, but primarily because it weakens the disciple's ability to lift the heart to the Lord at this vital moment. The lustful glance, the wandering eye, the furtive photograph, are wrong in great part because they train the soul for adultery and treat the beauty of another as an object of coveting and possession, but primarily because they weaken the disciple's ability to focus every sense on the thanksgiving, celebration, and transformation of the Eucharist. But likewise the eradication of desire, the iron-fisted discipline of the will, the imposition of listless compliance, are wrong when they mean that the disciple can find inside no surge of passionate longing at the moment in the liturgy when God is about to give his people everything they need to follow him. Hearts were made with one purpose above all: to be lifted to the Lord when he comes in transforming grace.

The second significant dimension of this moment in the liturgy relates to the conviction that when disciples respond to Jesus' command to "Do this," his will is done in heaven as it is on earth. It is an act of discipline, if not a fulfillment of longing, for the members of the congregation to lift their hearts; but the point of doing so is that this is a moment of entry into heaven, a moment when God makes his people alive together with Christ, and raises them up with him, and makes them "sit with him in the heavenly

places with Christ Jesus" (Ephesians 2.5–6). Those congregations who articulate the words of both Revelation 4 ("Holy, Holy, Holy Lord, God of
power and might") and Matthew 21 ("Blessed is he who comes in the name
of the Lord") during the Eucharistic Prayer identify specifically that God's
people are raised to heaven just as God's Son came to earth.

This moment in the liturgy is a rehearsal of heaven on earth. All God's
purposes are fulfilled – his people worship him, are his friends, and are
about to eat with him. And all that God's people need to be able to be God's
friends and eat with him has been provided. They have become one body,
with sins forgiven, reconciliation made, peace restored, God's word proclaimed and discerned, faith affirmed, and needs heard. God's purpose has
been fully communicated to his people and it has been fully embodied in
their life. The veil between earth and heaven is being drawn aside, and the
simple actions of sharing food anticipate the beautiful simplicity of life with
God forever. This is a moment of revelation, for the true life of the saints is
"hidden with Christ in God" (Colossians 3.3), and now it is made plain.
Christ is being revealed through the taking, breaking and sharing of bread
and wine, and "When Christ who is your life is revealed, then you also will
be revealed with him in glory" (Colossians 3.4).

If this glimpse of heaven is the moment of greatest desire, then it is also
the moment of greatest aching. For this is where the location of the
Church, still in exile from heaven, is most acute. Christ is about to come
among them through the Holy Spirit, but the true communion, the true
reunion of the body of Christ with its head, lies in heaven. So this lifting of
hearts is both a transportation to heaven, and also a rehearsal for heaven. It is
a taste of the firstfruits and an anticipation of the full banquet. It reminds the
Church that it is like a football team playing away from home, with perhaps
a hostile crowd and a host of pitfalls to be encountered; but also that it will
one day come to its home turf, and to the saints and angels singing their
name as they at last find their true seamless fluency. These moments in the
liturgy name the location of the Church, in a world pervaded by God,
which can yet not be called home. The fact that the Eucharist can be celebrated there describes what it means to call the world good; the fact that no
Eucharist can be everything the heavenly banquet will be names the ways in
which the world cannot be called home.

The Church aches not only because it is away from home, but also
because it is not one. It cannot fully lift its heart because its heart is broken.
The scandal of the disunity of the Church is fundamentally a Eucharistic
matter. If the Church cannot be one before God, it cannot fully receive
everything God has to give it through the Eucharist. God wants his people
to worship him, to be his friends, and to eat with him. But when they

cannot eat together they cannot fully be friends and thus they cannot fully worship. Nonetheless, since heaven is one, lifting hearts to heaven must be one way in which Christians seek to restore unity. If they truly hope to sit and eat with God, they prepare to be placed beside some unexpected companions.

Giving Thanks

Once again the a summary of the Gospel is rehearsed – after the introduction to confession, the sermon, and the Creed, now in the thanksgiving, the grand narrative of salvation is summoned to surround the vital moments of transformation. The people of God are gathered around a table, ready to eat with him. Now, in this final rendition of the heart of God's story, they are in an attitude not so much of penitence, or of truth-seeking, or of faith (although none of these is absent), but of glory and praise.

This part of the liturgy continues what was begun in the offering. If the offering reassembles creation around the table where God's people eat with him, then the thanksgiving reorders those people's lives so they see this as the fundamental work that defines all other work. Everything the Church does is designed to bring all humankind, indeed all creation into companionship with God epitomized in the sharing of food at his table. And thus all work is an analogy of this definitive work. It is not that work is co-creation, it is that work is appropriate participation in finding a place and a role and a fulfillment as God's companion – worshiping God, being his friend, and eating with him – and enabling others to do the same. Giving thanks does not exhaust what needs to be said about work. For it is not until the dismissal that the question of vocation, of *what* work, specifically arises. But the question that finds its definition in the Great Thanksgiving is not so much the question of *what* as the question of *how*.

Such an understanding of work begins in gratitude. It is an honor to participate in the Eucharist, it is an honor to have an analogous role to play in serving people and communities in relation to their mental and spiritual (worship), emotional (be his friends), and physical (eat with him) needs. To have mental, spiritual, emotional, and physical abilities that may find expression, purpose, and fulfillment in helping people and communities to flourish – this is to discover in oneself very precious qualities that are to be treasured as gifts. Just as in the Eucharist Christians discover their definitive form of work is to give thanks, so in return in every aspect of life a significant form of thanksgiving is to work. To work is to develop and discipline the gifts of God to attend to the mental, spiritual, emotional, and physical needs of others and thereby to meet a good number of one's own similar needs meanwhile.

And what are those needs? The Eucharist is likewise a training for what those needs are – they are, narrowly, for worship, friendship, and food, and, more broadly, for community, for forgiveness, for joy, for silence, for truth, for a place in a truthful story, for faith, for hope, for love and reconciliation, for a way of offering one's gifts, for an ordering of desire – in other words, for all the things the Eucharist brings. The Eucharist trains Christians to see need as God sees it. The congregation gets used to what God provides, and come over time to need what God faithfully gives, and to shape all other wants and desires around this perception of this definitive ordering of needs. And in the paradigm of eating together, the Eucharist offers a goal for all work – a goal of plenty, of harmony, and of relationship with God and one another. By such a goal may the worth of specific kinds of work be judged.

In return work clarifies what it means to be Church. Work is always praise and thanksgiving, but calling the life of the Church "work" reminds Christians that they should expect Church to be hard. It is hard because it requires discipline, to the task, to the agreed method, and to the colleagues – those to whom one gives orders, those from whom one receives orders, and those with whom one works as a team – with whom the task is to be attempted. Although it is hard, task-oriented discipline is still a gift, because aimless freedom is seldom experienced as a gift (any more than purposeless discipline). Discipline arises from necessity – whether the difficulty of dealing with raw materials, the difficulty over overcoming logistical obstacles, the difficulty of engaging the frailty of human character, or the difficulty of confronting outright hostility and opposition. Such necessity constitutes all human activity – the praise and thanksgiving of the Eucharist as much as the marketing of new computer software or the harvesting of the cash crop before the onset of the rains. Although for many the Eucharist is an expression of the life of the Sabbath, if it is to be the transforming social practice on all the levels I have described, it is bound to be hard, to require discipline, and to take on other characteristics generally associated with work. Work – and the Eucharist – will not always be an experience purely of resurrection. There are times when both may be an ordinary, less exalted experience of incarnate humanity. And there are times when both may be an experience of the cross. It is this that keeps the Eucharist human, and thus a celebration of the humanity of Christ.

The thanksgiving prayer within the Eucharist governs Christians' attitudes to work in two further ways. On the one hand, the Great Thanksgiving counterbalances work when work becomes too much. Work may, for example, become a substitute for family, when a person displaces real family relationships, and invests their entire emotional well-being in their continued employment by a particular organization. Work may become an alternative church, when it seeks to epitomize an ideal community, or demands the soul of its members, or sets itself the task of putting the whole of society straight. Work may become a rival gospel, when an ideology takes over the minds of a staff team or a whole profession, creating new nostrums whose efficacy no one can challenge. Or work may become a god – when it really does become everything, the defining and controlling force in a person's life. The Great Thanksgiving identifies all of these perversions as kinds of idolatry – for thanksgiving allows Christians to align their deepest needs with the gifts God abundantly gives, and thus brings freedom, whereas these distortions are each a response to need that leads a person into slavery.

On the other hand the Great Thanksgiving challenges Christians when work becomes not too much, but too little. Work becomes too little when a member of an organization has little or no respect for where the organization is going or how it is run. Such a sentiment may constitute a healthy skepticism about whether the organization contributes to the spiritual, emotional, mental, or physical needs of the world in any significant way – or even contributes to heightening those needs by worsening people's lives rather than enhancing them. Staying in such an organization without working for change quickly leads to a cynicism that corrodes the body and poisons its bloodstream. Work also becomes too little when a member of an organization, while respecting the system, has little respect for colleagues and thus fiddles expenses or subverts the structure in some other hidden way. Work becomes too little when a person experiences unemployment. While there are things worse than unemployment, it is rare that other ways of serving entirely replace work as a key aspect of the expression of human thanksgiving and thus fulfillment. The Great Thanksgiving, by portraying the definitive work of the Christian, addresses the flawed thankfulness that arises when work becomes too little. For the unemployed person, it reasserts that their true identity is found as God's companion, around God's table, worshiping, being his friend, and eating with him. For the person skeptical about their organization or their role in it, it displays the glory and goal of true work, by which God, through sacrament and story, gives his people everything they need to follow him, when they thankfully offer to him all the gifts they have received for him to use in reordering the lives of communities and persons. If this sacrifice of thanks and praise is not really made in the sacrament, it is scarcely a Eucharist; and if a sacrifice of thanks and praise is not properly made in the workplace, work disintegrates from an analogy of the Great Thanksgiving into a parody of idolatry or exploitation.

Remembering

Remembering is about actions and words. In the Eucharist, God's people recall the saving events that transformed the world and their place in it; and they re-enact those events. Both the words and the actions are significant.

The *words* of remembering locate the Church in time. The words recall the Last Supper, and thus identify the hinge of history, the events of the passion and resurrection of Christ. In recalling the Last Supper these words remember that that meal itself recalled a previous meal, the Passover, and its corresponding saving events, the Exodus and the establishing of the covenant. God acted in delivering his people from slavery and bringing them to freedom in the Promised Land, assuring them of his presence and faithfulness and giving them a guide for keeping their freedom. Now, in Jesus, God had acted again, this time decisively, to deliver his people from all that held them in slavery and to offer all the peoples of the world life with him forever.

So remembering means first of all acknowledging that the key events of history have already happened. This simple statement has enormous importance for ethics. For it locates the heart of ethics in particular events with universal significance. This differs in a number of ways from the way ethics is frequently understood. Ethics is not primarily about what is being discovered – it is about what has been revealed. It is not primarily about now – it is primarily about then (those events that constitute the hinge of history, which took place in the first century). It is not primarily about our actions – it is primarily about God's actions displayed in Jesus. It is not primarily about likely consequences of our present decisions – it is primarily about ultimate implications of God's eternal decision. It is not primarily about us acting now lest the worst might happen – it is about how God acted when the worst (the rejection and death of his Son) did happen. It is not about understanding the nature of things, and acting rightly or wrongly in relation to their inherent quality – it is about seeing the nature of all things transformed by Christ. It is not about being effective in a world of givens – it is about being faithful in a world where all has been made gift.

The Eucharist locates the Church after the decisive events of history – creation, covenant, Christ – have happened, but before the full consummation has come about. It remembers and anticipates. It embodies heritage and destiny. "On the night before he died . . . " signals the looking back; "I will never again drink of the fruit of the vine until that day . . . " signals the anticipation. It thus epitomizes the way every action of the Church or the Christian is similarly located between the decisive and the ultimate, between the historically definitive and the transcendentally unknown – between the revealed character of God and the final glory of his company. Ethics names the ways the Church seeks to embody the transformation brought about by Christ and to point to the consummation promised in final glory; and the definitive paradigm of this embodiment is the Eucharist itself. This is what it means to seek to make the whole world a Eucharist: it means to strive to order every aspect of creation in the light of the transformation in Christ and the consummation in heaven.

Remembering the words of institution, the words in which Jesus identified his future presence in the Church, defines the way Christians think about memory. The Last Supper becomes the prism through which Christians perceive the past. This means the Church's memory can never become detached from its intimate bond with the Jews, for the Last Supper is characterized by the recollection of God's saving purpose in the Exodus, his faithfulness to the Sinai covenant, and his promise to bring their long exile to an end. It means the Church's memory can never overlook its bond with suffering, for the body of Christ is no sooner identified than it is broken. It means the Church's memory can never forget its own sin, for the agony of Judas' betrayal and the quickly broken promises of Peter and the other disciples ripple through the narrative. The defining moment of memory is a body of flawed Jewish people discovering the identity and mission of Christ and realizing that in his suffering lay the renewal of God's covenant and the transformation of their status before him. Every moment in history is thereafter defined by the degree to which it discloses the identity and mission of Christ, the nature and embodiment of God's covenant through him, the transformation of suffering and sin in relation to the paradigm of the cross, and the new life and community made possible through these saving events.

These are among the ways the words of remembering shape the ethic of the Church. As for the *actions* of remembering, I refer to the fourfold gestures of taking, blessing, breaking, and giving (Dix 1945). These, of course, re-enact Jesus' fourfold action at the Last Supper:

> While they were eating, he took a loaf of bread, and after blessing it he broke it, gave it to them, and said, "Take; this is my body." Then he took a cup, and after giving thanks he gave it to them, and all of them drank from it. He said to them, "This is my blood of the covenant, which is poured out for many."
>
> (Mark 14.22–4)

The significance of these four actions becomes clearer in the light of Jesus' own story. For he took human nature in his incarnation, and his human flesh bore the divine character in material form. In his ministry, through words of wisdom, question, and command, and through gestures of compassion, challenge, and miracle, he blessed humanity and the whole creation. In his agonizing death and the harrowing exposure of human sin that it entailed, he was broken for the life of the world. And in his resurrection and perhaps most especially in the coming of his Holy Spirit, he gave and shared new life with all who trusted in him. Thus the fourfold action epitomizes the way Jesus' life is made present in the Church.

There are strong hints in the resurrection appearances – at Emmaus, in the upper room, by the Galilean lakeshore – that it was in this fourfold action in relation to food that the identity of the risen Jesus was made known to the dumbfounded disciples. This then becomes the definitive series of actions that identifies the birth, ministry, death, and resurrection of Christ and affirms his presence with the Church as its living Lord. Thus this series of actions comes to define what the Church understands by prophecy. Prophecy is the practice of drawing on the revelation of God in the past to identify his action in the present. "Therefore every scribe who has been trained for the kingdom of heaven is like the master of a household who brings out of his treasure what is new and what is old" (Matthew 13.52). The prophet brings out of the treasure-house of God's story the fresh discoveries of his revelation for today. This may be in the form of words, but it may even more vividly be in the form of actions or gestures. The Eucharist is the definitive prophetic action, because it identifies the whole life and work of Christ in such a way that it declares Christ's living presence today. It is a demonstration of how God gives his people everything they need: for everything is taken, blessed, broken, and given. This is how everything is made new.

Whenever a community act in such a way that their gestures point back to the transforming events of Christ's death and resurrection and point forward to the eschatological fulfillment of God's promises, their actions may be described as prophetic. The point of a prophetic action is not to change the world but to display the manner in which the world is changed by God. Thus, for example, during the Vichy regime in France during the 1940s, villagers in Le Chambon-sur-Lignon took in Jewish escapees from across central Europe, gave them hospitality, and found ways to spirit them along the perilous journey to Switzerland. The point was not that such actions would end the Holocaust or win the war, but that such gestures demonstrated the self-giving love of God revealed in Christ and offered a foretaste of the fellowship to be perfected in heaven (Wells 1998, 134–40). Likewise, as we saw in Chapter Ten, under the Pinochet regime in Chile, members of the Sebastian Avecedo Movement against Torture took to performing impromptu street liturgies, in which they would gather outside a known place of torture and recite names of the torturers and their victims. Again, the point was not directly to end the torture or bring down the regime, but to identify the courage of the oppressed, express the anger of God against their oppressors, and to point to the truthfulness of the day when all secrets would be revealed (Cavanaugh 1998, 273–7). On a rather more modest level, one local church in a deprived neighborhood in Britain found that it was attracting four times as many children as adults – in a culture where the children were accustomed to appearing without the company of their parents. So the church decided to give over its principal worship area to the children and take the adults into a side room. Again the point was not to solve the social problems of the area by educating (or converting) the children, but gently to alert the neighborhood, and other churches in the area, to the God who displaces the mighty and exalts the humble.

The prophetic claim of the Eucharist is that there is no part of life – no part at all – that may not be brought within this saving cycle of taking, blessing, breaking, and giving. This claim derives from the more familiar claim that there is no aspect of life that is not incorporated in Christ's birth, ministry, death, and resurrection. Prophecy demonstrates the ways in which this incorporation takes place. The significance of the Eucharist in relation to prophecy is that it keeps prophecy embodied in action – rather than simply, for example, verbal critique – and that it keeps prophecy Christological – in that the fourfold action focuses entirely on the person and work of Christ. So the "Eucharistic" test of all prophecy is whether that prophecy points to an embodied social practice, and whether that prophecy is shaped entirely around the pattern of God disclosed in Christ.

Inviting

If the words and actions of remembering enable the Church to identify the presence of Jesus in the Eucharist, the corresponding moment of invocation enables Christians to identify the activity of the Holy Spirit. This is a defining moment for companionship with God, because it is the moment when the three understandings of the body of Christ – Jesus, the Church, and the Eucharistic bread – coalesce. The Church meets to discover Jesus in the transforming practice of sharing food. This is the moment when the past, future, and present of the Church are united. The Last Supper, the eschatological banquet, and the local celebration are made one as the Holy Spirit makes the incarnate Jesus and the coming Lord present in the sharing of food.

The prayer of invocation asks that the Holy Spirit will do among the congregation what Jesus did at Cana. At Cana, in transforming water into wine,

Jesus took the simple and earthy, and made it extraordinary and heavenly; he drew back the veil of mortality, and for a moment offered a glimpse of divine glory; he saved his people from lack and scarcity, and offered them abundance; he anticipated the marriage of heaven and earth, and revealed God's purpose of saving the best till last. He epitomized everything that is meant by "Emmanuel" – God with us. The invocation asks that the Holy Spirit will do all these things, and bring heaven to earth in the form of bread and wine and in the sharing of food in companionship with God.

This is the place where Christians discover what is meant by holiness. The definition of holiness involves a number of dimensions, each of which may be derived from this moment in the Eucharist.

Holiness is not a quality in the self, it is the gift of the Holy Spirit. It is not a static condition, but the manifestation of God through the material of flesh and blood, just as the coming of the Holy Spirit in the liturgy is the manifestation of God through the material of bread and wine. Holiness does not define itself, but takes its meaning from its relation to the events of Christ's life, ministry, death, and resurrection, as disclosed in the Eucharist. Just as Christ took, blessed, broke, and shared the bread, so he took and blessed human nature, was broken, and thus gave his life for the world; and likewise the holy life is one that God has taken in order to bless, and broken in order to give for the life of the world. Holiness, as defined by the Eucharist, is not a momentary state, but a gift that is received through the repeated faithful practice of joining in confession, praise, Scripture study, intercession, reconciliation, peacemaking, thanksgiving, and remembrance, as well as being open to the transformation of the Holy Spirit. Its goal is not so much good actions as good people. It is not an individual pursuit, but one of companionship; just as the Eucharist gathers together an assembly of disparate people, so in the prayer of invocation the longing is that the Holy Spirit will make holy not just the elements of bread and wine but the people who receive them, so that holiness may be revealed through the unity of the Church in the bond of peace. Holiness is not just an inner condition – the prayer of invocation is that the congregation become a kingdom of priests, a corporate witness that participates in the reconciliation of the world to God. And finally, the Eucharist defines holiness in that it offers a specific practice, the sharing of food, to embody the longing for life with God. Holiness is fundamentally about abundance, because it about disciples forgetting their narcissistic self-fascinations in the sheer glory of God's goodness.

This is also the place where Christians discover what is meant by power. If holiness perhaps represents a caricature of the "pious" understanding of Christian ethics, power perhaps epitomizes the "realist" understanding of the discipline. While the distinction may be illegitimate, the significant point here is that both find their paradigm at this point in the liturgy.

The defining moment in a theological understanding of power is the day of Pentecost. The disciples are enjoined to "stay here in the city" until they have "been clothed with power from on high" (Luke 24.49). At Pentecost they are indeed clothed with power from on high. The disciples are given everything they need to worship God, to be his friends, and to eat with him. This moment defines what Christians understand by power, in that it comes from God, and it is the capacity to achieve what God intends. It is not a quality in the self, and it is not a quality that enables the self's aggrandizement; it is the capacity to realize God's reign in present circumstances, to swathe materiality with the life-giving Spirit, to infuse communities and peoples with the ways of justice and peace. In other words, it is the ability to live without the constraint of sin, death, and evil – to embody the life made possible by the death and resurrection of Christ. This is exactly what the Holy Spirit offers – an infusion of all that is made possible in Christ.

The gifts of the Spirit clothe the people of God with this transforming power. And the gift of the Spirit whose regular reception becomes the practice through which all other gifts are understood is the Eucharist. At the Eucharist the Holy Spirit is invited to come down, in a re-enactment of Pentecost, to make the process of sharing food the means of receiving all the gifts of the Spirit – all the benefits of Christ. This prayer is an elaborate definition of power. It is, first of all, a prayer. All intercessory prayer is an invocation of God; prayer is an act of recognition of God's sovereignty, a demonstration that all power comes from God. The prayer is an invitation, not an instruction. It is an embodiment of the relationship of creature to creator, in no position to apply force but confident that asking will lead to receiving – when power lies in the hands of grace. Second, the prayer is directed initially toward the common food – bread and wine. Control over the production and distribution of food constitutes one of the most significant forms of power. This moment in the liturgy is a proclamation that God has control over the food that meets the deepest needs of his people. As at Cana, as at the feeding of the 5,000, what began as a modest offering was transformed into abundant, overflowing bounty, so at this moment the prayer asks that God show his power in flooding the world with grace. Next, this demonstration of power through the distribution of food is for the building up of the Church. This epitomizes the purpose of all power, which is a gift intended to strengthen the agents of God's glory in the world. All gifts are to be evaluated by whether they build up the Church: this gift builds up the Church in a definitive way. This is a gift that liberates, rather than destroys. Just as the manna was a gift to liberate the children of

Israel from fear for their own survival and to guarantee the presence of God among them, so this moment in the liturgy expresses the way God is present in the Church today, giving his people everything they need and delivering them from fear. As a gift of God, power is therefore good. The exercise of power is not to be avoided as inherently corrupting. However any power that is not exercised as demonstrated through this moment in the liturgy – is not attributed to God, is experienced as force rather than authority, is not intended to build up the people subject to it, does not liberate but destroys, creates fear rather than plenty – such power enslaves, and this enslavement engulfs not just the people but the powerful too.

One aspect of the power defined at the Eucharistic table remains to be noted. This power is vested in a humble loaf (or wafer) of bread, an item about to be broken in two. If the elements – the people – the world is about to be clothed with power from on high, that power is the power proclaimed by a crown of thorns, a scourged savior, a broken body. The power of the cross is a power revealed in weakness. The power demonstrated in the Eucharist proclaims that when the Holy Spirit comes upon disciples, they have everything they need, but they are invariably broken before those gifts can be fully shared for the life of the world. This is where the power of the saint differs from the power of the hero (Wells 2004, 42–4).

Breaking Bread

If this is the moment in the liturgy when the Lord's Prayer is said, then the Lord's Prayer becomes like a collect, focusing all the work of the preceding prayers. And this is very appropriate, because the Lord's Prayer is a proclamation that God gives his people everything they need to worship him, to be his friends, and eat with him.

The prayer's first petition is for present needs: "Give us." It is a prayer for manna, for daily bread. Provision of daily bread frees the Church from one kind of slavery, the slavery of hunger. It is a statement that bread fundamentally comes from God, that anxiety over "your life, what you will eat or what you will drink, or about your body, what you will wear" (Matthew 6.25) is a matter of faith, and that this kind of prison is a prison of one's own making. Placing this prayer for food in the context of the Eucharist expresses once again the way, through the Eucharist, God gives food, and through the giving of food, gives his people everything they need. So the prayer becomes "May we receive every day what you give us today." Eating with God, being God's companions, is not just the eschatological aspiration of the Church, not just the direction of the Eucharist – it is the aim and purpose of every Christian's life every day. "Give us each day the presence and friendship of a companion at table" is a prayer for "bread" to symbolize everything Christians need and desire from God.

The prayer's second petition is for the healing of past wounds: "Forgive us." This is deliverance from a second kind of slavery, the slavery of sin. To be short of food is a pitiful condition. But how much more miserable is to have abundant food but not to be able to eat it because of social division. This is the predicament from which the Lord's Prayer in the context of the Eucharist seeks definitive salvation. If eating with God and one another requires bread, then being God's friends and the friends of one another requires forgiveness. The Eucharistic Prayer defines the way Christians think about memory: but if memory is going to yield the trust that is necessary for friendship, it needs to be accompanied by reconciliation. And just as food fundamentally comes from God, so forgiveness fundamentally springs from God. It is God who forgives his companions, and it is only in the strength and liberation of that forgiveness that they can ask for a second blessing, the blessing to forgive one another. The Eucharist embodies the purpose of forgiveness: for without reconciliation it is not possible to be friends, and without being friends it is not possible to eat together – with one another or with God. If disciples want to eat with God they have to be able to eat with one another. That is the lesson of the Eucharist.

The prayer's third petition is for disarming the unknown: "Deliver us." The slavery in question here is the slavery of fear. And the Church's response to fear is worship.

> If our God whom we serve is able to deliver us from the furnace of blazing fire and out of your hand, O king, let him deliver us. But if not, be it known to you, O king, that we will not serve your gods and we will not worship the golden statue that you have set up.
>
> (Daniel 3.17–18)

The Church has abundant food and corresponding gifts for today; it has been liberated from the oppression of past sins committed by and inflicted upon it. Does it dare to take up the offer of companionship, of being God's friends and eating with him? Temptation, testing, evil – these name the forces that may still be stronger than the community that has abundant gifts and is released from the curse of sin. These are the shadows that overawe Christian ethics, the fightings within and fears without that make the ethical task seem so daunting. And the central response to these mighty forces is to name and proclaim a mightier one – to worship the God of Jesus Christ, to invoke the power of the Spirit. Here, in the Lord's Prayer, is displayed the kernel of the argument of this whole book: that in Jesus, the Church, and the Eucharist, God gives his people everything they need to worship him, to be his friends, and to eat with him. They find food through calling on God to meet their present needs, they find friendship by calling on God to forgive their sins and empower them to forgive others', and they find faith by calling on God to manifest his power within and without in worship. Thus they become God's companions.

In one local congregation, there was a profound sense of striving for personal holiness, but a more inhibited air when it came to the corporate identification of shared faith. On one occasion the person presiding at the Eucharist described how she had on many occasions worshiped in France. She told how at this moment in the Mass, she had invariably noticed how all the members of the congregation held hands to say the Lord's Prayer. She commented how sporting heroes in big matches would stand in a line with arms around each others' shoulders to sing the national anthem. This was a way of showing they were a team – that they stood or fell together – that they were one body. "So let's hold hands together to say the Lord's Prayer," she said. "Because we are one body. And the Lord's Prayer is our national anthem."

Having been taken and blessed, the bread is now broken. The breaking of the bread is celebrated in the Emmaus story as the moment of revelation, the moment when two lost souls became God's companions. Just as on the road the two disciples had listened as Jesus explained how the Messiah must suffer, and then at supper they had perceived their companion as that same suffering servant, now resurrected, so at the Eucharist the congregation first rediscover the true nature of Jesus' person and mission, and then see the crucifixion and resurrection vividly portrayed in the breaking and sharing of bread.

This is the moment in the liturgy where wrath and mercy meet. On the one hand this is the bread of scarcity – of limited resources, of selfish greed, of cruelty, of breaking the bodies of others, of misusing the gifts of creation, of murder, of raging hatred and bitter enmity: of sin. On the other hand this is the bread of abundance, of limitless love, unending forgiveness, ceaseless forbearance, steadfast endurance, relentless delight, the tender embrace of the beloved child: of grace. The bread of sorrow and the bread of joy: and at this moment the anger and the love of God break his heart, as they did on the cross. And this is how God's people come to share his life: they enter the broken heart of God. They become his companions in the breaking of the bread.

Here is the moment that defines Christians' understanding of violence. Violence has no definition in and of itself: it receives its definition by analogy to all that Christ endured. In the background to the passion are the paths that Jesus rejected: collusion with the Roman and Jewish authorities, the gentle path of persuasion and half-truth and postponed integrity; and withdrawal to the desert, a quest for righteousness removed from a personal encounter with political power. In the foreground are the forces that put Jesus to death: the short-term calculations and temptations of militarily-dominated government, the pleadings and manipulations of institutional religion and the sharp edge of bigotry, the ebb and flow of nationalism and the insidious appeal of racism, the fear and frenzy of the mob and the consequent trampling of justice (Yoder 1994). And at the center lies the broken body of Christ.

The broken body of Christ crystallizes both the manner of God's sovereignty over his creation, and the ultimate purpose of that sovereignty. If God's sovereignty genuinely is the grain of the universe, the whole orientation of creation, then God's love, notably his love of enemies, is the most powerful force of all: thus the power of violence and the power of money are revealed for what they really are, not dominant but ultimately weak. The love displayed on the cross – enacted in the breaking of the bread – is the most powerful force in the universe, because it is the way the sovereign God chooses to make his character known. Meanwhile the portrayal of this sovereign love in the breaking of the bread at the Eucharist discloses the ultimate purpose of that sovereign power expressed in love: and that purpose is to share food with his people – to call them to worship him, be his friends, and eat with him. This key moment in the liturgy displays the Church's understanding of violence, of God's character, and of the ultimate purpose of creation: it portrays the method, results, and conclusion of salvation.

At the two defining moments in Jesus' life, his birth and his death, he is utterly powerless – so powerless that he cannot use his arms. At his birth, his arms are strapped to his sides by swaddling clothes – Luke's Gospel relates this twice, and the angels tell the shepherds that this will be the "sign." And later at Jesus' death his two hands are nailed to either end of a horizontal beam, and as he dies in agony he cannot even wipe his own brow or scratch an itch or waft away a fly or mosquito. These are the most intimate moments in Jesus' life, and at both moments, by nails and by swaddling clothes, he is, literally, disarmed. Jesus is God disarmed. The disarmed and disarming love of God. This is the sovereignty disclosed at the breaking of the bread. This is the heart of the Church's perception of violence.

Sharing Food

All the preceding elements of the liturgy meet their consummation in the sharing of food. The significance of gathering is disclosed in the practice of eating together. The goal of reconciliation with God and one another is manifested in the common meal. The anticipation of heaven conveyed in the glory of praise and lifting of hearts is embodied in the banquet of the kingdom. The understanding of Scripture, as for the Emmaus disciples, is made plain in the context of the breaking of the bread. The confession of faith is given its climax in the enactment of the goal of revelation – that God's people might worship him, be his friends, and eat with him. The offering of need and gift is transformed through the prism of the Eucharistic prayer so that those who have offered their differences receive – and digest – the same things. And most of all, the prayer that Christ in his life and death, his resurrection and exaltation might live in and through the elements of bread and wine finds its true purpose in the ingestion of those elements by the Church, so that the members of the congregation may become the body of Christ, and he might live in and through the Church.

Sharing food is a proclamation and a practice, a witness and a discipline. I shall consider its role as revelation before going on to examining its significance as gift.

As revelation, sharing food offers Christians the discovery that God gives them everything they need. This is a proclamation of abundance. The discovery is that the more food is shared, the more food there is: like the sorcerer's apprentice, the congregation finds that breaking bread in two means twice as much bread, not half as much. The inspiration for such a discovery is the feeding of the 5,000, where the role of the disciples was to ensure everyone received the abundant bread available, and to collect up the leftovers so that nothing was wasted. And there were 12 baskets of bread that no one could eat.

Thus the sharing of food is the way the Church comes to understand economics. Integral to the Church's understanding of economics is the practice of hospitality and the virtue of generosity. Generosity is the assumption that, since one has freely received, therefore one may freely give. And the embodiment of this pattern of giving and receiving is, once again, in the Eucharist. The members of the congregation have handed over the firstfruits of their labor and have received back the firstfruits of the resurrection. What reason is there not to be generous?

Sharing food proclaims the abundance of food. But it also proclaims the abundance of places at the table. As Christians gather around the table, they learn to look around them as they eat, and speculate on whether these are the people with whom God predicts they will spend eternity, or whether he has other people in mind, and if so, why those people are not present now. Just as Christians discover when reading Scripture that they need to be a diverse and rainbow congregation if they are truly to hear everything the Scripture has to tell them, so now at the distribution of food they discover that they need to incorporate a great number and range of people – especially the hungry – if they are to be able to eat all the food that God has given them.

Everyone is called to a place around the table, whatever their gender, their race, their class, whatever their orientation, their physical health or ability, their mental health or ability, whatever their social or criminal history. And this is not because everyone has a *right* to be there. It is because the Church *needs* everyone to be there. The Church does not need everyone to be there so as to ensure Christ will be present: the Holy Spirit is not dependent on human cooperation. The reason the Church needs everyone to be there is first so that it can hear the Scripture fully, second so that it can offer all of creation, not just a small segment, in thanksgiving, and third so that it can eat and drink all that has been given to it so that *nothing is wasted*. The crisis of the Church is the crisis not of scarcity, but of abundance: the Church is not thirsty but drowning. It is not that God has withheld his gifts, but that the Church has been given too much. Thus the Church is desperate, not to find sources of nourishment when God's Spirit falls short, but to share and distribute and offer God's superabundant gifts universally so that nothing is wasted.

This is the picture of society enacted at this moment in the liturgy: that the abundant gifts of God should ensure that everyone, every created being, should receive enough, and that every being should be so stirred by receiving that they in turn give generously, give everything. This thoroughgoing pattern of offering and receiving, this spinning spiral of mutual enjoyment and treasuring, this virtuous circle of never-ending provision – this is the embodiment of God's call to his people to worship him (the offering), to be his friends (the sharing), and to eat with him (the receiving). It is not so much that God desires Christians to match his sacrifice with their sacrifice; it is more that he moves Christians to respond to his fulsome pouring-out with their own kenotic imitation. This is the economics of generosity, the politics of love.

One local congregation found it difficult to decide whether they should sit, stand, or kneel to receive communion. Kneeling seemed appropriate to some, because it embodied humility. But some said that, without an altar rail, it asked too much of people with disabilities. It seemed that sitting was the posture that stressed equality, because everybody looked and felt much the same. But it was felt that, besides being too comfortable, remaining in one's seat suggested that God made the whole journey, with almost no response from his people. Standing in a circle became the norm. It stressed the differences of height, age, and physical ability, and it made it necessary for some to rest on the strength of others. Though some said they felt unworthy to stand, others pointed out the Christ had enabled, even commanded them to stand, and that standing was a symbol of resurrection. By standing in a circle, the congregation realized they did not just eat of one body – they were one body.

If sharing food is revelation, it is also gift. It is gift because it is a practice that shapes a community. Just as parents learn to love the children they have been given, so the community learns to want the gifts God gives it. And if the proclamation of sharing food is about economics, the gift of sharing food is about unity.

This gift of unity is expressed in the single word, "communion." Communion embodies the way Christians perceive they are invited to become and remain one. Communion means most importantly that Christians share a belief that they have a *place at God's table*. Communion means being God's intimate friend – and this is characterized by eating with him. Christians make the bold claim that they are invited to occupy the fourth place at God's table, along with the members of the Trinity itself. Communion secondarily involves a shared sense of the importance of sitting at table *with one another*. When Christians eat together they act on the commission of the Son and in the company of the Spirit – and their worship is present to the Father. A further, third understanding is a shared sense of the *discipline and order* required for this special act – Baptism, the faithfulness of the participants, the training, character, and order of those leading the liturgy, the vertical reconciliation of the confession, and the horizontal reconciliation of the peace. And finally there is a fourth common understanding of the *practices* of this special act – greeting, celebrating in praise, giving thanks, listening to Scripture, preaching, confessing the faith through the Creed, interceding, sharing God's gifts, being blessed, and being sent out.

The Eucharist offers a pattern of unity through a perception of the hierarchical and sequential nature of these four shared understandings. For most problems that arise in a community touch on one or more of these shared understandings of communion. A problem with one of the elements does not invalidate the others – on the contrary, it is probably only through a shared understanding of the others that a problem in one of the elements can be overcome. It is only when there is no shared understanding in any of the four areas that communion seems lost. For example, in churches where the person and character of the leader is regarded as especially significant, issues such as the ordination of women and the acceptance of homosexual relationships in clergy households stretch some people's perception of some aspects of the third understanding, that of discipline and order. But a greater grasp of what is shared through having a place at God's table, sharing that place with one another, and engaging together in a transforming pattern of practices ought to put these differences in perspective. Likewise a difference on the question of the divinity of Christ may seem to make communion impossible due to the significance of sitting at table with the Trinity, but a remarkable fellowship in regard to the other three understandings – sitting with one another, discipline and order, and transforming practices may still be found.

It is very important to remember that the first understanding, the invitation to eat with God at God's table – communion with God the Trinity – is the point of creation and redemption. It is what the universe was made for, what Christ died for. But there is a clear warning that if Christians cannot meet the terms of the second understanding – sitting at table together – they have little chance of enjoying the fellowship of God eternally. The purpose of the third and fourth understandings of communion – discipline and order and an agreed pattern of practices – should help Christians carry out the second one – sitting and eating together – not make it more difficult. Communion is impaired if it is simply not possible to carry out the whole pattern of shared practices, the fourth understanding; for example greeting is impaired if the Church condones the exclusion of some on racial grounds, and sharing God's gifts may seem absurd if the Church is meanwhile condoning grotesque economic inequalities. But the severing of communion is a grave and drastic matter, and should only be accepted if all communication on all four levels has proved impossible.

After sharing food, for the third time the congregation lapses into silence. The first time, after the glory of praise, the members of the congregation pondered how far they had come since the service began – gathered, made into the Church, forgiven, transported by worship. The second time, after the proclamation of the word, the members of the congregation sought to discern God's voice now that the past, present and future of the world and their lives had been renarrated through Scripture and sermon, such that they were now no longer strangers and aliens, but companions and friends. And now, a third time, silence reigns, and the members of the congregation digest the significance and relish the wonder of entering God's life and eating with him. They have been given everything they need. What will they now be asked to do? That is the perennial question of ethics, and that is the burden of the final part of the liturgy.

Chapter Twelve

GOING

The liturgy has reached its climax in the sharing of food. Sharing food looks back to the foundational event of the Last Supper, and forward to the anticipated heavenly banquet. It is the definitive practice that cannot be carried out without gathering together in the present. Sharing God's life by breaking bread in his company epitomizes what is understood by worshiping God, being his friends, and eating with him. It is the living portrayal of being God's companions.

What remains is to confirm the pattern of the Eucharist as the habit of the Church – to clothe the congregation with the practices of faith so that they make the whole world a Eucharist. Making the whole world a Eucharist means following the pattern set out in the five chapters of this part of the book. It means extending God's invitation to all, ordering the life of the many in relation to God's revelation in Christ, bringing all to repentance, and joining creation's praise. It means proclaiming the truth of God through the history of the world and the dynamics of the universe and sharing discernment within the silence of God. It means articulating human need and working for human reconciliation. It means restoring a good relationship between humanity and its ecological home, stirring the heart, setting about work in a spirit of thanksgiving, discovering power under the authority of the Spirit, confronting evil with confidence in the sovereignty of God, and sharing in the generous economy of God so that nothing of his bounty is wasted. Making the whole world a Eucharist is the fulfillment of the call to become God's companions. God has given his people everything they need to make the whole world a Eucharist. The completion of the liturgy simply reinforces what has already been given, by offering a practice, a confirmation, and a purpose.

Washing Feet

In John's description of the Last Supper the Church reads of one practice that sums up all the others. Jesus washes the disciples' feet, and thus sets a pattern for servant discipleship. The great mystery of contemporary liturgy is that the washing of feet is so seldom practiced. Once again, if God gives his people everything they need to follow him by giving them Jesus, the Church, and the Eucharist, if they do not embrace the whole of what the Eucharist involves they are in no position to complain that they have not been given everything they need.

Washing feet is a vital gift of God to his people. It illuminates all three of God's primary gifts – Jesus, the Church, and the Eucharist – because it embodies the Gospel, shapes community, and defines mission.

To say, first, that washing feet embodies the Gospel is to highlight the role Jesus' washing of the feet of his disciples plays in the fourth Gospel.

> Jesus, knowing that the Father had given all things into his hands, and that he had come from God and was going to God, got up from the table, took off his outer robe, and tied a towel around himself. Then he poured water into a basin and began to wash the disciples' feet and to wipe them with the towel that was tied around him . . . After he had washed their feet, had put on his robe, and had returned to the table, he said to them, "Do you know what I have done to you? . . . I have set you an example, that you also should do as I have done to you."
>
> (John 13.3–5, 12, 15)

There can be no question that the "table" in this account represents heaven, the "outer robe" represents the trappings of divinity, and the "towel" represents the human nature of Jesus. This is evidently an enactment of the incarnation and exaltation of Christ, a microcosm of the whole Gospel – confirmed by the words "knowing that he had come from God and was going to God." In between come the broad dimensions of the Gospel – ministry (footwashing), teaching ("One who has bathed does not need to wash, except for the feet, but is entirely clean"), prophecy ("For he knew who was to betray him; for this reason he said, 'Not all of you are clean'"), questioning ("Do you know what I have done to you?"), command ("If I, your Lord and Master, have washed your feet, you also ought to wash one another's feet"), controversy ("Peter said to him, 'You will never wash my feet'"), and confrontation ("Unless I wash you, you have no share with me").

Thus when disciples wash one another's feet, they enact the most succinct summary of Jesus' whole career that the New Testament offers – a performance of the celebrated hymn of Philippians 2.5–11. Here, perhaps more distinctively than anywhere else in the liturgy, Christians may perceive the significance of sacrifice. Sacrifice is not primarily identified with offering – the "sacrifice" of time, possessions, money, firstfruits, for the sake of the worship of God. This would be a propitiatory reading of sacrifice. Neither is sacrifice primarily identified with the broken body of Christ (portrayed in the breaking of the bread), as a view of the atonement that strongly emphasized the death of Jesus would have it. It is true that the congregation's participation in the sacrifice of Christ is a witness to the definitive sacrifice, and a protest against all calls for sacrifice (of reluctance to kill, for example). The whole shape of the Old and New Testaments presents Jesus' sacrifice as only making sense as the *last* sacrifice, the one who finally took away sin and inaugurated the peaceful flourishing of all creation in God's company. The sacrifice of the Son of God is the sacrifice to end all sacrifice. So the war to end all wars was not the First World War: it was the cross. The good news of the cross is fundamentally that the war is over.

But footwashing denotes a third, perhaps most significant dimension of sacrifice. Sacrifice is focused on the moment when Jesus "got up from the table, took off his outer robe, and tied a towel around himself." It is the moment when Jesus relinquished the limitless range of options open to him, and chose a single path. It is more about Bethlehem than Calvary. Sacrifice is the consequence of following a call: it is an accounting for the roads not taken. Sacrifice is still an integral part of the Christian life, yet it is not a pyre on which a first-born creature burns to appease an angry potentate, but a sober estimate of the personal and corporate cost of following a distinct path and leaving the rest to God. Temptation – the agony of Gethsemane – pleads that one can make a choice, follow a call, and still leave all the options open. Sacrifice names the discovery that the call to follow Christ still maps out a path via the way of the cross. God's sacrifice is the same as God's choice: never to be except to be for us in Christ. Our sacrifice mirrors God's, when it is the commitment never to seek any god that is different from the God revealed in Christ. This is enacted every time the disciple leaves the Eucharistic table, lays aside a robe, and puts on a towel.

To say, second, that washing feet shapes community is to highlight the way this practice brings together the water of Baptism with the meal of the Eucharist. Once it has also been established that this practice is a microcosm of the Gospel, then the reasons for describing it as a vital gift of God to his people are transparent: it combines Scripture with the two foundational sacraments, and thus it must be close to the heart of the Church's practice.

The baptismal overtones of the footwashing episode are not hard to discern: not only does Jesus use water, and perceive washing one part of the body as tantamount to washing the whole. He also makes such a washing essential to being part of the community ("Unless I wash you, you have no share with me"), and, most pertinently of all, in what surely must be a reference to the unrepeatability of Baptism, he says "One who has bathed does not need to wash, except for the feet, but is entirely clean." And all this takes place "during supper." One could almost say that every aspect of God's gifts to his people crystallize in this moment: Jesus, Church and Eucharist, Scripture and Sacrament, worship, friendship, and the sharing of food. It is all here.

But one thing is explicitly here that is only implicitly evident in Baptism and Eucharist. That is the status reversal of the lord and master stooping to wash feet. Whereas the primary role of God's people in Baptism and Eucharist is through the Holy Spirit to receive the gifts of God made possible by Christ, the washing of feet commands Christians actively to embody the ministry of Christ in a concrete act of humble service. And that act of humble service is inherently socially subversive, not so much in being deliberately confrontational but more in its playful turning of the world upside-down. When Mary of Bethany anointed Jesus' feet and wiped them with her hair she was commended for it; in a similar incident in Mark's Gospel the woman is described as having done "a beautiful thing" (Mark 14.6). Footwashing inspires the Church to take on the basest of roles in society and transform them into beautiful things. It inspires the most senior of office-holders to incarnate themselves in the lives of their subordinates. It inspires them to challenge every lofty mark of status to examine whether that status genuinely exists for the sake of service, and to tease every fine garment for whether it can be adapted to accommodate a towel and a basin. Earlier I challenged a notion of equality that was based at the Lord's table, because I argued that the Church needs everyone at the Lord's table primarily because there was so much food there, given by God, that the Church couldn't bear to have any wasted lest God withhold his gifts in future – thus the more hungry mouths, the more sincere human need incorporated in the Church, the more faithful it could be to the abundance of God. If the Church is to have a notion of equality it belongs not at the altar but in the practice of washing feet: for here disciples discover that there is no fundamental hierarchy, simply a call to all Christians to attend to the most intimate, least attractive, and most shameful gestures of mutual care. This is a model of interdependent community, subversive, playful, imaginative, physically (but not sexually) intimate, and faithful.

In one local congregation there was a week of activities for all ages leading up to Easter. At the end of the whole program, after food had been shared and thanks had been expressed, regrets articulated, and moments of joy celebrated, every participant gathered in a large circle, children alternating with adults. As a song began, each child turned to the adult on their left, and began to stroke or otherwise treasure one of their feet or shoes. As the verse ended, each child climbed through the legs of their neighboring adult and stood up, whereupon the "new" adult knelt to caress the foot or shoe of the child. At the end of the next verse, the adult continued anti-clockwise and the child continued clockwise, and roles were again reversed. The whole circle proceeded to "wash" one another's feet. No words were exchanged – just the repeated shared words of the song. Thus did one community discover the surprise and playfulness of the new commandment.

In the same congregation there was an elderly retired minister who had not been seen for a few days. The senior pastor called to see him and found that the old man's bowels had given way, and there were discarded clothes and the results of diarrhea all over the house. The pastor considered who was to blame, who should take responsibility, how the man's dignity could be rescued: but then had to admit that his careful professional distance was an avoidance of his simple vocation. He got down on his knees, took soap and a towel, and began to clean the floor, the clothes, and finally the old man himself.

To say, third, that washing feet defines mission builds on this aspect of status reversal and also highlights the location of this practice toward the end of the liturgy, after the sharing of food and before the sending out. It confirms that if making the whole world a Eucharist is too broad or vague a commission, the place to start is by washing feet. Washing feet means beginning with human touch, and trusting the encounters that gentle touch may provoke. It means not fearing taboos, daring to accompany shunned people, and being willing to help people engage parts of themselves they would rather ignore. It means seeing the person through the soiled barriers, much as a parent or caregiver sees a child with love, rather than a full diaper with disgust. It means never seeing another person as beneath oneself, since they are never lower than Christ. Archbishop Oscar Romero famously said "our task is to put feet on the Gospel": this task is never more appropriately performed than in washing feet.

Being Blessed

In many congregations this is a moment reserved for making announcements and sharing information. Locating these notices at this point in the liturgy perfectly illustrates how the Eucharist gives Christians so many gifts for ordering their life of discipleship. For the notices invariably indicate specific ways in which the community is being called upon to respond to need or opportunity. And when this information follows the definitive form of God's presence (sharing food) and the definitive form of ministry (washing feet), and precedes the activity of being sent out, it finds a context that illuminates the commitments involved.

In one local church the notices used to come just before the sending out. On one occasion the priest shared with the congregation that a group of young girls had been trying for several days to persuade her to let them use the church building to dance in on a Saturday. She asked the congregation for suggestions. The church building was often surrounded by clamoring children and a number of the congregation found their incessant attention intimidating. It was difficult to find enough adults to staff the youth program the church needed to put on to maintain good relationships with the local young people. After a pause, one woman aged 86 put up her hand and said "I'll sit with those girls if you like." After a few weeks, one of the children's mothers took over and set up a dance club that flourished for three years. Challenged by the call to go and do likewise, the elderly woman proved to be a stirring example to the rest of the congregation. If an 86-year-old could be a youth worker, everyone could.

The two remaining activities appropriately conclude the liturgy because they summarize what in organizational terms might be called the minutes of this meeting and the agenda for the next. Being blessed draws a line under all that has been achieved in this encounter with God, and being sent out expresses all that now, in the light of this corporate experience of revelation, remains to be done. Blessing alludes to themes of creation and goodness, dismissal refers to themes of transformation and vocation: together, they complete the pattern of worship, friendship, and sharing food that form Christians as God's companions.

For Christians blessing is not primarily promising something that lies tantalizingly in the future, such as a quiverful of children or a burgeoning property portfolio. Blessing rather confirms something already given in the past. What has already been given is the gift of God in Christ, his engrafting of the Church into God's covenant with Israel, his conquest of death and evil through cross and resurrection, his securing of humanity's place at the right hand of the Father through his coming as one like us, and the gift of the Holy Spirit to clothe the Church with everything it needs to follow God in Christ. In the shape of the liturgy the members of the congregation have experienced these blessings in the transforming forgiveness and reconciliation with God and one another, in the proclamation of a liberating story to envelop the frailty of their lives with the embrace of grace, and in the sharing of the common loaf to embody the providential care of God expressed in daily bread.

The place the Church looks to understand the notion of blessing most of all is the Beatitudes. Just as the congregation needs to ask "Do we dare to say the Creed?" because those who declared faith in the scriptural narrative are quickly tested, so the congregation may well ask, "Do we dare to seek blessing?" For those blessed are the poor in spirit, those who mourn, the meek, those who hunger and thirst for righteousness, the merciful, the pure in heart, the peacemakers, and those who are persecuted for righteousness' sake. This is not just about acquiring more flocks and houses and descendants. Likewise if the members of the congregation look around at the end of the service, and realize that these are the kinds of people who are present, they will discover that they have already been blessed.

The archetypal scriptural notion of blessing is found in the call of Abraham – "in you all the families of the earth shall be blessed" (Genesis 12.3). The fulfillment of blessing comes in finding that one has been a blessing to others. This, in addition to its role as summarizing the events of the liturgy, is why the blessing is appropriately placed immediately before the dismissal. For the congregation is about to turn around, to "re-turn" to the world out of which it was gathered and formed as the Church, and the members of the congregation are about to be sent out to be a blessing for that world. Like Jacob, they have wrestled with God: and they will not let him go until they receive a blessing.

The activity of being blessed therefore reminds the Church of its purpose – to be a blessing. And the retrospective nature of the blessing points to how that blessing is to be carried out – by making the whole world a Eucharist.

Being Sent Out

One local church had near the entrance a photograph of a golden retriever. The photograph reminded the congregation that, like the retriever puppy, they discovered their mission in going and coming back. Just as the dog's owner would throw a stick or a ball into the thicket or undergrowth or lake and both owner and dog would take great delight in the adventures the dog would have before the hurled item was safely retrieved, so at the dismissal God throws something significant out from the gathered assembly, away into the neighborhood and wider world, and, together with the members of the congregation, enjoys the process by which that gift of word or food or gesture or time returns at the occasion of the next Eucharist, doubtless with surprises and discoveries and insights attached to it.

For the Eucharist is a process, not just an event. It is a constant to and fro, a sending-out and a gathering-back. Each celebration ends with a commissioning ("Go therefore"), each new celebration begins with a sense of what has been discovered, where God has been met in the time since the last gathering. When Jesus sent out the 70, he invited them to bring back stories of what the Holy Spirit had done – and he was delighted by what they had discovered.

> Jesus rejoiced in the Holy Spirit and said, "I thank you, Father, Lord of heaven and earth, because you have hidden these things from the wise and the intelligent and have revealed them to infants; yes, Father, for such was your gracious will." . . . Then turning to the disciples, Jesus said to them privately, "Blessed are the eyes that see what you see! For I tell you that many prophets and kings desired to see what you see, but did not see it, and to hear what you hear, but did not hear it."
>
> (Luke 10. 21, 23–4)

And this offers a complementary perspective on the mission to make the world a Eucharist: for in return, those who have gone to make the world a Eucharist bring back the wisdom and understanding of the Kingdom that combine to help the Church hear the Scripture better and share communion better.

This is the teleological goal of mission: that not only will the whole world be brought to worship God, be his friends, and eat with him, but, in the meantime, the discoveries and surprises encountered in mission and ministry will enrich the Church so it is more fully able to enjoy, receive, and employ the gifts God has given it. Being sent out is about creating a virtuous circle of mission, practice, discovery, reflection, worship, and renewed mission, in which a key dimension is the way the Eucharist offers a shape for mission. Disciples practice seeking out the ways of God in the most benighted corners of the world: they strive not only to "celebrate the Eucharist" in those places, aspiring to repentance, truth-telling, need-sharing, mutual reconciliation, footwashing and the other disciplines of sharing food; they strive also to meet resources in those places that enrich their practice of repentance, their hearing of the gifts and demands of the Gospel, their awareness of human need, and their commitment to reconciliation, their understanding of the depth of human and divine suffering, and their discernment of distinctions between sadness and sin, their ability to wash feet as well as have their own feet washed, and their perception of what broken and shared bread, poured and passed wine, may really mean.

The dismissal completes the role of the thanksgiving. In the thanksgiving, the members of the congregation discover that the definitive form of work is praise, that when they stand together to remember and give thanks they embody the purpose for which they were made. But in the dismissal they rediscover the ministry, not so much of the Eucharist, but of Baptism: that is, their own vocation. Vocation is primarily defined by Baptism, but that moment of commissioning that is part of Baptism is re-enacted at this point of the Eucharist. Disciples have brought different experiences to the gathering, and confessed different sins; but they have received the same forgiveness and heard the same Gospel. They have brought different needs and offered different gifts at the table but they have received the same gift in return. They have stood together in the same act of remembrance and thanksgiving but are now sent out to different ministries in the week ahead.

And how will they know if those ministries have been faithful? If they follow the mission statement of the Church. And what is the mission statement of the Church? It is to make the world a Eucharist. On the day of judgment, the Father will recognize his children if they look like his Son. Likewise in the discernment of faithful service, the Church recognizes those practices that look like a Eucharist – that gather people and form them as one body, that reconcile and open lives to repentance and forgiveness, that proclaim truth and reveal God's story, that embrace need and unleash gifts, that express thanks and are open to the Holy Spirit, that share food and wash feet. The fact that there is a period of time – a week, maybe less, sometimes more – between Eucharists affirms that the dismissal is a commission to make partnerships with those who are not against Christ, and to discover ways in which such people may turn out to be for him. In such partnerships – neighborhood action, community regeneration, institution-forming, action for justice, relief of poverty, support for those with particular needs, and countless more – Christians learn what it means to be salt and light, to be distinct yet among (Matthew 5.13–16). They develop the practice of service, remembering that even the Son of Man came not to be served but to serve. They learn the disciplines and techniques of cooperating with people of very different principles and stories, of resolving conflict without violence and standing beside the weak and afflicted. And yet the fact that Christians return to the Lord's table, after an interval, expresses the nature and limitations of such partnerships. Partnerships illuminate, clarify, embody, test out, share, and enrich the practice of the Eucharist: but the Eucharist defines the purpose and possibility of all partnerships, because it discloses the contours of work and vocation.

In one local church, when the time had come for the priest to leave for another post, and the final Eucharist was almost complete, he went to each member of the congregation and offered to wash their feet. Some washed his in return. Each person laid hands on one another in a great chain around those who laid hands on him, and gave him a blessing, calling on God to bless other people through him the way they had found blessing in the years just past. And finally he walked to the door of the church, and turned to face the people he had served and loved for many years: and they dismissed him, with the words, "Go in peace." Much was unfinished; many were unreconciled; countless were yet to find faith; much justice remained undone; fragility still reigned despite the glory that shone out. Yet these had been his companions; with them he had seen the abundance of God. He had received a blessing, everything he needed to worship God, be his friend, and eat with him. And so he departed, resolved to make elsewhere the Eucharist he had found there.

WORKS CITED

Aquinas, Thomas. *Summa Theologica*, translated by the Fathers of the English Dominican Province, 5 volumes (New York: Benziger, 1948)

Archbishops' Council. *Common Worship: Services and Prayers for the Church of England* (London: Church House Publishing, 2000)

Bailey, Kenneth. *Poet and Peasant* (Grand Rapids, MI: Eerdmans, 1976)

Barnes, Michael, SJ. *Theology and the Dialogue of Religions* (Cambridge: Cambridge University Press, 2002)

Barth, Karl. *Table Talk*, edited by J.D. Godsey (Edinburgh and London: Oliver and Boyd, 1963)

Bausch, William J. *Telling Stories, Compelling Stories: Thirty-Five Stories of People of Grace* (Mystic, CT: Twenty-Third Publications, 1991)

Benedict, Saint. *The Rule of St Benedict for Monasteries*, translated by Bernard Basil Bolton (Godalming: Ladywell, 1970)

Berryman, Jerome. *The Complete Guide to Godly Play*, 5 volumes (Denver, CO: Living the Good News, 2004)

Bowker, John. *Problems of Suffering in the Religions of the World* (Cambridge: Cambridge University Press, 1975)

Bretherton, Luke. "Tolerance, Education and Hospitality: A Theological Proposal," *Studies in Christian Ethics* 17/1 (2004): 80–103

Brueggemann, Walter. *Genesis* (Atlanta, GA: John Knox Press, 1982)

Bruner, Frederick Dale. *Matthew: Volume 1: The Christbook: A Historical/Theological Commentary* (Dallas, TX: Word, 1987)

Byatt, A.S. *Still Life* (London: Penguin, 1986)

Cardenal, Ernesto. *Love in Practice: The Gospel in Solentiname*, translated by Donald D. Walsh (London: Search Press, 1977)

Cavanaugh, William T. *Torture and Eucharist: Theology, Politics, and the Body of Christ* (Oxford: Blackwell, 1998)

——*Theopolitical Imagination: Discovering the Liturgy as a Political Act in an Age of Global Consumerism* (Edinburgh: T. & T. Clark, 2002)

Chacour, Elias (with Mary E. Jensen). *We Belong to the Land: The Story of a Palestinian Israeli who Lives for Peace and Reconciliation* (San Francisco: HarperSanFrancisco, 1992)

Dix, Gregory. *The Shape of the Liturgy* (London: Dacre, 1945)

Donovan, Vincent J. *Christianity Rediscovered: An Epistle from the Masai* (London: SCM Press 1982)

Ford, David F. *The Shape of Living* (Grand Rapids, MI: Zondervan, 2002)

Forrester, Duncan B. "Violence and Non-Violence in Conflict Resolution: Some Theological Reflections," *Studies in Christian Ethics* 16/2 (2003): 64–79.

Fox, Michael V. *Character and Ideology in the Book of Esther* (Columbia, SC: University of South Carolina Press, 1991)

Giles, Gordon. *The Harmony of Heaven* (Oxford: Bible Reading Fellowship, 2003)

Hardy, Daniel and Ford, David F. *Praising and Knowing God* (Philadelphia, PA: Westminster, 1985)

Hauerwas, Stanley. "Some Theological Reflections on Gutierrez's use of 'Liberation' as a Theological Concept," *Modern Theology* 3/1 (1986): 67–76

—— *With the Grain of the Universe: The Church's Witness and Natural Theology: Being the Gifford Lectures Delivered at the University of St Andrews in 2001* (Grand Rapids, MI: Brazos Press, 2001)

—— and Wells, Samuel (eds). *The Blackwell Companion to Christian Ethics* (Oxford and Cambridge, MA: Blackwell, 2004)

—— and Willimon, William H. *Resident Aliens: Life in the Christian Colony* (Nashville, TN: Abingdon, 1989)

Hebert, A.G. *Liturgy and Society: The Function of the Church in the Modern World* (London: Faber, 1935)

Howard-Brook, Wes. *Becoming Children of God: John's Gospel and Radical Discipleship* (Maryknoll, NY: Orbis, 1994)

Hutter, Reinhard. *Suffering Divine Things: Theology as Church Practice* (Grand Rapids, MI: Eerdmans, 2000)

Ignatieff, Michael. "Articles of Faith," *Index on Censorship* 25/5 (1996): 110–22

Jasper, R.C.D. and Bradshaw, Paul F. *A Companion to the Alternative Service Book* (London: SPCK, 1986)

Jenson, Robert. *Systematic Theology, Volume 2: The Works of God* (Oxford: Oxford University Press, 1999)

Jones, James. *Jesus and the Earth* (London: SPCK, 2003)

Kant, Immanuel. *Religion Within the Limits of Reason Alone*, translated by T.M. Greene and H.H. Hudson (New York: Harper and Row, 1960)

Lohfink, Gerhard. *Jesus and Community: The Social Dimension of the Christian Faith* (Philadelphia, PA: Fortress, 1984)

Loughlin, Gerard. *Telling God's Story: Bible, Church and Narrative Theology* (Cambridge: Cambridge University Press, 1996)

McCullum, Hugh. *The Angels Have Left Us: The Rwanda Tragedy and the Churches* (Geneva: World Council of Churches, 1995)

Milbank, John. *The Word Made Strange: Theology, Language, Culture* (Oxford: Blackwell, 1997)

—— *Being Reconciled: Ontology and Pardon* (London: Routledge, 2003)

Muir, Edwin. *The Complete Poems of Edwin Muir: An Annotated Edition*, ed. Peter Butter (Aberdeen: Association for Scottish Literary Studies, 1991)

Myers, Ched. *Binding the Strong Man: A Political Reading of Mark's Story of Jesus* (Maryknoll, NY: Orbis, 1988)

Preston, Geoffrey. *Faces of the Church*, ed. Aidan Nichols (Grand Rapids, MI: Eerdmans, 1997)

Stibbe, Mark. *John* (Sheffield: Journal of the Society of the Old Testament Press, 1993)

Tutu, Desmond. *No Future without Forgiveness* (London: Rider, 1999)

Tyler, Anne. *Saint Maybe* (London: Vintage, 1992)

Volf, Miroslav and Bass, Dorothy, eds. *Practicing Theology: Beliefs and Practices in Christian Life* (Grand Rapids, MI: Eerdmans, 2002)

Wannenwetsch, Bernd. *Political Worship: Ethics for Christian Citizens* (Oxford: Oxford University Press, 2004)

Wells, Samuel. *Transforming Fate into Destiny: The Theological Ethics of Stanley Hauerwas* (Carlisle: Paternoster, 1998; reissued Eugene, OR: Cascade, 2004)

—— "How Common Worship Forms Local Character," *Studies in Christian Ethics* 15/1 (2002): 66–74

—— *Community-Led Estate Regeneration and the Local Church* (Cambridge: Grove Booklets, 2003)

—— *Improvisation and the Drama of Christian Ethics* (Grand Rapids, MI: Brazos and London: SPCK 2004)

Witherington III, Ben. *Grace in Galatia: A Commentary on St Paul's Letter to the Galatians* (Edinburgh: T. & T. Clark, 1998)

Yoder, John Howard. *The Original Revolution* (Scottdale, PA: Herald, 1971)

—— *The Priestly Kingdom: Social Ethics as Gospel* (Notre Dame, IN: University of Notre Dame Press, 1984)

—— *The Politics of Jesus: Behold the Man! Our Victorious Lamb*, second edition (Grand Rapids, MI: Eerdmans, 1994)

—— *Body Politics: Five Practices of the Christian Community Before the Watching World* (Scottdale, PA: Herald, 2001)

—— *The Jewish/Christian Schism Revisited*, edited by Michael G. Cartwright and Peter Ochs (London: SCM Press, 2003)

Young, Frances. *Face to Face: A Narrative Essay in the Theology of Suffering* (Edinburgh: T. & T. Clark, 1990)

INDEX